Dangerous Weather

A Change in
the Weather

Dangerous Weather

A Change in the Weather

Michael Allaby

ILLUSTRATIONS by Richard Garratt

☑®
Facts On File, Inc.

A Change in the Weather

Facts On File, Inc.
132 West 31st Street
New York NY 10001

Library of Congress Cataloging-in-Publication Data

Allaby, Michael.
   A change in the weather / Michael Allaby; illustrations by
Richard Garratt.
       p. cm.—(Dangerous weather)
Includes bibliographical references and index.
   ISBN 0-8160-4790-1 (acid-free paper)
   1. Climatic changes. 2. Meteorology. 3. Paleoclimatology. I. Title.
QC981.8.C5A435 2004
551.6—dc21   2003009535

Facts On File books are available at special discounts when purchased in bulk
quantities for businesses, associations, institutions, or sales promotions. Please
call our Special Sales Department in New York at (212) 967-8800 or
(800) 322-8755.

You can find Facts On File on the World Wide Web at
http://www.factsonfile.com

Text design by Erika K. Arroyo
Cover design by Nora Wertz
Illustrations by Richard Garratt

Printed in the United States of America

VB Hermitage 10   9   8   7   6   5   4   3   2   1

This book is printed on acid-free paper.

Contents

Preface

Several years have passed since the publication of the first edition of the *Dangerous Weather* series of books. Much has happened during that time and my friends at Facts On File and I felt it would be appropriate to revise all of the books in the series in order to bring them up to date.

As we began to prepare the new editions, it occurred to us that none of the books so much as mentioned climate change, yet in the minds of many people this is the single most important environmental issue of our time. Omitting the topic from a series of books about the atmosphere might make it seem that we were either ignorant or uncaring. First, though, we had to decide whether the subject would fit into the overall concept of the series. Is it "dangerous weather"?

Obviously, it is "weather." Is it dangerous? If some of the more alarming predictions were to come true, many people would be at risk. Sea levels might rise, causing flooding in coastal areas. Agricultural yields might decrease, causing food prices to rise. Some people would suffer, although the suffering would not be shared equally—it never is. So we decided that, yes, climate change can be considered dangerous. It is a suitable topic for a book on *Dangerous Weather.*

Climate change is not new. Climates are changing constantly and they have been very different at times in the past. How do we know this? The book explains how scientists reconstruct the climates of the distant past. You will read about ice ages and what triggers them, and about the warm weather in medieval times, when Scandinavian farmers settled in Greenland and England was a major wine producer. You will learn about the Little Ice Age, when they held fairs on the River Thames in London, England, and about their link with the number of sunspots.

Present climate change is due, or mainly due, to greenhouse gases. The book explains the greenhouse effect and the factors influencing it, such as the cycling of carbon, the albedo, or brightness, of the Earth, and the islands of heat that surround cities. You will also learn about the response to climate change through the work of the Intergovernmental Panel on Climate Change and the United Nations Framework Convention on Climate Change and its Kyoto Protocol. Predictions of future climate change are based on computer models. You will read about these and how they are made. Finally, the book discusses what climate change may mean in terms of its effects on sea levels, agriculture, and wildlife.

Sidebars throughout the book provide more detailed explanations of technical matters. You will find sidebars on such topics as adiabatic cooling and warming, latent heat, ice cores, blackbody radiation, and many more.

Measurements are given in familiar units, such as pounds, feet, miles, and degrees Fahrenheit, throughout the book, but in each case I have added the metric or scientific equivalent. All scientists now use standard international units of measurement. These may be unfamiliar, so I have added them, with their conversions, as an appendix.

You will find suggestions for further reading listed at the end of the book. The sources include a number of books that you may find useful, but a much larger number of web addresses. If you have access to a computer, these will allow you to learn more about climate change quickly and free of charge.

My friend and colleague Richard Garratt designed and prepared all of the diagrams and maps that illustrate this book. As always, I am deeply grateful to Richard for his skill in translating my crude drawings into such accomplished artwork.

I am grateful, too, to Frank K. Darmstadt, my editor at Facts On File, for his hard work, cheerful encouragement, and patience.

If *A Change in the Weather* encourages you to pursue further your interest in atmospheric science it will have achieved its aim and fulfilled my highest hopes for it. I hope you enjoy reading the book as much as I have enjoyed writing it for you.

—Michael Allaby
Tighnabruaich
Argyll, Scotland
www.michaelallaby.com

Introduction

What is climate change?

Imagine a typical day in spring. When you wake in the morning and look from the window, the sky is cloudy and gray. A while later it begins to rain, but then, toward the middle of the morning, the sky begins to look lighter in the west. The rain eases and then stops. Patches of blue sky appear and grow larger as the gray cloud thins and dissipates. By afternoon the Sun is shining and the air feels warm. There is a short, light shower in the early evening, and then a beautiful sunset, with a red sky that promises a fine day tomorrow.

Sunshine and showers; blue skies and gray skies; rain, snow, and hail; and wind and calm are all aspects of ordinary day-to-day weather. The weather can change in the course of a day—perhaps several times. It also changes with the seasons. As summer arrives, spring showers and sunshine give way to warmer weather and longer periods of sunshine. These changes occur regularly. We know they are coming and can prepare for them. We check the heating during the summer to make sure it will keep us warm in winter—because we know winter will come. We have winter clothes that are thicker and warmer than those we wear in summer. Maybe we have two sets of tires for the car, one for driving in summer and the other for use in winter, when the roads are covered with ice and snow.

Weather changes all the time. That is why we have weather forecasts. After all, if the weather always stayed the same we would know what it would be like tomorrow and forecasts would be pointless. The scientists who prepare weather forecasts are called *meteorologists* and the scientific study of weather is *meteorology*. A "meteor" is any phenomenon that happens in the air. Rain, clouds, dust storms, and anything else you can think of that happens naturally in the air is a meteor. The word comes from the Greek *meteōron*, which means "lofty," and *logos*, which means "account," so meteorology is an account of things that happen in the air.

Aristotle (384–322 B.C.E.) was the first person to use the word. He was a Greek philosopher and scientist who wrote on many subjects. Among the 47 of his works that survive, one is called *Meteorologica*—literally, "an account of lofty things." It is Aristotle's attempt to explain weather phenomena. He gave us our word *meteorology* and, with it, the idea that such things as clouds, rain, hail, wind, thunder, lightning, and storms can be explained—that they have natural causes and we can understand them. He rejected the traditional explanation, which was that they are caused by the gods, who use the weather to reward or punish humans or simply as a plaything. You cannot explain the supernatural, so in this view you cannot explain the weather, either. Most of Aristotle's explanations were incorrect, but what really matters is that he taught his students to learn about the natural world by observing it closely rather than relying on traditional stories about what other people thought happened. Aristotle gave us the scientific study of weather and the name for it.

Weather is not the same as climate

Of course, your spring day would not be one of rain, sunshine, and a gorgeous red sunset if you lived in Qaanaaq. Qaanaaq used to be called Thule. It is a town of about 600 people in northern Kalaallit Nunaat (the modern name for Greenland). Gazing from your bedroom window on an April morning in Qaanaaq you would see clear, blue skies and a great deal of ice and snow. By early afternoon, the temperature might rise as high as 0.5°F (−17.5°C). It might snow, but this is very unlikely. During April, Qaanaaq receives an average of about 2 inches (40 mm) of snow—when melted, this is equivalent to 0.2 inch (4 mm) of rain. So whatever outdoor activity you had planned for the day you would know that almost certainly the weather would stay fine, and also that you would need to dress warmly. There is only one useful piece of information a weather forecast could provide—the strength of the wind. A strong wind will blow loose, powdery snow from the surface to create a blizzard. You would not want to be caught unawares in a whiteout.

If you lived in Riyadh, the capital of Saudi Arabia, you could look forward to a fine, warm April day. Around dawn, the temperature is probably about 64°F (18°C) and by lunchtime it will have risen to about 89°F (32°C). This will not be too unpleasant, however, because the air is dry and rain is not very likely.

These differences between the weather on any particular day in Qaanaaq, Riyadh, and your own hometown reflect differences in climate. Although the weather in each place varies from day to day and season to season, it does so only within certain limits. Qaanaaq never experiences a scorching-hot day, and the sea never freezes along the coasts of Arabia.

The climate of a place is the average weather it experiences over a long period. On one April day some years ago, the temperature in Qaanaaq reached 37°F (3°C); it has also fallen to −26°F (−32°C). These temperatures really were recorded, but they are included in calculating the average, and the average weather is a more useful guide to the type of climate.

Because they describe average weather, climates can be given names. Most of Arabia has a desert climate, for example, and Kalaallit Nunaat has a polar climate. The classification of climates is complicated, however, and there are several classification systems. Climatology is the scientific study of climates and the scientists who practice it are climatologists. Meteorology and climatology are related but distinct branches of science.

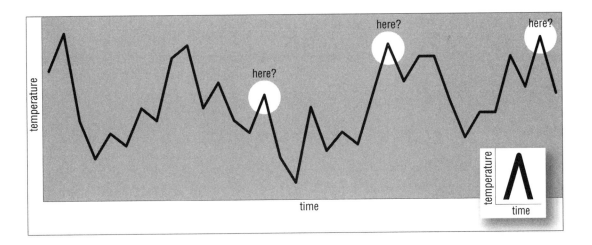

Climates also change

Weather changes from day to day. Climates also change, but much more slowly. There have been times in the past when they were very different from the climates of today. The land where Chicago now stands once lay beneath a thick ice sheet and the climate was like that of central Kalaallit Nunaat. Beneath the streets and squares of London, England, scientists have found the fossilized remains of hippopotamus and elephants, animals that live in tropical climates.

    The world's climates are still changing, but so gradually that detecting the change is difficult. Changes that take place over a few years can be very misleading. It may be true that average temperatures have risen or fallen over the last half-century or so, but this does not mean they will continue to move in the same direction. As the illustration shows, fitting a short-term trend into a long-term pattern is largely a matter of guesswork. That is why the study of past climates is so important—without the historical record, predictions are very unreliable.

    Climatology and meteorology are distinct, but both are based on our understanding of the way the atmosphere behaves in response to warm sunshine, the rotation of the Earth, and its contact with the continents and oceans. Climatology and meteorology are atmospheric sciences.

It is difficult to interpret a record of temperature over a short period. The record (inset) may show the temperature rising and falling. but where does this fit into the long-term climate record?

HOW THE ATMOSPHERE PRODUCES OUR WEATHER

Composition and structure of the atmosphere

Climates can and do change. This is true of all climates, not only those of our own planet. Other planets in the solar system that possess atmospheres also have climates and at various times in the past those climates have been different from the way they are now.

Venus has an atmosphere that is about 100 times denser than ours and the temperature at the surface is high enough to melt lead (see the sidebar "Atmospheres of Earth, Venus, and Mars" on page 2). Until recently, scientists believed that Venus had a very stable climate. They thought that the high surface temperature was due to the strong greenhouse effect (see the section "Greenhouse gases and the greenhouse effect," on pages 94–104) produced by the massive atmosphere. Now they are not so sure. Photographs of the surface of Venus taken in the early 1990s by the *Magellan* spacecraft show a pattern of cracks. There are similar cracks on Earth, although they are much smaller. On Earth, the cracks are found in basalt rocks that were erupted from a volcano and then cooled slowly. The pattern on Venus indicates that over very long periods the surface temperature has risen and fallen by about 360°F (200°C).

It is unlikely to have been volcanic activity that caused the cracks on Venus, but they may be the result of chemical changes in the atmosphere. If, for example, sulfur dioxide in the atmosphere reacted with substances at the planet's surface, this would remove sulfur dioxide, reducing the greenhouse effect. As the atmosphere cooled, more carbon dioxide would be absorbed into the surface rocks, further reducing the temperature. Whatever the reason, Venus has experienced climate change in the past and may experience it again in the future. Far from being stable, temperatures could rise or fall by hundreds of degrees from their present values.

Mars was not always a cold desert

Mars has a cold climate, although in summer the temperature can reach 80°F (27°C) in parts of the Tropics. There is weather on Mars, despite its thin atmosphere. From time to time dust storms blanket vast areas—

Atmospheres of Earth, Venus, and Mars

Venus and Mars are our neighbors in the solar system. Both planets possess atmospheres, but these atmospheres are very different from the atmosphere of Earth and the three planets have very different climates.

Our own atmosphere is 78.08 percent nitrogen by volume, 20.95 percent oxygen, and 0.93 percent argon, with minute traces of a range of other gases, including carbon dioxide, which accounts for about 0.04 percent. There is also a variable amount of water vapor. It is the water vapor that produces most of the features of the Earth's climates. The average atmospheric pressure at the Earth's surface is 14.7 lb. in.$^{-2}$ (100 megapascals, MPa, or 1 bar) and the average surface temperature is 59°F (15°C).

Earth is the third planet, counting outward from the Sun. Mercury (with no atmosphere and therefore no climate) is the first and Venus the second. Venus is almost the same size as Earth, but slightly less massive (its mass is 81.5 percent of Earth's mass). Its atmosphere is much more massive than our own and the surface atmospheric pressure is about 1,470 lb. in.$^{-2}$ (1,000 MPa, 100 bar). The atmosphere is 96.5 percent carbon dioxide and 3.5 percent nitrogen, with small traces of carbon monoxide, sulfur dioxide, water vapor, argon, and helium.

Venus is permanently shrouded in cloud, extending from about 28 miles (45 km) above the surface to a height of nearly 43 miles (70 km), with layers of haze both below and above the clouds. The clouds themselves are composed mainly of sulfuric acid. The dense atmosphere and clouds combine to produce a very strong greenhouse effect. The surface temperature is about 850°F (454°C).

Mars is the fourth planet and so farther from the Sun than Earth. It is also smaller—about half the size of Earth. Its atmosphere is very thin, producing a surface pressure of about 0.9 lb. in.$^{-2}$ (600 pascals, Pa; 6 millibars, mb). Martian air is 95.3 percent carbon dioxide, 2.7 percent nitrogen, 1.6 percent argon, 0.13 percent oxygen, and there are traces of water vapor, neon, krypton, and xenon.

The average surface temperature is –67°F (–55°C). Temperatures at the surface range from –207°F (–133°C) high in the polar mountains in winter to 80°F (27°C) in dark regions in the Tropics in summer.

sometimes they cover the entire planet. Then the sky is pink. More often, though, the sky is dark blue and cloudy. The clouds are made from crystals of water ice. The surface temperature rises during dust storms and falls when the dust settles and the sky is clear.

This is the present climate, however, and it was not always so cold and dry. Surface features closely resemble riverbeds and shorelines, and scientists suspect that is what they are. If so, there were times in the past when the climate of Mars was warmer than it is today. Rivers flowed, there were lakes and shallow seas, and perhaps rain fell from the sky.

How Earth acquired its three atmospheres

We know that our own climate can change, but we tend to assume that the atmosphere itself has always been the same as it is today, composed almost entirely of nitrogen (78 percent) and oxygen (21 percent). That is wrong. Our present atmosphere is the third atmosphere the Earth has possessed.

The first atmosphere is the one that cloaked the planet while it was forming, around 4.5 billion years ago. At that time rocks were continually smashing into the surface, and each time this happened the impact generated enough heat to vaporize some of the ingredients. The resulting gases formed the atmosphere. Most space rocks contain some water, and comets contain so much they are sometimes called "dirty snowballs." Consequently, the first atmosphere was mostly water vapor, with small amounts of hydrogen, nitrogen, carbon monoxide, and carbon dioxide. Heat from the repeated impacts—like the heat that warms a nail after prolonged hammering—meant the atmosphere was much too hot for water to exist as a liquid. The water vapor remained a gas, and there were no clouds.

Then the Earth was involved in a major collision with a body about the size of Mars. This smashed both bodies and as gravity drew the fragments together again, they assembled themselves not as one body, but as two: Earth had acquired its Moon. The atmosphere also returned, but by now the Earth was sufficiently massive, and its interior was hot enough, for volcanoes to begin erupting. There were many more active volcanoes than there are now and the gases they released became part of the atmosphere.

As more and more rocks hit the Earth, Moon, Venus, and Mars and became part of them, the number of rocks orbiting the Sun decreased, and so the bombardment eased. This allowed the Earth to cool. After a time it had cooled sufficiently for water vapor to start condensing. Clouds formed and it began to rain. Almost all of the atmospheric water fell to the surface, where it filled the low-lying areas to form vast oceans. At the same time, the atmosphere also lost its hydrogen. Earth's gravity was insufficient to retain this lightest of all gases and little by little it drifted away into space. The atmosphere then probably consisted of about 95 percent carbon dioxide and 3 percent nitrogen, with small amounts of carbon monoxide and other gases. This was much like the atmospheres of Venus and Mars, and it was much denser than our present atmosphere. The surface air pressure was probably around 365 lb. in.$^{-2}$ (2,500 MPa, 25 bar).

Carbon dioxide then reacted with water and with calcium and magnesium in the surface rocks to form carbonates. These accumulated in the oceans, where they formed sediments that were slowly compressed and heated until they were transformed into carbonate rocks, such as limestone. After some hundreds of millions of years, this process removed a great deal of carbon dioxide and reduced the surface pressure. This in turn slowed the reactions and the atmosphere stabilized. Earth then had its second atmosphere, still consisting mainly of carbon dioxide.

How oxygen accumulated

At that time the Sun was young and weak. The thermonuclear reaction in its core had made it start to shine, but it was about 25 percent to 30 percent dimmer and cooler than it is today. Nevertheless, this was enough to warm the surface layers of water and to provide light for the first cells to begin manufacturing sugars by photosynthesis. Those cells were cyanobacteria and they lived in microbial mats; the fossil remains of those mats are called *stromatolites*. Oxygen is a by-product of photosynthesis and cyanobacteria released it.

By around 2.1 billion years ago the atmosphere contained oxygen—about 15 percent of the amount it contains now—and the amount was increasing. The ozone layer formed in the stratosphere when the air contained 1 percent of its present concentration of oxygen. Ozone is a form of oxygen in which each molecule comprises three oxygen atoms (O_3) rather than the two (O_2) of ordinary oxygen.

Photosynthesis was producing the oxygen, but no one knows for sure how it came to accumulate, because photosynthesis is always accompanied by respiration. Photosynthesis removes carbon dioxide from the air and releases oxygen, but respiration releases energy by oxidizing carbon back into carbon dioxide, which is released into the air. When organisms die their tissues are decomposed by organisms that use their carbon as a source of energy, releasing it by respiration. Consequently, respiration removes the oxygen from the air and returns the carbon dioxide, so the composition of the air remains unchanged.

The first photosynthesizers lived in water. Most scientists think that when these single-celled organisms died, a small proportion of their material—about 0.1 percent—sank to the bottom and was buried in mud. This prevented further decomposition and would have allowed oxygen to remain in the atmosphere.

Other scientists believe a second process may have contributed. Modern microbial mats, very similar to those that existed more than 2 billion years ago, release large amounts of hydrogen at night, when photosynthesis ceases and so no oxygen is being released. Some of the hydrogen would have been used by other organisms, but a proportion would have risen through the atmosphere and escaped into space. Hydrogen is released by breaking the bonds that hold water molecules together: $H_2O \rightarrow H + OH$. In the presence of oxygen, the water molecule reforms: $4H + O_2 \rightarrow 2H_2O$, but at night, when oxygen was not being released, this reaction would not have taken place, allowing the oxygen to accumulate.

Oxygen continued to accumulate and the amount of carbon dioxide continued decreasing until the atmosphere reached its present composition. This is the Earth's third atmosphere, the one it has had for about 600 million years, during which time its composition has not changed. The table on page 5 lists the gases that constitute our present atmosphere.

Layers of the atmosphere

There is no clearly defined top to our atmosphere. About 90 percent of it lies between the surface and a height of about 10 miles (16 km). Above

COMPOSITION OF THE PRESENT ATMOSPHERE

Gas	Chemical formula	Abundance
Major constituents		
nitrogen	N_2	78.08%
oxygen	O_2	20.95%
argon	Ar	0.93%
water vapor	H_2O	variable
Minor constituents		
carbon dioxide	CO_2	365 p.p.m.v.
neon	Ne	18 p.p.m.v.
helium	He	5 p.p.m.v.
methane	CH_4	2 p.p.m.v.
krypton	Kr	1 p.p.m.v.
hydrogen	H_2	0.5 p.p.m.v.
nitrous oxide	N_2O	0.3 p.p.m.v.
carbon monoxide	CO	0.05–0.2 p.p.m.v.
xenon	Xe	0.08 p.p.m.v.
ozone	O_3	variable
Trace constituents		
ammonia	NH_3	4 p.p.b.v.
nitrogen dioxide	NO_2	1 p.p.b.v.
sulfur dioxide	SO_2	1 p.p.b.v.
hydrogen sulfide	H_2S	0.05 p.p.b.v.

(p.p.m.v. means parts per million by volume; 1 p.p.m. = 0.0001 percent. p.p.b.v. means parts per billion by volume; 1 p.p.b. = 0.0000001 percent.)

this height, the remainder of the atmosphere extends to at least 350 miles (550 km) from the surface. Beyond that it merges imperceptibly with the molecules and atoms of interstellar space and the outer fringes of the solar atmosphere.

The density of the air decreases rapidly with height, so that the molecules in its outermost reaches are so widely scattered that they rarely collide with one another. Air temperature also changes with height. If you climb a mountain you will find the air is colder the higher you go, and even near the equator there are mountains that have snow on their peaks. So we are used to the idea that the higher you climb the colder you will feel. This is true while you remain fairly close to the surface,

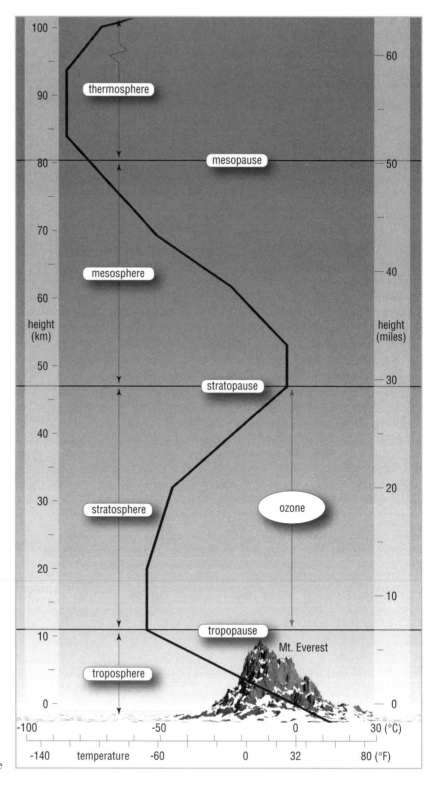

Atmospheric structure

but there are other regions of the atmosphere where the temperature increases with height—eventually to about 1,830°F (1,000°C) when you reach an altitude of 310–620 miles (500–1,000 km). As the diagram shows, the atmosphere is arranged in layers, one above another, and the layers are produced by the way temperature changes with height within them.

Troposphere and tropopause

The lowest layer, extending to about 10 miles (16 km) over the equator, seven miles (11 km) over middle latitudes, and five miles (8 km) over the poles, is the *troposphere*. This is the region where the air is constantly being mixed and where all the world's weather happens.

It is also the layer in which the temperature decreases with height. Its upper boundary, known as the *tropopause*, is the height at which the temperature ceases to decrease as you climb higher. This means that air that is rising because it is warmer and therefore less dense than the air around it meets a barrier in the form of air at the same density. The air can rise no farther and so the tropopause forms a very real boundary.

The average temperature at the tropopause ranges from –85°F (–65°C) at the equator to –22°F (–30°C) at the poles. The temperature is higher at the poles than at the equator because the tropopause is lower there, so air cannot rise so high and its temperature cannot fall so low.

Stratosphere and stratopause

The layer above the tropopause is called the *stratosphere*—because Léon-Philippe Teisserenc de Bort (1855–1913), the French meteorologist who discovered and named it, thought that at this height the atmospheric gases separated into layers, or strata, according to their masses. This was incorrect, but the name stuck.

Temperature remains constant with height through the lower stratosphere, but it begins to increase with height above about 12 miles (19 km) and the rate of increase accelerates above 20 miles (32 km). The temperature at the upper boundary of the stratosphere, known as the *stratopause*, is sometimes higher than 32°F (0°C). The warming is due to the absorption of ultraviolet (UV) radiation by oxygen and ozone.

The stratopause is at about 34 miles (55 km) over the equator and the poles and about 31 miles (50 km) over middle latitudes. It is higher in winter than in summer. The air pressure at this height is about 0.015 lb. in.$^{-2}$ (0.100 pascal, Pa; 1 millibar, mb).

Mesosphere and mesopause

The stratopause is a region where temperature remains constant with height. The atmospheric layer above it is the *mesosphere*, extending to a height of about 50 miles (80 km). At the top of the mesosphere the air pressure is about 0.00015 lb. in.$^{-2}$ (1 Pa; 0.01 mb)—one-millionth of the pressure at sea level.

Temperature remains constant with height at the stratopause, but then decreases. The temperature at the upper boundary, the *mesopause*, varies widely. In winter it can be as low as –148°F (–100°C), but in summer it can reach –22°F (–30°C). Air at this height warms in summer, because this is where incoming UV radiation first strikes oxygen molecules. The molecules absorb *photons*—units of light. This supplies enough energy to break the molecules apart: $O_2 + photon \rightarrow O + O$. The reaction warms the air.

Some of the atomic oxygen (O) drifts down into the stratosphere, where it takes part in further reactions in which ozone (O_3) is formed and then broken apart again ($O + O_2 + M \rightarrow O_3$; $O_3 + photon \rightarrow O_2 + O$; $O_3 + O \rightarrow 2O_2$). Ozone formation requires a catalyst (M). This process forms the *ozone layer* and it absorbs most of the incoming UV radiation at certain wavelengths.

Thermosphere, exosphere, and ionosphere

The mesopause separates the mesosphere from the *thermosphere*. This is the uppermost layer of the atmosphere. It has no precise upper boundary, but there is enough air to exert a measurable amount of drag on spacecraft even more than 155 miles (250 km) above the surface. In the lower part of the thermosphere the air contains some atomic oxygen (O) as well as molecular nitrogen (N_2) and oxygen (O_2). Atomic oxygen predominates above about 125 miles (200 km).

The temperature increases with height, due to the absorption of UV radiation by atomic oxygen, and may reach 1,800°F (1,000°C). Temperature is a measure of the speed atoms and molecules are traveling, which is a measure of the energy they possess. Atoms and molecules are so widely scattered in the thermosphere, however, that they do not warm satellites orbiting at this height.

There is a region beyond the thermosphere known as the *exosphere*. It extends from about 300 miles (480 km) to about 450 miles (725 km) above the Earth's surface. The air in this region consists mainly of atomic oxygen (O), helium (He), and hydrogen (H). Hydrogen constantly drifts away into space. It is replaced by the breakdown of water vapor (H_2O) and methane (CH_4) near the mesopause.

The region of the atmosphere from the base of the mesosphere to a height of about 620 miles (1,000 km) is also known as the *ionosphere*. It is where solar radiation supplies sufficient energy to separate the electrons from some atoms. This is known as *photoionization*, and atoms that have lost one or more electrons are *ions* and carry positive charge. The ionosphere is where interactions with solar particles (the *solar wind*) in the Earth's magnetic field produce aurorae—the northern and southern lights. The ionosphere also reflects radio waves, making it possible to transmit radio signals directly over long distances.

GENERAL CIRCULATION OF THE ATMOSPHERE

Although the Sun is more than 100 times larger than Earth, it is also a very long way away—about 93 million miles (150 million km). At this distance it appears quite small in the sky. It radiates heat and light in all directions, but because of the distance, most of its radiation misses Earth altogether. As the diagram shows, we receive only a small fraction of it, and the radiation that we do receive falls only on the area of the surface directly facing the Sun. Some places are exposed to more intense sunlight than others and, because the Sun radiates heat as well as light, that is why they have warmer climates.

Imagine a huge disk with the Sun at its center and the Earth traveling around the edge, so that the edge marks the path of the Earth's orbit. This disk is known as the *plane of the ecliptic*. At noon, a person standing at a point where the plane of the ecliptic intersects the surface will see the Sun directly overhead. That point rests on a line marking a circle around the Earth, and the closer you are to that line, the warmer and sunnier the climate is likely to be—or would be if the solar energy did not produce such a large amount of cloud and rain.

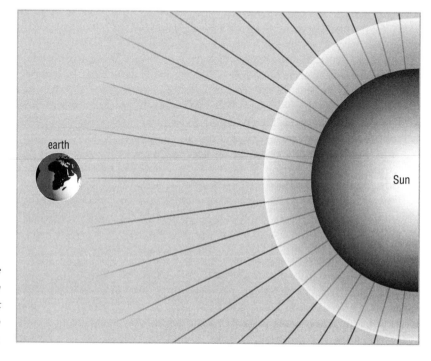

Solar radiation. Because of the distance between the Sun and Earth, most of the Sun's radiation misses us.

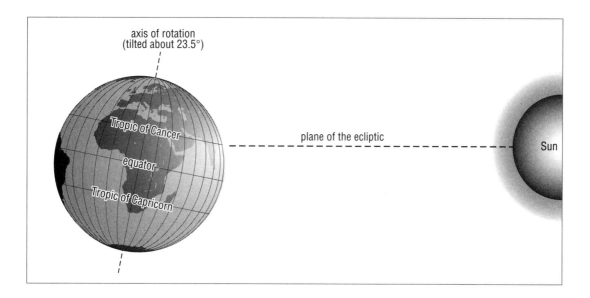

Seasons and Tropics

If the Earth were upright, so its north-south axis of rotation intersected the plane of the ecliptic at a right angle, the plane of the ecliptic would divide the Earth exactly at the equator. The person wishing to stand directly beneath the Sun could choose any point on the equator to do so. In fact, though, the Earth's rotational axis is tilted from the vertical by 23.5°. Consequently, as the Earth travels around its orbit, the Sun appears to move north and south, and it is directly overhead at the equator on only two days each year. Those days are known as the equinoxes and at present they fall on about March 21 and September 23 (the date varies by a day or two from year to year). They are called equinoxes—from a Latin word meaning "equal nights"—because when the Sun is directly above the equator it is above the horizon for precisely 12 hours and below it for precisely 12 hours as seen from anywhere on Earth.

The Sun is farthest from the equator at the solstices—June 21 and December 23—when it appears overhead at noon at a point on a circle in latitude 23.5° N or S. These circles, shown in the illustration, are known as *Tropics*. The dates of the solstices change (see the section "Milutin Milankovitch and his astronomical cycles" on pages 52–60), but in ancient times the Sun was in the constellation of Cancer at the June solstice and in the constellation of Capricorn at the December solstice, and that is how the Tropics earned their names. The northern circle is the tropic of Cancer and the southern circle is the tropic of Capricorn. Not surprisingly, the latitude of the Tropics is the same as the angle of tilt of the Earth's rotational axis.

The combination of the axial tilt and the Earth's orbit produces our seasons, as shown in the diagram. When the Sun is over the tropic of Can-

Why the Sun is overhead in the Tropics. As the Earth travels around the Sun in the course of a year, the line where the plane of the ecliptic meets the surface—and therefore where the Sun is directly overhead at noon—moves from the tropic of Cancer, across the equator, to the tropic of Capricorn, then back again.

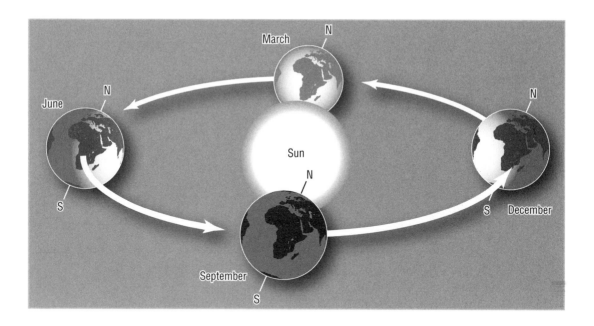

Seasons and the Earth's
orbit. Because of the tilt
of the Earth's axis, when
it is summer in one
hemisphere it is winter
in the other. As the Earth
travels around the Sun,
these alternate.

cer, the Northern Hemisphere is more intensely illuminated than the Southern Hemisphere, and it is summer in the north. During summer, there are more hours of daylight than there are hours of darkness. On the longest day of the year, New York (40.72° N) enjoys 15 hours 6 minutes when the Sun is above the horizon. (Daylight lasts longer than this because light is scattered by the atmosphere, and so the Sun provides some illumination even when it is a few degrees below the horizon.) Inside the Arctic Circle, at 66.5° N, there is a period in midsummer when the Sun does not sink below the horizon at all—the time of the "midnight Sun." When it is summer in one hemisphere, it is winter in the other and the hours of darkness exceed the hours of daylight. The shortest day in New York lasts for 9 hours, 15 minutes, and inside the Arctic Circle the Sun does not rise above the horizon at all, although scattering of light means that the Arctic "darkness at noon" is twilight rather than total darkness.

Why Earth is not like the Moon

When the Sun is below the horizon none of its radiation falls directly on the surface. The temperature falls, but it does not fall so far as it does on the Moon. There, the temperature on the dark side can fall to –243°F (–153°C), while on the sunny side it can rise to 273°F (134°C). The Earth and Moon are close together and formed together (see the section "Composition and structure of the atmosphere" on page 1.) The difference in temperatures cannot be due to the distance of the two bodies from the Sun. In fact, it is due entirely to the fact that Earth has an atmosphere and oceans, while the Moon has no oceans and an atmosphere so tenuous that it exerts no influence whatever. Without our atmosphere and oceans, daytime and nighttime temperatures on Earth would be similar to those on the Moon.

The atmosphere reduces these extremes of temperature in two ways: it stores heat and it transports heat. Air accumulates heat during the day and releases it at night. This prevents daytime temperatures from rising very high and nighttime temperatures from falling very low (see the section "Greenhouse gases and the greenhouse effect" on pages 94–104). Temperatures are moderated in this way everywhere on Earth, regardless of latitude. The transport of heat, on the other hand, reduces temperatures in equatorial regions and increases them in polar regions.

Trade winds and Hadley cells

Air over the equator is heated strongly by contact with the warm surface. The warm air rises all the way to the tropopause. There, trapped beneath the tropopause, it moves away from the equator. Cooler air flows toward the equator at low level, to take its place.

Moving air tends to turn in a circle. This is called *vorticity* and it is why the water usually forms a spiral, or vortex, when it flows out of a bathtub. As the cool air moves toward the equator its vorticity swings it to the right in the Northern Hemisphere and to the left in the Southern Hemisphere. The resulting surface winds, shown in the diagram, blow from the northeast on the northern side of the equator and from the southeast on the southern side. These are the trade winds. They are the most dependable winds on Earth.

The trade winds were well known to mariners in the days of sailing ships, and in the 17th and 18th centuries scientists tried to discover why they are so reliable. Their calculations led them to propose what we now

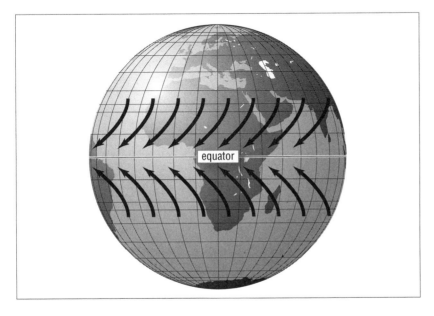

equator

Trade winds

call the *general circulation of the atmosphere* (see the sidebar "George Hadley and Hadley cells" below). This is a description of the way air moves. Its modern form, the *three-cell model*, is greatly simplified and quite often the air is not moving in the way it describes. Nevertheless, it provides a broadly accurate picture of the atmosphere.

Hadley believed there was just one cell in each hemisphere. In fact there are three. What he thought was a single cell covering an entire hemisphere affects only the Tropics.

Air rises over the equator. It is very moist, because oceans cover most of the equatorial region. As it rises the air cools and its water vapor condenses. This produces the heavy rainfall of the Tropics. It also releases

George Hadley and Hadley cells

When European ships began venturing far from their home ports, into the Tropics and across the equator, sailors learned that the trade winds are very dependable in both strength and direction. They made use of them and by the end of the 16th century their existence was well known. Many years passed, however, before anyone knew why the trade winds blow so reliably. Like many scientific explanations, this one developed in stages.

Edmond Halley (1656–1742), an English astronomer, was the first person to offer an explanation. In 1686 he suggested that air is heated more strongly at the equator than anywhere else. The warm equatorial air rises, cold air flows in near the surface from either side to replace it, and this in-flowing air forms the trade winds. If this were so, however, the trades on either side of the equator would flow from due north and south. In fact, they flow from the northeast and southeast.

There the matter rested until 1735. In that year George Hadley (1685–1768), an English meteorologist, proposed a modification of the Halley theory. Hadley agreed that warm equatorial air rises and is replaced at the surface, but he suggested that the rotation of the Earth from west to east swings the moving air, making the winds blow from the northeast and southeast.

Hadley was right about what happened, but not about the reason for it. This was discovered in 1856 by the American meteorologist William Ferrel (1817–91), who said the swing is due to the tendency of moving air to rotate about its own axis, like coffee stirred in a cup.

In accounting for the trade winds, Hadley had proposed a general explanation for the way heat is transported away from the equator. He suggested that the warm equatorial air moves at a great height all the way to the poles, where it descends. This vertical movement in a fluid, driven by heating from below, is called a *convection cell* and the cell Hadley described is known as a *Hadley cell*.

The rotation of the Earth prevents a single, huge Hadley cell from forming. What really happens is more complicated. In various equatorial regions, warm air rises to a height of about 10 miles (16 km), moves away from the equator, cools, and descends between latitudes 25° and 30° N and S. These are the Hadley cells. When it reaches the surface in the Tropics, some of the air flows back toward the equator and some flows away from the equator.

Over the poles, cold air descends and flows away from the poles at low level. At about latitude 50° it meets air flowing away from the equatorial Hadley cells. Where the two types of air meet is called the *polar front*. Air rises again at the polar front. Some flows toward the pole, completing a high-latitude cell, and some flows toward the equator until it meets the descending air of the Hadley cell, which it joins.

There are three sets of cells in each hemisphere. This is called the *three-cell model* of atmospheric circulation, by which warm air moves away from the equator and cool air moves toward the equator.

latent heat (see the box "Latent heat and dew point" on page 32). The latent heat warms the surrounding air, causing it to continue rising.

When air and water move away from the equator they are deflected by the Coriolis effect, often abbreviated as CorF because it was once thought to be a force rather than a simple consequence of the rotation of the Earth (see the sidebar "The Coriolis effect" on page 16). The magnitude of the CorF is zero at the equator and reaches a maximum at the North and South Poles. Air that rises over the equator is unable to cross the tropopause, so the constant stream of rising air pushes it away from the equator, heading due north and south. It then becomes subject to the CorF. This deflects it, so by the time it reaches about latitude 25° N and S it is moving more from west to east than toward the pole. At the same time, the warm air is radiating its heat into space and cooling. As its temperature decreases, the density of the air increases. The two effects combine to "pile up" increasingly dense air. Eventually the air is denser than the air beneath it, and it subsides all the way to the surface. This happens in latitudes 25°–30° in both hemispheres.

Descending air is compressed and warms adiabatically (see the sidebar "Adiabatic cooling and warming" on page 34). The air lost most of its moisture during its ascent, when its temperature was decreasing. As it descends and warms, its capacity for holding moisture increases and its relative humidity—the amount of water it carries as a percentage of the amount needed to saturate it—falls. By the time it reaches the surface, the air is hot and very dry. The subsiding air produces several regions of high surface pressure, with air flowing out of them. This prevents moist air from entering and ensures that the affected regions have a dry climate. These regions comprise the belts of subtropical deserts that girdle the Earth in both hemispheres. They include the Sonoran, Sahara, Arabian, Middle Eastern, and Thar Deserts in the Northern Hemisphere and the Kalahari and Australian Deserts in the Southern Hemisphere.

Air flows away from the subtropical high-pressure regions in both directions: toward the equator and toward the pole. The air flowing toward the equator becomes the easterly trade winds and air flowing away from the equator becomes the mid-latitude westerly winds.

This equatorial and tropical circulation comprises the Hadley cells. There are several of these in each hemisphere—usually about five in winter and four in summer. They coincide with subtropical high-pressure regions that are separated by low-pressure regions.

The trade winds from the north and south meet at the *Intertropical Convergence Zone* (ITCZ). This is a region of low surface pressure, and it contains areas where the winds are light and often do not blow at all. These regions are called the *doldrums*.

Polar and Ferrel cells

Extremely cold, dense air also subsides over the North and South Poles. It produces the two polar high-pressure regions. Air flows out from them and is deflected to become the polar easterly winds.

The Coriolis effect

Any object moving toward or away from the equator and not firmly attached to the surface does not travel in a straight line. As the diagram illustrates. It is deflected to the right in the Northern Hemisphere and to the left in the Southern Hemisphere. Moving air and water tend to follow a clockwise path in the Northern Hemisphere and a counterclockwise path in the Southern Hemisphere.

The French physicist Gaspard Gustave de Coriolis (1792–1843) discovered the reason for this in 1835, and it is called the *Coriolis effect*. It happens because the Earth is a rotating sphere, and as an object moves above the surface, the Earth below is also moving. The effect used to be called the Coriolis "force," and it is still abbreviated as CorF, but it is not a force. It simply results from the fact that we observe motion in relation to fixed points on the surface.

The Earth makes one complete turn on its axis every 24 hours. This means every point on the surface is constantly moving and returns to its original position (relative to the Sun) every 24 hours, but because the Earth is a sphere, different points on the surface travel different distances to do so. If you find it difficult to imagine that New York and Bogotá—or any other two places in different latitudes—are moving through space at different speeds, consider what would happen if this were not so: the world would tear itself apart.

Consider two points on the surface, one at the equator and the other at 40° N, which is the approximate latitude of New York and Madrid. The equator, latitude 0°, is about 24,881 miles (40,033 km) long. That is how far a point on the equator must travel in 24 hours, which means it moves at about 1,037 MPH (1,668 km/h). At 40° N, the circumference parallel to the equator is about 19,057 miles (30,663 km). The point there has less distance to travel and so it moves at about 794 MPH (1,277 km/h).

Suppose you planned to fly an aircraft to New York from the point on the equator due south of New York (and could ignore the winds). If you headed due north, you would not reach New York. At the equator you are already traveling eastward at 1,037 MPH (1,668 km/h). As you fly north, the surface beneath you is also traveling east, but at a slower speed the farther you travel. If the journey from 0° to 40° N took you six hours, in that time you would also move about 6,000 miles (9,654 km) to the east, relative to the position of the surface beneath you, but the surface itself would also move, at New York by about 4,700 miles (7,562 km). Consequently, you would end not at New York, but (6,000 − 4,700 =) 1,300 miles (2,092 km) to the east of New York, way out over the Atlantic, somewhere due south of Greenland.

The size of the Coriolis effect is directly proportional to the speed at which the body moves and the sine of its latitude. The effect on a body moving at 100 MPH (160 km/h) is 10 times greater than that on one moving at 10 MPH (16 km/h). Sin 0° = 0 (the equator) and sin 90° = 1 (the poles), so the Coriolis effect is greatest at the poles and zero at the equator.

The polar easterlies and mid-latitude westerlies meet along the boundary between polar and tropical air. This is known as the *polar front*. At the top of the polar front, close to the tropopause, the temperature difference on either side is very large. It produces the *polar front jet stream*, which is a strong, high-level wind blowing from west to east in both hemispheres.

Air rises along the polar front. Some of the air flows back toward the pole, where it cools and subsides once more. This produces a second set of cells, called the *polar cells*.

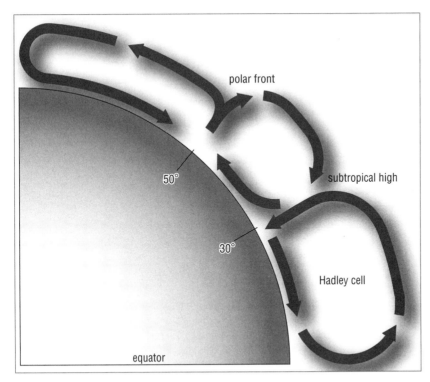

polar front

subtropical high

50°

30°

Hadley cell

equator

Three-cell model. The tropical (Hadley) and polar cells are directly driven by convection. The middle-latitude (Ferrel) cell is indirect, because it is driven by the polar and tropical cells.

Some of the air flows toward the equator. Over the Tropics it meets the high-level air of the Hadley cells and subsides with it. This forms a third set of cells. Their existence was discovered by the American meteorologist William Ferrel (1817–91) and they are known as *Ferrel cells*.

There is another region of light surface winds, known as the *horse latitudes*, where the subsiding air reaches the surface and divides. Historically, ships often carried cargoes of horses. If the ships were becalmed, supplies of drinking water sometimes ran short. Horses often died of thirst when this happened, and their bodies were thrown overboard, hence the name.

The Hadley cells and polar cells are *direct cells*, driven by convection and the subsidence of cold, dense air. The Ferrel cells are *indirect cells*, driven by the direct cells to the north and south of them. Together, the Hadley, Ferrel, and polar cells comprise the three-cell model shown in the diagram.

Between them, these cells transport warm air away from the equator and cool air toward the equator. Without them, tropical temperatures would be much higher than they are and polar temperatures much lower.

TRANSPORT OF HEAT BY THE OCEANS

Edmonton, Alberta, and Dublin, Ireland are in almost the same latitude (53.58° N and 53.37° N respectively). July is the warmest month in Edmonton, with an average daytime temperature of 74°F (23°C), and January is the coldest month. The average nighttime (coldest) temperature in January is –4°F (–20°C). July is also the warmest month in Dublin, with an average daytime temperature of 67°F (20°C), and January is the coldest month, with nighttime temperatures of 34°F (1°C).

Edmonton is warmer than Dublin in summer and very much colder in winter. The difference between the highest and lowest temperatures—the *temperature range*—is 78°F (43°C) in Edmonton, but in Dublin it is only 33°F (19°C). Why is the climate of Edmonton so much more extreme than that of Dublin?

Both cities receive most of their weather from air that moves from west to east. Air over Edmonton has crossed the Rocky Mountains and the hills of western Alberta. Dublin's air has crossed the much shorter distance from the western coast of Ireland. Edmonton lies deep inside a continent. Dublin is on the coast of an island. This simple geographic fact—the distance between the city and the ocean—explains the difference in their climates.

Oceans exert a huge influence on climate. Even though continental cities such as Edmonton lie a long way from the nearest coast, the distant ocean nevertheless modifies their weather considerably.

Ocean currents

Like the atmosphere, ocean currents transport heat. Instead of transporting it by means of vertical cells, in which air rises, moves horizontally, and subsides again, the oceans transport it by a system of surface and deep currents.

Ocean currents have names, many of which are familiar. Most people have heard of the Gulf Stream, for example, and perhaps of the California and Labrador Currents. There are also the Kuroshio and Oyashio Currents which affect the weather in Japan, and the Peru Current which flows northward parallel to the western coast of South America carrying nutrients that sustain a vast population of plankton, fish, seals, and seabirds. During an El Niño (see the sidebar "El Niño" on page 19), the South Equatorial Current which ordinarily carries warm water away from South America and toward Asia weakens or even reverses direction. The West

Wind Drift, also known as the Antarctic Circumpolar Current, is the only ocean current that flows all the way around the world. It moves through the Southern Ocean around the continent of Antarctica, where there is no large land mass to interrupt it.

There are many currents. Their names make them easier to remember, but also obscure an important fact. Despite having individual names, the major ocean currents are not separate. They are all linked into a global pattern of currents forming a closed loop that is known as the Great Conveyor. It is shown on the map.

El Niño

At intervals of between two and seven years, the weather changes across much of the Tropics and especially in southern Asia and western South America. The weather is drier than usual in Indonesia, Papua New Guinea, eastern Australia, northeastern South America, the Horn of Africa, East Africa, Madagascar, and in the northern part of the Indian subcontinent. It is wetter than usual over the

(*continues*)

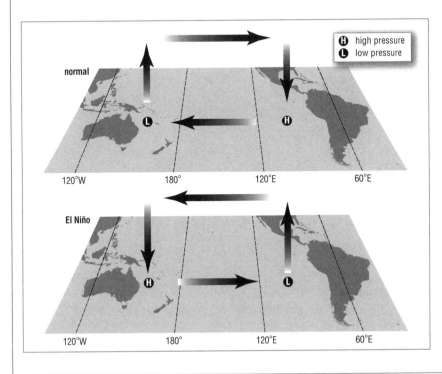

El Niño. A reversal of pressure distribution allows warm water to flow eastward.

(*continued*)

central and eastern tropical Pacific, parts of California and the southeastern United States, eastern Argentina, central Africa, southern India, and Sri Lanka. The phenomenon has been occurring for at least 5,000 years.

The change is greatest around Christmastime—midsummer in the Southern Hemisphere, of course. That is how it earned its name of El Niño, "the Christ child," in Peru, where its effects are most dramatic. Ordinarily, the western coastal regions of South America have one of the driest climates in the world, but El Niño brings heavy rain. Farm crops flourish, but many communities rely on fishing, and the fish disappear.

Most of the time the prevailing low-level winds on either side of the equator are the trade winds, blowing from the northeast in the Northern Hemisphere and from the southeast in the Southern Hemisphere. At high level the winds flow in the opposite direction, from west to east. This is known as the Walker circulation, in memory of Sir Gilbert Walker (1868–1958), who discovered it in 1923. Walker also discovered that air pressure is usually low over the western side of the Pacific, near Indonesia, and high on the eastern side, near South America. This pressure distribution helps drive the trade winds, and the trade winds drive the Equatorial Current that flows from east to west, carrying warm surface water toward Indonesia. The warm water accumulates around Indonesia, in a warm pool.

In some years, however, the pressure distribution changes. Pressure rises over the western Pacific and weakens in the east. The trade winds then slacken. They may cease to blow altogether or even reverse direction, so they blow from west to east instead of east to west. This causes the Equatorial Current to weaken or reverse direction. Water then begins to flow out of the warm pool, moving eastward, and the depth of warm water increases off the South American coast. This suppresses upwelling cold water in the Peru Current and deprives fish and other marine life of the nutrients in the cold water. Air moving toward South America is warmed and carries a great deal of moisture. This brings heavy rain to the coastal region. This is an El Niño.

In other years the low pressure deepens in the west, and the high pressure in the east rises. This accelerates the trade winds and Equatorial Current, increasing the rainfall over southern Asia and the dry conditions along the South American coast. This is called La Niña. The periodical change in pressure distribution is known as the Southern Oscillation, and the complete cycle is an El Niño–Southern Oscillation (ENSO) event. The diagram illustrates how this happens.

Thermohaline circulation and North Atlantic Deep Water

At the edge of the Arctic Circle, where water freezes at the ocean surface, it is the process of freezing that drives the Great Conveyor. Ice is less dense than liquid water; that is why ice floats. Water becomes denser as its temperature decreases and it reaches its maximum density at a little above freezing. Freshwater is densest at 39.2°F (4°C) and seawater is densest at 35.6°F (2°C). The sea loses heat into the very cold air. This chills the sea surface and increases the density of the uppermost layer of water.

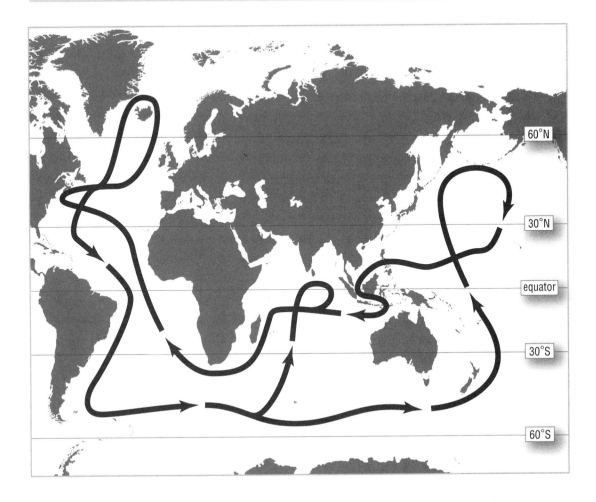

The Great Conveyor. A system of ocean currents carries cold water toward the equator and warm water toward the poles, strongly influencing climate.

When salt water freezes its salt is stripped from it. A water molecule is arranged with its two hydrogen atoms separated by an angle of 104.5°, so they are both on the same side of the oxygen atom. The oxygen side of the molecule carries negative charge (written as O^-) and the hydrogen side carries positive charge (H^+).

Salt is sodium chloride (NaCl). Each of its atoms is charged and the salt molecule is held together by a *covalent bond* between them: Na^+Cl^-. When a salt molecule dissolves in water, the polar water molecules pull its sodium and chlorine apart. Na^+ then attaches to the O^- of a water molecule and Cl^- attaches to H^+. The diagram illustrates the process. When the water freezes, however, its molecules bind together, the H^+ of one molecule linking to the O^- of its neighbor. This leaves no room for the Na^+ and Cl^-. They are detached from the water molecules and join together.

Ice therefore consists of freshwater. When sea ice forms, the water adjacent to the ice carries the salt that was "squeezed out" as the water froze. Adding more salt increases the density of the liquid water.

Water at the edge of the ice is denser than water farther away because its temperature is just above freezing and because it contains more salt. In the Norwegian Sea, this water sinks all the way to the ocean floor and flows south. Arctic bottom water (ABW) forms in the same way between Greenland and Norway. This dense water fills the basins of the Greenland and Norwegian Seas and spills through narrow channels in the submarine ridge that lies between Greenland, Iceland, and Scotland. It is then known as the North Atlantic Deep Water (NADW) and continues down the western side of the North Atlantic. Because it is driven by changes in the temperature and salinity of the water, this flow of water is often called the thermohaline circulation (THC).

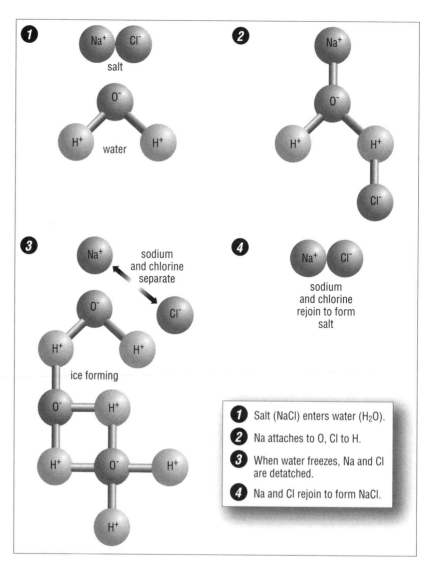

What happens when salt water freezes. 1. Salt (NaCl) enters water (H₂O). 2. Na attaches to O. Cl to H. 3. When water freezes. Na and Cl are detached. 4. Na and Cl rejoin to form NaCl.

The Great Conveyor

The NADW crosses the equator and continues down through the South Atlantic until it joins the West Wind Drift. This carries it toward the east. The NADW rises at intervals and mixes with the colder water of the West Wind Drift. These upwellings warm the air significantly between latitudes 60° S and 75° S.

Dense, very salt water also sinks near the edges of the ice shelves in the Ross and Weddell Seas. It forms the Antarctic Bottom Water (AABW), which merges with the NADW.

Part of the bottom water breaks away to flow northward into the center of the Indian Ocean, where it describes a loop that reverses its direction, so it is then flowing westward. The remainder of the current continues flowing eastward, then turns northward into the South-Pacific, wending its way among the islands and crossing the equator.

When it is approximately level with Japan, the bottom water rises to the surface. The ocean becomes shallower in that region of the Pacific, especially on the eastern (North American) side, and the strong westerly winds that blow around the Aleutian low—the semipermanent area of low pressure centered on the Aleutian Islands at about 50° N—carry away surface water. These factors combine to bring the deep water to the surface.

The water has now become a surface current, driven by the wind and carrying cold water southward, parallel to the western coast of North America. This is the California Current. Once it is in the latitude of Central America the current turns to flow westward. It is then known as the North Equatorial Current. Driven by the trade winds, the water absorbs heat as it flows through the northern tropic. When it reaches Indonesia, part of the current turns northward. It passes Japan as the warm Kuroshio Current, then heads eastward as the North Pacific Current, then turns south to rejoin the North Equatorial Current. Some of the water from the North Equatorial Current turns to the south near Asia, then flows eastward, close to the equator, as the Equatorial Countercurrent, and some spills through the Indonesian islands into the Indian Ocean.

The South Equatorial Current flows from east to west in the South Pacific, some of its warm water flowing south as the Agulhas Current parallel to the coast of Africa. The North Equatorial Current flowing across the North Atlantic becomes the warm Caribbean Current as it crosses the Caribbean. This is joined by the Antilles Current, a branch of the North Equatorial Current that washes the shores of the Great Antilles. As it approaches the Central American coast, the Caribbean Current turns to flow clockwise around the Gulf of Mexico and along the coast of Florida. It passes around the southern tip of Florida, then flows northward parallel to the coast. From the tip of Florida to Cape Hatteras, North Carolina, it is known as the Florida Current. Deflected by the Coriolis effect (see the sidebar "The Coriolis effect" on page 16), it then moves away from the North American coast to cross the Atlantic Ocean. The current is then known as the Gulf Stream.

The main part of the Gulf Stream turns southward in the middle of the ocean at the latitude of Spain and Portugal. It is then called the Canary (or Canaries) Current, which rejoins the North Equatorial Current. After this section breaks away, the remainder of the Gulf Stream continues in a northeasterly direction. It divides again in the latitude of northern Newfoundland and Great Britain. One branch, known as the North Atlantic Drift or North Atlantic Current, passes close to the west coast of Britain and then northern Norway, where it is known as the Norwegian (or Norway) Current. The other branch carries warm water toward Greenland (Kalaallit Nunaat). It meets and merges with the East Greenland Current which carries cold water southward, then flows around the tip of Greenland, up the western coast, and back into the Arctic Ocean.

The Atlantic Conveyor carries cold water away from the Arctic, gathers more cold water near Antarctica, and, after it has surfaced in the North Pacific and traveled through the Tropics, carries warm water into high latitudes. It exerts a major influence on climates.

When the Atlantic Conveyor flows very strongly, as it did between 1870 and 1899, and from 1943 to 1967, the number of Atlantic hurricanes increases, rainfall increases along the southern edge of the Sahara, El Niño events become less frequent (see the sidebar "El Niño" on page 19), and average temperatures decrease all over the world. In the periods 1900–42 and 1968–93 the Atlantic Conveyor flowed fairly weakly. There were more El Niño events, fewer hurricanes, less rainfall along the edge of the Sahara, and warmer temperatures.

Ocean gyres and boundary currents

Ocean currents are like rivers that flow through the water around them. They are quite distinct. "Kuroshio" means "black water" and the Kuroshio Current is clearly visible as a stream less than 50 miles (80 km) wide moving at up to 7 MPH (11 km/h).

When an ocean current moves toward or away from the equator, the Coriolis effect influences its direction. Currents start to turn as they approach continents. The Coriolis effect intensifies as currents move farther from the equator. This makes them turn more, until they are flowing across the ocean. This brings the currents close to the continent on the opposite side. They are deflected again, this time toward the equator, so that eventually they follow an approximately circular path, called a *gyre*. There is a gyre in each of the major oceans. They turn clockwise in the Northern Hemisphere and counterclockwise in the Southern Hemisphere.

Gyres also affect the climate by transporting heat away from the equator. They pass close to the continents on either side of each ocean as *boundary currents*. Boundary currents on the western side of the ocean carry

Why the Arctic is warmer than the Antarctic

Vostok is the name of a Russian research station in Antarctica, located at about 78.75° S. Qaanaaq is a small town in northern Greenland (Kalaallit Nunaat), at 76.55° N. The maps show their locations.

They are in similar latitudes, but they have very different climates. At Vostok, January is the warmest month, when the average temperature is −26°F (−32°C). The coldest month is August, with an average temperature of −90°F (−68°C). At Qaanaaq, the average temperature ranges from a high of 46°F (8°C) in July to a low of −21°F (−29°C) in February.

(continues)

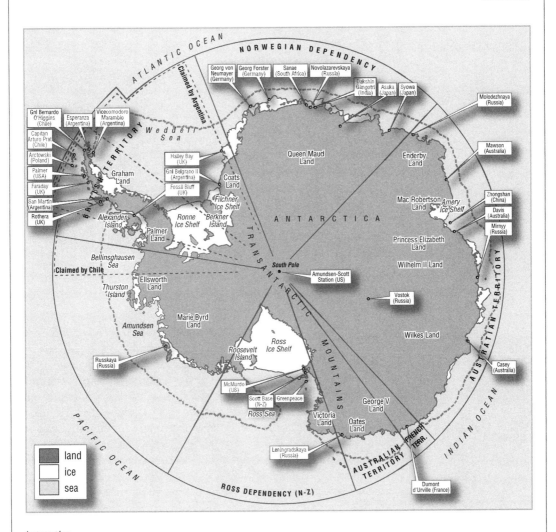

Antarctica

(continued)

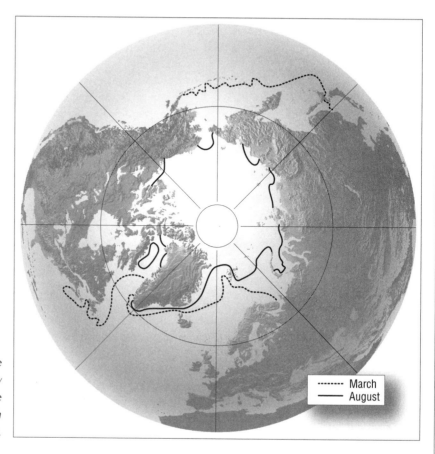

--------	March
———	August

Arctic Basin. The broken lines show the edges of the sea ice in March and August.

warm water away from the equator in both hemispheres. The magnitude of the Coriolis effect increases with distance from the equator. Combined with the increased force of the wind driving the currents as they enter the belt of middle-latitude westerlies and the friction between the currents and the adjacent water, the strengthening of the Coriolis effect makes western boundary currents narrow and fast-moving. This effect is known as *western intensification*. The Gulf Stream, for example, is about 50 miles (80 km) wide and flows at about 1.3–2.2 MPH (2.1–3.5 km/h), transporting about 1,942 million cubic feet of water per second (55×10^6 $m^3 s^{-1}$).

Eastern boundary currents flow toward the equator. They move out of the influence of the westerly winds, the Coriolis effect decreases with increasing distance from the pole, and friction with the adjacent water decreases as the current slow. This makes the currents broad and slow-moving. The Canary Current is 600 miles (1,000 km) wide and flows at

Both places are dry, despite all the snow and ice. Qaanaaq has an annual rainfall (it falls as snow in winter, of course, but is converted to the equivalent amount of rainfall) of 2.5 inches (64 mm). Vostok has 0.2 inch (4.5 mm).

The temperature range is similar for both: 64°F (36°C) at Vostok and 67°F (37°C) at Qaanaaq. The difference is that Vostok is much colder than Qaanaaq. This is because Qaanaaq is on the coast, albeit the coast of an ocean that is frozen over for much of the year, while Vostok is in the interior of a large continent. The North Pole is located in the Arctic Ocean, and the Arctic Basin is sea surrounded by Eurasia, North America, and Greenland (Kalaallit Nunaat).

A large ice sheet covers East Antarctica, where Vostok is located. Air subsiding into the permanent Antarctic high-pressure region flows outward as a bitterly cold, extremely dry wind that blows almost incessantly. This combined with its elevation—Vostok is 13,000 feet (3,950 m) above sea level, on top of the thick ice—is what gives Vostok its cold, dry climate.

The continent also receives 7 percent less solar radiation than the Arctic does, because in the middle of winter (June) the South Pole is 3 million miles (4.8 million km) farther from the Sun than the North Pole is in the middle of its winter (December).

Qaanaaq is at sea level, but that is not the principal reason for its warmer climate. It is warmer because of the sea. Ocean currents carry warm water into the Arctic Basin. The sea is frozen for most of the year, but there are gaps in the ice—called *leads*—that appear and disappear. Winds move the ice, piling it up in some places and leaving it thin in others. Heat escapes from the ocean where there are open water surfaces, but ice insulates the areas it covers. The sea temperature never falls below 29°F (−1.6°C); below this temperature the water approaches its greatest density and sinks below warmer water that flows in at the surface to replace it. When the air temperature over the water falls below the temperature of the sea surface, heat passes from the water to the air. This warmer air then moves across the ice. Consequently, air temperatures over the entire Arctic Basin are much higher than they would be if there were land rather than sea beneath the ice. The coldest temperature recorded over the ice in the Arctic is −58°F (−50°C), and over most of the Arctic Basin the average temperature ranges between about 4°F (−20°C) and −40°F (−40°C). On July 21, 1983, the temperature at Vostok fell to −128.6°F (−89.2°C).

about 0.22–0.67 MPH (0.35–1.08 km/h), carrying 565 million cubic feet of water per second (16×10^6 m^3 s^{-1}).

Air that crosses a boundary current is affected by the contact. If it is a western boundary current, the air becomes warmer and gathers more moisture. If it is an eastern boundary current, the air cools and some of its moisture condenses to form cloud or fog. The frequent fogs of San Francisco are due to the condensation of moisture in warm Pacific air that crosses the nearby California Current. Western boundary currents produce less effect in middle latitudes, because there the weather systems usually travel from west to east, so they move from land to sea on the eastern sides of the continents.

EVAPORATION AND CONDENSATION AND HOW THEY PRODUCE OUR WEATHER

Weather consists mainly of water, or the lack of it. Water moves into the air from the oceans and from the surface of lakes, rivers, and wet ground. It falls from the air as precipitation—rain, drizzle, sleet, snow, hail, fog, frost, and dew. Its constant movement between the surface of the land and sea and the atmosphere constitutes the *hydrologic cycle*. The diagram illustrates this.

A staggering amount of water is involved. Each year, approximately 89 million billion (89×10^{15}) gallons (336×10^{15} liters) evaporate from the ocean surface and 17×10^{15} gallons (64×10^{15} liters) evaporate from the land surface or from plants (transpiration). About 79×10^{15} gallons (300×10^{15} liters) fall as precipitation over the oceans and 26×10^{15} gallons (100×10^{15} liters) over land. About 9.5×10^{15} gallons (36×10^{15} liters) flow from the land back to the sea.

This is a very large quantity of water, but it amounts to only a small proportion of the total amount of water on Earth. The oceans hold 97 percent of all the water on the planet. Of the remaining 3 percent, more than half is frozen and held in the polar icecaps and glaciers and about 0.5 percent is held in the ground, but either bound firmly to mineral particles or located so deep below the surface as to be beyond our reach. The moisture in the air and clouds, together with the water or ice falling at any given time as precipitation and the water flowing through rivers and streams, in ground water, and stored in lakes, amounts to about 4 billion billion (4×10^{18}) gallons (15×10^{18} liters). That is approximately 0.005 percent of the total.

Despite sometimes feeling so wet, in fact the air contains very little water. Over a desert, the very dry air often contains almost no water vapor, and even in the wettest places, such as the humid Tropics, it seldom accounts for more than about 4 percent of the air by volume. Knowing the amount of water that is moving through the cycle at any particular time and its location in the cycle makes it possible to calculate the length of time an individual water molecule spends in each part of the cycle. It remains in the ocean for about 4,000 years. Once it falls onto land, the molecule spends around 400 years at or close to the land surface. It spends a much shorter time traveling between sea and land, however. A water molecule remains in the atmosphere for an average of only 10 days.

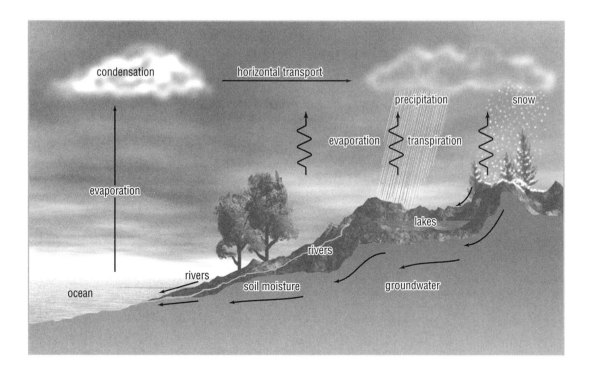

The water molecule and the hydrogen bond

Movement requires energy and it is the Sun that supplies the energy for the movement of water from the ocean to the land—the hydrologic cycle. Once the water is moving, particular physical properties of air and water interact to produce our weather.

A water molecule comprises one atom of oxygen and two of hydrogen (H_2O). The three atoms share electrons. That is what binds them together, but it does so in such a way that lines drawn from the two hydrogen atoms to the center of the oxygen atom meet at an angle of 104.5°. Both of the hydrogen atoms are on the same side of the oxygen atom, and their electrons—a hydrogen atom has only one electron—are on the side adjacent to the oxygen atom. Electrons carry negative electromagnetic charge and protons carry positive charge. This arrangement of the atoms makes the water molecule *polar*: although the molecule carries no charge overall, there is a positive charge on the hydrogen side, from the proton that is the hydrogen nucleus, and a negative charge on the oxygen side, where the two hydrogen electrons are held.

In liquid water, the hydrogens (H^+) of one molecule link to the oxygens (O^-) of neighboring molecules by the attraction of opposite charges.

The hydrologic cycle. Water evaporates from the ocean and surface water on land and enters the air by transpiration from plants. It is transported horizontally by air movements, either as atmospheric moisture or, after condensation, as clouds. It falls as precipitation, and precipitation falling on land returns to the oceans through rivers and groundwater.

The resulting links are called *hydrogen bonds*. Liquid water consists of short strings of molecules held together by hydrogen bonds. They are constantly moving, at speeds that increase as the temperature of the water rises. Their bonds are constantly breaking and reforming, and the groups are able to slide past one another freely so that the overall mass of them has no shape or structure. Liquid water will fill every corner of any vessel it is poured into. Indeed, this is a defining characteristic of any liquid.

Breaking the bond: evaporation

A molecule in a mass of liquid water is pulled by the molecules around it, but it is pulled equally strongly from every direction. If it is at the surface of a body of liquid, however, it is pulled from the sides and from below, but not from above, so it is not quite so securely held. If it can acquire a little more energy, the molecule will move faster and faster until the hydrogen bonds linking it to its neighbors break and the molecule is free to enter the air.

It then enters the layer of air immediately above the surface. This *boundary layer* contains water molecules that left the liquid earlier. There is a limit to the number of water molecules the layer can hold, and if the arrival of more takes the total above the limit—the water vapor in the layer is then said to be *saturated*—some molecules will return to the water. Although, strictly speaking, it is the water vapor that is saturated, we usually think of saturation in terms of the air holding the water vapor and talk of the air being saturated.

If a water molecule enters air that is cooler than the water surface it escaped from, it loses energy and as soon as it approaches another water molecule a hydrogen bond forms between them. That is why the molecule returns to the body of water. If the air above the water is dry, however, the water molecule can remain. Air is dry either because it contains very few water molecules, in which case they rarely approach each other closely enough to form groups linked by hydrogen bonds, or because it is warm, in which case the molecules are moving too rapidly for hydrogen bonds to form. When the air above a water surface is dry, water molecules will pass through the layer immediately above the water surface, enter the air beyond that layer, and disperse. The amount of water vapor in the air will increase and the amount of liquid water will decrease. This is evaporation.

Specific heat capacity

When any substance absorbs heat, its temperature rises. The amount of heat that must be absorbed to produce a one-degree rise in temperature varies from one substance to another. It is known as the *specific heat capac-*

ity of the substance, usually denoted by the symbol *c*, and is measured as the units of heat that must be absorbed for a one-degree increase in temperature. The scientific units are joules per gram per kelvin and are written as J g^{-1} K^{-1}. Alternatively, the units can be given as calories per gram per degree Celsius (1°C = 1K), written as cal g^{-1} °C^{-1}.

Specific heat capacity also varies slightly with temperature. When quoting values for *c*, therefore, it is necessary either to show them as a table, with values at a range of temperatures, or to specify the temperature to which the given value applies. The table below shows the specific heat capacities of several substances at specified temperatures, using both sets of units.

The table shows that water has the highest specific heat capacity of any common substance. One gram of fresh water at 59°F (15°C) must absorb 1 cal (4.19 J) of heat in order to raise its temperature by 1.8°F (1°C) and one gram of seawater at 62.6°F (17°C) must absorb 0.94 cal (3.93 J). This is almost twice as much heat as ice must absorb and approximately five times as much as most rocks must absorb. Consequently, the land, made from rock and sand, heats much faster than the sea during the day and during the summer. That is why, on a hot day, the sand may burn your feet as you run across it, but when you plunge into the lake or sea, the water feels cool. In winter the reverse happens, and the lake or sea remains warmer than the land for several months, because it takes a long time for the water to lose the warmth it absorbed in summer.

Water's capacity for absorbing a large amount of heat without raising its temperature is one of its most important properties, and it greatly affects climates. Air that passes across the ocean will be warmed by contact with it in winter and cooled in summer. Maritime climates, found in lands adjacent to the ocean, have a narrower temperature range than continental climates.

SPECIFIC HEAT CAPACITIES (c) OF COMMON SUBSTANCES

Substance	Temperature		c	
	°C	°F	J g^{-1} K^{-1}	cal g^{-1} °C^{-1}
freshwater	15	59	4.19	1.00
seawater	17	62.6	3.93	0.94
ice	−21−−1	−5.8–30.2	2.0–2.1	0.48–0.50
dry air	20	68	1.006	0.2403
basalt	20–100	68–212	0.84–1.00	0.20–0.24
granite	20–100	68–212	0.80–0.84	0.19–0.20
white marble	18	64.4	0.88–0.92	0.21–0.22
quartz	0	32	0.73	0.17
sand	20–100	68–212	0.84	0.20

Latent heat and adiabatic cooling and warming

Water also absorbs heat when it evaporates. This heat supplies the energy needed to break the hydrogen bonds that hold molecules together. Because it is used to break the hydrogen bonds between individual molecules, this heat does not raise the temperature of the liquid water. It is known as *latent heat*, because it appears to be hidden (see the sidebar "Latent heat and dew point" below).

Heat energy that is absorbed when water evaporates is released when the hydrogen bonds form once again and the water vapor condenses into liquid. Water vapor condenses when it (or the air containing it) becomes satu-

Latent heat and dew point

Water can exist in three different states, or phases: as gas (water vapor), liquid (water), or solid (ice). In the gaseous phase, molecules are free to move in all directions. In the liquid phase, molecules join together in short "strings." In the solid phase, molecules form a closed structure with a space at the center. As water cools, its molecules move closer together and the liquid becomes denser. Pure water at sea-level pressure reaches its densest state at 39°F (4°C). If the temperature falls lower than this the molecules start forming ice crystals. Because these have a space at the center, ice is less dense than water and, weight for weight, has a greater volume. That is why water expands when it freezes and why ice floats on the surface of water.

Molecules bond to one another by the attraction of opposite charges and energy must be supplied to break those bonds. The molecules absorb this energy with no resulting change in their temperature, and the same amount of energy is released when the bonds form again. This energy is called *latent heat*. For pure water, 600 calories of energy are absorbed to change one gram (1 g = 0.035 oz.; 600 cal g^{-1} = 2,501 joules per gram; joules are the units scientists use) from liquid to gas (evaporation) at 32°F (0°C).

This is the *latent heat of vaporization*, and the same amount of latent heat is released when water vapor condenses. When water freezes or ice melts, the *latent heat of fusion* is 80 cal g^{-1} (334 J g^{-1}). Sublimation, the direct change from ice to vapor without the water passing through the liquid phase, absorbs 680 cal g^{-1} (2,835 J g^{-1}), equal to the sum of the latent heats of vaporization and fusion. Deposition, the direct change from vapor to ice, releases the same amount of latent heat. The amount of latent heat varies very slightly with temperature, so this should be specified when the value is given. The standard values given here are correct at 32°F (0°C). The diagram illustrates what happens.

Energy to supply the latent heat is taken from the surrounding air or water. When ice melts or water evaporates, the air and water in contact with them are cooled, because energy has been taken from them. That is why it often feels cold during a thaw and why our bodies can cool themselves by sweating and allowing the sweat to evaporate.

When latent heat is released by freezing and condensation, the surroundings are warmed. This process is very important in the formation of storm clouds. Warm air rises, its water vapor condenses,

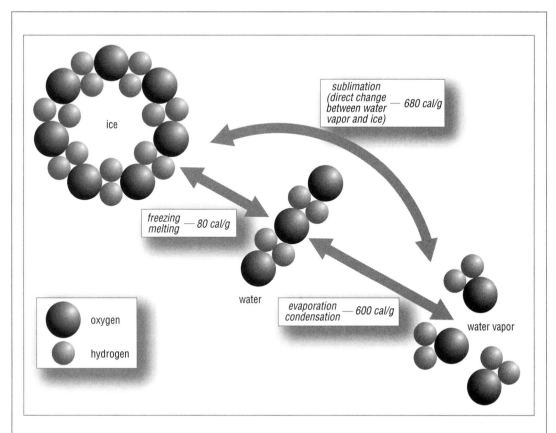

Latent heat. As water changes between the gaseous, liquid, and solid phases, the breakage and formation of the hydrogen bonds linking molecules release or absorb energy as latent heat.

and the release of the latent heat of condensation warms the air still more, making it rise higher.

Warm air is able to hold more water vapor than cool air can, and the amount of water vapor air can hold depends on its temperature. If moist air is cooled, its water vapor will condense into liquid droplets. The temperature at which this occurs is called the *dew point* temperature. It is the tempera-ture at which dew forms on surfaces and evaporates from them.

At the dew point temperature, the air is satu-rated with water vapor. The amount of moisture in the air is usually expressed as its *relative humidity* (RH). This is the amount of water present in the air, expressed as a percentage of the amount needed to saturate the air at that temperature.

rated, and saturation occurs when the air temperature falls below a thresh-old known as the *dew point*. When the temperature decreases, water mole-cules lose energy and move more slowly, and when they meet they remain close to one another long enough for hydrogen bonds to form between them. The *relative humidity* (RH) is the amount of water vapor present in a unit volume of air expressed as the percentage of the amount that is needed to reach saturation *at that temperature.* If the amount of water vapor remains constant, RH decreases as the air warms and increases as it cools.

Air cools if it is made to rise. It will rise by convection if it is heated by contact with a warm surface, or if it is forced to rise over high ground—a process called *orographic lifting*—or by *frontal lifting* if cold air pushes beneath warm air at a weather front and lifts the warm air. Regardless of the surrounding temperature, rising air cools and subsiding air warms. This is called *adiabatic* cooling and warming (see the sidebar "Adiabatic cooling and warming" below). Adiabatic cooling reduces the temperature of rising air, and if the temperature falls below the dew point temperature, water vapor

Adiabatic cooling and warming

Air is compressed by the weight of air above it. Imagine a balloon partly inflated with air and made from some substance that totally insulates the air inside. No matter what the temperature outside the balloon, the temperature of the air inside remains the same.

Imagine the balloon is released into the atmosphere. The air inside is squeezed between the weight of air above it, all the way to the top of the atmosphere, and the denser air below it.

Suppose the air inside the balloon is less dense than the air above it. The balloon will rise. As it rises, the distance to the top of the atmosphere becomes smaller, so there is less air above to weigh down on the air in the balloon. At the same time, as it moves through air that is less dense, it experiences less pressure from below. This causes the air in the balloon to expand.

When air (or any gas) expands, its molecules move farther apart. The amount of air remains the same, but it occupies a bigger volume. As they move apart, the molecules must "push" other molecules out of their way. This uses energy, so as the air expands its molecules lose energy. Because they have less energy they move more slowly.

When a moving molecule strikes something, some of its energy of motion (kinetic energy) is transferred to whatever it strikes, and part of that energy is converted into heat. This raises the temperature of the struck object by an amount related to the number of molecules striking it and their speed.

In expanding air the molecules are moving farther apart, so a smaller number of them strike an object each second. They are also traveling more slowly, so they strike with less force. This means the temperature of the air decreases. As it expands, air cools.

If the air in the balloon is denser than the air below, it will descend. The pressure on it will increase, its volume will decrease, and its molecules will acquire more energy. Its temperature will increase.

This warming and cooling has nothing to do with the temperature of the air surrounding the balloon. It is called *adiabatic* warming and cooling, from the Greek word *adiabatos,* meaning impassable.

Adiabatic cooling and warming. Effect of air pressure on rising and sinking air. Air is compressed by the weight of air above it. A "parcel" or "bubble" of air is squeezed between the weight of air above and the denser air below. As it rises into a region of less dense air, it expands. As it sinks into denser air, it contracts.

will start to condense to form clouds. The height at which this happens is known as the *lifting condensation level*. Condensation releases latent heat, which warms the adjacent air. This can be enough to make the air continue rising, with further condensation leading to towering clouds of the cumulus and cumulonimbus types.

Potential temperature

There is an apparent paradox, however. When a fluid cools, its molecules move closer together, increasing its density. If a rising fluid, such as air, grows colder it must become denser, and it cannot rise above fluid that is less dense. Yet temperature decreases with height throughout the troposphere (see the section "Composition and structure of the atmosphere," on page 1). It seems to follow that air at the top of the troposphere must be

Potential temperature

Cold air is denser than warm air, because its molecules are closer together. Consequently, a given volume of cold air has a greater mass than a similar volume of warm air and it weighs more. Warm air rises because it is less dense than the cold air above it. The cold, dense air sinks beneath the warm, less dense air and pushes it upward.

Air temperature decreases with height. If you climb to the top of a mountain you expect the air to be colder there. High mountaintops are covered in snow, even in summer, and climbers take warm clothes with them. Why is it, then, that the cold, dense air at the top of a mountain, or at the top of the troposphere, does not simply sink to the surface? How does it manage to stay up?

To answer that you must imagine what would happen to the air if it did descend. Suppose, for example, that the air is fairly dry, with no clouds in the sky, and the temperature near ground level is 80°F (27°C). Near the tropopause, 33,000 feet (10 km) above the surface, suppose the air temperature is –65°F (–54°C). The air near the tropopause is dense, because of its temperature, but this really means it is denser than the air immediately above it. Because air is very compressible, its density also decreases with height.

If the high-level air were to subside all the way to ground level, as it descended it would be compressed and it would heat adiabatically (see the sidebar "Adiabatic cooling and warming" on page 34). Because it is dry, the air would warm at the dry adiabatic lapse rate (DALR). The DALR is 5.4°F per 1,000 feet (9.8°C per 1,000 m). As the air descends 33,000 feet (10 km) its temperature will rise by 5.4 × 33 = 178.2°F (98°C). Add this increase to its initial temperature, and its temperature when it reaches the ground will be 178.2 – 65 = 113.2°F (44°C). This is much warmer than the actual ground-level temperature of 80°F (27°C). The air could not reach the ground because it would be less dense, and therefore lighter, than the air below.

The temperature that air at any height above the surface would have if it were subjected to sea-level pressure of 1,000 mb (100 kPa, 29 in. of mercury) and warmed adiabatically as it was compressed is known as its *potential temperature* (usually symbolized by ϕ, which is the Greek letter phi). Potential temperature depends only on the actual pressure and temperature of the air. Meteorologists calculate the potential temperature of air to determine its stability.

denser than the air below it. Why, then, does it not sink to the surface? The solution to this puzzle involves the concept of *potential temperature*—not the actual temperature of the air, but the temperature it would have if it were brought down to sea level and warmed adiabatically during its descent (see the sidebar "Potential temperature" on page 35).

Evaporation and condensation transport water. Without them life on land would be impossible because there could be no precipitation to deliver water. These processes also affect the temperature locally by producing clouds that shade the surface (see the section "How bright is the Earth?" on pages 113–120) and by absorbing and releasing latent heat. The movement of moist air transports heat as well as moisture. Water that evaporated in one place is carried to a cooler region where it condenses, releasing its latent heat. This reduces temperature extremes by cooling warm regions and warming cool regions.

Water or the lack of it produces our weather. It also produces the world's climates, and changes in climate involve changes in moisture—climates become moister or drier, sometimes with dramatic consequences.

CLIMATES OF THE PAST

Revealing the past

Climates are changing constantly, but slowly. Even the present global warming, which many people fear may eventually amount to a significant shift in climate, is measured by the extent to which temperatures might rise over the course of a century. The timescales are longer than a human lifetime. This makes them difficult to comprehend, because the weather we experience today is little different from the weather our grandparents knew, so it is hard to detect any change at all.

If we are to understand them, we need to compare changes that may be occurring now with changes that have taken place in the past. This presents us with a further problem. Written records of the weather are few and far between, and most of them describe conditions in particular places that are widely but unevenly scattered. There are some old weather records for parts of Europe and North America, but many fewer for Africa and Asia, and none at all for the oceans outside the main shipping routes. To make matters worse, records from different places and different times are not based on standardized measurements. Different instruments were used, and readings were taken in different ways and at different times of day, so it is difficult to compare the records from one place with those from another. It is almost impossible to draw conclusions from them about the climates of entire continents, far less that of the whole world.

Inadequate though they are, even these records provide information about only the last few centuries. Accounts of the weather in the 19th or even the 17th centuries may be useful, but accounts earlier than that are very sparse and usually refer only to extraordinary events, such as severe storms or droughts, that are neither typical nor very helpful. Obviously, there are no written records of any kind to tell us what the weather was like or how the climate was changing hundreds of thousands of years ago. Yet we need to know about processes that operate over thousands of years.

We need other, more reliable sources of information. Obtaining it seems impossible, but it is not. *Paleoclimatologists*—scientists who study the climates of ancient, prehistoric times—use *proxy measurements* to reveal details of climate. These are not measurements of temperature or precipitation, but of things that were caused by the weather and from which the weather conditions can be deduced.

Tree rings

Tree rings are probably the best-known source of proxy data. Tree trunks and branches grow thicker each year as well as longer. This thickening is known as *secondary growth* and it takes place just below the outer bark, where new cells are formed. In some tree species the new cells that form in spring are much larger than the cells formed in late summer. When the cells die and turn into the heartwood of the tree, this difference is preserved. The big spring cells can be seen as a pale ring and the late summer cells as a dark ring adjacent to it. One pair of rings represents one year's growth. Not all trees produce rings in this way, though there are often other annual changes that can be used in the same way.

Counting the rings in the trunk is a way of determining the age of the tree. Aging a tree in this way is known as *dendrochronology*. Living trees are dated by removing a narrow core of wood, drilled from the bark to the center of the trunk, and examining it under a microscope. The oldest living trees are bristlecone pines (*Pinus longaeva*, sometimes mistakenly given the name of a related but shorter-lived species, *P. aristata*) that grow in arid regions of California and Nevada, usually at elevations above 7,500 ft. (2,300 m). Several are more than 3,000 years old, and one is believed to be about 4,900 years old. Correlating tree-ring data from living trees with rings from dead trees lying in the same area produces a record going back about 8,200 years.

Most trees do not live so long, of course, but dead tree trunks are sometimes preserved for several centuries, and they can provide information about the climate. Like any plant, a tree grows more or less vigorously depending on the weather, and this affects the annual rings. If the weather is really bad, the tree may not grow at all that year. If it is excellent, the tree will put on a large amount of growth. Tree rings in cores taken from living trees can be counted and compared with recent—and reliable—weather records. This reveals the way tree-ring formation reflects the weather conditions. This information can then be applied to rings taken from trees that have been dead a long time to reveal what the weather was like year by year.

Radiocarbon dating

Tree-ring dating is all very well while the tree is alive, but if the rings come from a dead tree, how can scientists know which years they refer to? The first step in answering that question is to find out when the tree died by means of radiocarbon dating.

Neutrons (particles with no electromagnetic charge) are constantly bombarding the Earth as components of the cosmic radiation that reaches us from space. Some of the neutrons hit nitrogen atoms in the atmosphere. When this happens, the nitrogen nucleus, with seven protons and a relative atomic mass of 14, written as $^{14}_{7}N$, gains a neutron and loses a proton. This transforms it into $^{14}_{6}C$, an unstable form of carbon that decays to $^{12}_{6}C$, the common and stable form, with a half-life—the time required for half of a sample to decay—of 5,730 ± 30 years. The two forms, or *isotopes*, are usually known as ^{14}C or carbon-14 and ^{12}C or carbon-12.

All living organisms absorb both isotopes, so the ratio of $^{14}C:^{12}C$ in their tissues is the same as that in the atmosphere. When an organism dies it ceases to absorb carbon, but its ^{14}C continues to decay to ^{12}C, altering the ratio. Comparing the ratio in the sample with that in the air now makes it possible to calculate the time that has elapsed since the organism died. This technique is known as *radiocarbon dating* and it can be used to date samples up to about 70,000 years old.

The method assumes that the $^{14}C:^{12}C$ ratio has remained the same throughout history, but in fact it is known to have changed. Radiocarbon dates over the last 8,000 years have been corrected by reference to bristlecone pine rings. Measuring the ratio present in bristlecone pines rings, dating the rings by dendrochronology, and then calculating the amount of ^{14}C decay over that time allows scientists to reconstruct the original atmospheric ratio. This provides a means for correcting radiocarbon dates obtained from samples.

Pollen and beetles

Ancient tree trunks are fairly uncommon, but pollen is abundant in many soils, and especially in bogs. Pollen grains remain viable for only a short time—a matter of hours in the case of grasses—but their tough outer coats, called *exines*, resist decay for thousands of years. Exines vary in shape and size and are marked with patterns. These characteristics make them very distinctive. Palynologists—scientists who study pollen grains—can often identify the genus, or even the species in some cases, of the plant that produced the pollen in a sample.

A sample is likely to contain pollen from a number of plant species, so the palynologist can compile a list of the plants that grew in a particular place at a time that can be dated either by radiocarbon or in some other way. Once scientists know what plants were growing they can tell what the environment and climate were like. For example, pines, spruces, firs, birches, and aspens are typical of the forests that stretch across Canada from the Pacific to the Atlantic. If pollen from these trees is found in soil samples collected over a fairly wide area, it suggests the climate was much like the present Canadian climate.

Beetles are also climate indicators. They seem to turn up anywhere and everywhere, but in fact many species are extremely particular about where they live, because they can tolerate only a narrow range of temperatures. Beetles do not live very long, of course, but, like pollen exines, their wing cases, or *elytra*, are made from a tough material that is often preserved in the ground long after their owners have died. The elytra identify the species, and knowing the species often tells the scientist the range of temperatures in that place at the time when the beetle lived there.

Seabed sediment

Information about past climates can also be obtained from the thick layer of sediment that covers the ocean floor. The sediment—scientists call it *ooze*—consists largely of the shells of tiny organisms called *foraminifera* or *forams* for short. These were once living either on the surface of the ooze or in the water immediately above it. The species can be identified from their fossilized shells and, because each species could survive only at a certain water temperature, the presence of particular species is a clear indication of the historical temperature of the water.

Ocean sediments have been accumulating for a very long time. This means that by drilling vertically into the ooze and extracting a core, paleoclimatologists can obtain a record of water temperature going back for hundreds of thousands of years. Sediment accumulates on the ocean floor at a known rate, so the age of a sample taken from a core can be calculated from its distance below the surface.

Ice cores

Cores are also taken from the ice sheets covering Greenland and Antarctica (see the sidebar "Vostok, GISP, and GRIP on page 41). Polar ice sheets are made from compacted snow—the ice is not made by freezing water, the way you make ice cubes. It is never warm enough for snow to melt in either Greenland or Antarctica, so each year's snow lies on top of the snow that fell in previous years. The weight of all that snow compresses the lower layers, packing the snowflakes tightly together. Cores drilled from the ice retain marks, rather like tree rings, that indicate each year's snowfall. They are not so clear or reliable as tree rings, so it is difficult to date samples to the year, but there are approximate dates for ice-core samples up to 200,000 years old.

Ice cores contain dust that fell with the snow. Strong winds raised the dust over the continents and carried it all the way to the ice sheet. Rain would have washed it from the air to the ground before it reached the ice sheet, so the amount of dust present in an ice-core sample is related to the amount of precipitation in higher latitudes at the time when the sample formed. Samples that contain a large amount of dust are made from snow that fell when the world climate was dry. If climates were dry, less water must have been evaporating from the surface and then condensing to form clouds. Less evaporation suggests the climate was colder. So large amounts of dust mean the climate was cold, and if the ice contains little or no dust, the climate was warm and wet.

The ice also contains biological material, such as spores and pollen grains, and volcanic particles and gases. All of these "impurities" in the ice help scientists to compile an overall picture of conditions in the remote past.

Vostok, GISP, and GRIP

Vostok is the name (the word means "east") of a Russian research station in Antarctica, at the geo-magnetic South Pole, 78.46° S, 106.87° E, and at an elevation of 11,401 feet (3,475 m), on the surface of the East Antarctic ice sheet. The station was opened on December 16, 1957. Work began in 1980 on

(continues)

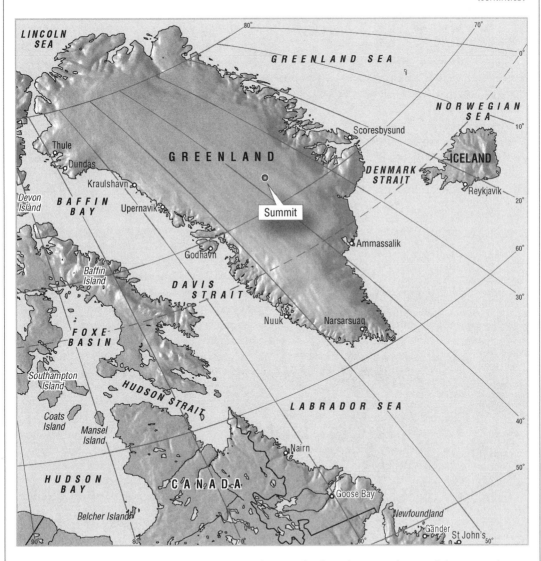

Summit, Greenland. Summit is the highest point on the Greenland ice sheet. It is the site of the GISP and GRIP projects.

(*continued*)

drilling through the ice sheet at a point near the station that is 11,444 feet (3,488 m) above sea level. A core of ice was removed from the borehole. In 1985 drilling reached a depth of 7,225 feet (2,202 m). It was impossible to drill this hole deeper, but drilling of a second hole began in 1984. In 1989, this became a joint Russian-French-U.S. project. In 1990 the hole (and core) reached a final depth of 8,353 feet (2,546 m). A third hole, started in 1990, reached 11,887 feet (3,623 m) in 1998.

The Vostok ice cores contain a record of climate that goes back about 420,000 years. So far, analysis has revealed the record over the last 200,000 years.

The Greenland Ice Sheet Project (GISP) is a U.S. program, sponsored by the National Science Foundation (NSF), to retrieve ice cores from the Greenland ice sheet. The first core reached bedrock at a depth of about 9,843 feet (3,000 m), and in 1988 the NSF Office of Polar Programs authorized the drilling of a second hole, GISP2. This was completed on July 1, 1993, after the drill had penetrated five feet (1.55 m) into the underlying bedrock. The ice core was 10,018.34 feet (3,053.44 m) long. Ice at the base of the core is about 200,000 years old, and analysis of the GISP2 core has yielded a detailed record of climate over more than 110,000 years.

The Greenland Ice Core Project (GRIP) is a European program organized through the European Science Foundation and funded by the European Union and Belgium, Denmark, France, Germany, Iceland, Italy, Switzerland, and the United Kingdom. Drilling began in January 1989, and on August 12, 1992, it reached bedrock at 9,938 feet (3,029 m), where the ice is about 200,000 years old.

GISP2 and GRIP are located close to Summit, the highest point on the Greenland ice sheet (chosen to provide the longest cores), at 72.6° N 38.5° W. The map shows its location.

Freshly fallen snow lies loosely, with many air spaces between snowflakes and grains. When the snow is compacted into ice, some of these air spaces remain as tiny bubbles in the ice. It is possible to extract the air from these bubbles by melting the ice under carefully controlled conditions. Analysis of the air reveals its composition. Climate scientists are especially interested in the amount of carbon dioxide and methane it contains. These are "greenhouse" gases that affect air temperature.

Oxygen isotopes and "heavy" water

Water molecules from ice cores and shells taken from sediments have another story to tell. They contain oxygen of two different types and two different types of hydrogen.

Most chemical elements exist as two or more isotopes. Different isotopes of an element are identical chemically, but they have different atomic masses. Oxygen has three isotopes, two of which are important: ^{16}O and ^{18}O. Seawater contains 99.76 percent $H_2{}^{16}O$ and 0.2 percent $H_2{}^{18}O$. It also contains 0.03 percent HDO; the remainder contains the third oxygen isotope, $H_2^{17}O$. HDO is deuterium oxide or "heavy water," in which a deuterium (D) atom substitutes for one of the hydrogen atoms. The difference is that a hydrogen nucleus consists of a single proton and a deuterium nucleus consists of one proton and one neutron, so it is heavier by the weight of the neutron.

When water evaporates, more $H_2^{16}O$ enters the air than $H_2^{18}O$ or HDO, because both of these molecules are heavier than $H_2^{16}O$. A high rate of evaporation therefore depletes seawater of $H_2^{16}O$. Being heavier, cloud drops of $H_2^{18}O$ and HDO fall as precipitation sooner than drops of $H_2^{16}O$. Most rain and snow soon melt and the water returns to the ocean, but snow that falls onto the polar ice sheets remains there. Consequently, if the polar ice lasts for a very long time, the oceans become steadily more depleted of $H_2^{16}O$. When the ice melts, its accumulated $H_2^{16}O$ returns to the oceans and the original balance is restored.

Ice obtained from ice cores reveals the proportions of $H_2^{16}O$, $H_2^{18}O$, and HDO present in the water. This tells scientists more than simply whether or not the ice sheets were extensive at a particular time. The rate of seawater evaporation depends on the air temperature. When the temperature is high, more $H_2^{18}O$ and HDO evaporate. If these molecules become more abundant in the ice, it means the weather was warm in middle latitudes, which is where most of the water in polar ice caps originates. If $H_2^{16}O$ becomes more abundant, it means conditions were cooler in middle latitudes.

Carbonate from the seabed

The shells making up most of the ooze on the ocean floor also record changes in oxygen isotopes, though not of changes in the amount of HDO in water. They are made from calcium carbonate ($CaCO_3$). The carbonate is present in the water as bicarbonate (HCO_3), formed when atmospheric carbon dioxide (CO_2) dissolves to form carbonic acid ($CO_2 + H_2O \rightarrow H_2CO_3$) and the carbonic acid (H_2CO_3) then dissociates ($H_2CO_3 \rightarrow HCO_3 + H$). One of the oxygen atoms in $CaCO_3$ is derived from the water, and therefore a quantity of $CaCO_3$ will record the ^{16}O:^{18}O ratio in the water at the time the carbonate formed. If the proportion of ^{18}O is high, it means that ice was accumulating around the poles and depleting the water of ^{16}O. A fall in the ^{18}O content indicates that the ice sheets were melting.

By using all the means at their disposal, paleoclimatologists are gradually constructing a history of the world's climate that extends for hundreds of thousands of years into the past. This record makes it easier to compare today's climate with climates of the past and helps the climatologists who are trying to calculate what changes may occur in the future.

CLIMATE CHANGES THAT HAVE CHANGED HISTORY

Radiocarbon dating can be used to determine the age only of organic material—material that contains carbon and was once part of a living organism—and it cannot be used on samples that are more than about 40,000 years old. This is because 40,000 years is equal to about seven half-lives of ^{14}C. After seven half-lives, the sample contains less than 1 percent of the original ^{14}C. It is impossible to measure such a small amount precisely enough to provide a date and, even if that were possible, no one knows whether so long ago the atmosphere held the same proportions of ^{12}C and ^{14}C as it does today, so the date would be very unreliable.

There are other ways to date ancient materials by the decay of radioactive elements, however. These are used to determine the age of materials that are many millions of years old, and because they measure substances that occur naturally in rocks they are not limited to samples from once-living organisms.

Radiometric dating

All *radiometric dating* methods work in the same way as radiocarbon dating, by measuring the proportions of a radioactive element and the stable element into which it decays. One of the two isotopes of rubidium (^{87}Rb) decays to an isotope of strontium (^{87}Sr) with a half-life of 48 billion years (10 times the age of the solar system). Radioactive potassium (^{40}K) decays to argon (^{40}Ar) with a half-life of 1.277 billion years. The most widely used dating methods, however, are based on the decay of uranium (U) and thorium (Th).

Uranium has several isotopes, of which the most important are ^{235}U and ^{238}U. The most stable isotope of thorium is ^{232}Th. All of these decay to different isotopes of lead (Pb), but at different rates: ^{235}U decays to ^{207}Pb with a half-life of 0.704 billion years; ^{238}U decays to ^{206}Pb with a half-life of 4.468 billion years; and ^{232}Th decays to ^{208}Pb with a half-life of 14.05 billion years. There is another isotope of lead, ^{204}Pb, that is not the end product of radioactive decay. Any ^{204}Pb present on Earth was there when the Earth first formed. Scientists measure the proportions of each of the lead isotopes present in a sample, as well as the amounts of thorium and the uranium isotopes, and use these measurements to calculate the age of the sample.

Reading stalagmites

Victor Polyak and Yemane Asmerom, scientists at the University of New Mexico, used uranium-thorium dating to determine the age of the bands in stalagmites taken from caves in the Carlsbad Caverns National Park and Hidden Cave in the Guadalupe Mountains National Park, both in southwestern New Mexico. What they found was a clear link between changes in the local climate and the way of life of the people living there at the time. They found evidence of climate changes that had changed the course of history.

Water that falls as rain and then percolates through the soil is naturally slightly acid because of the carbon dioxide that dissolves in it to form carbonic acid (H_2CO_3). If the underlying rock is limestone, the acid may dissolve it away. Gradually the flow of water washes out enough rock to form a cave below ground. If the water table falls below the level of the cave floor, the cave will dry out, but water may continue to drip from the ceiling. This water contains dissolved minerals. As it evaporates into the dry air inside the cave, some of the minerals are left behind as deposits growing from the ceiling. They grow like icicles hanging downward. These are *stalactites*. Some of the water trickling down a stalactite drips to the floor of the cave and evaporates there. This leaves a mineral deposit that grows upward from the floor, as a conical mound called a *stalagmite*.

Stalagmites are fed by water dripping onto them. If the amount of water feeding them varies from time to time, that variation will be preserved as identifiable bands in the stalagmites—a thick band representing a rainy period and a thin band representing a dry period. Dr. Polyak and Professor Asmerom dated the bands in the stalagmites they studied and used the thickness of the bands—representing their rate of growth—to determine whether the weather was wet or dry in each year. In this way they compiled a year-by-year history of the climate of that part of New Mexico over the past 4,000 years.

They found that the climate became wetter around 4,000 years ago. Until about 3,000 years ago it was as wet as the present climate, or possibly somewhat wetter. Then it became wetter still and remained wetter than today's climate until around 800 years ago. After that the weather grew drier.

The Anasazi

The ancestors of the modern Pueblo peoples of New Mexico and Arizona moved into the Carlsbad Caverns region around 2000 B.C.E. Between that time and 1000 B.C.E. they changed from being nomads who obtained their food by gathering wild plants and hunting game and began establishing permanent settlements and cultivating crops. They made high-quality baskets, pottery, ornaments, and tools, and they wove fine cloth. We know them by the name Anasazi, a Navajo word that means "Ancient Ones" or "Enemy Ancestors."

At first the Anasazi lived below ground, in "pithouses" that they excavated. They started building above ground around 750 C.E. That is when the stalagmite evidence shows the climate becoming wetter—did the pithouses flood now and then?—and the archaeological evidence shows that their population increased. They grew corn and cotton. Cultivation of corn began around 1000 B.C.E., during a period when the climate was wet. It became drier between 300 C.E. and 700 C.E. That is when they started growing cotton and making pottery. During the 13th century the climate grew much drier and the stalagmites ceased growing. That is when many of the Anasazi settlements were abandoned and their inhabitants moved away in the tens of thousands to northeastern Arizona, western New Mexico, and along the watershed of the Rio Grande.

The 13th-century drought is also recorded in tree rings, and scientists knew about it long before Polyak and Asmerom produced their stalagmite record. There is doubt, though, that the drought would have been sufficient in itself to cause such a major change. Historical events seldom have single, simple causes, and many archaeologists believe the drought struck the Anasazi at a time of great cultural upheaval and possibly even a civil war.

Whatever the truth about the end of the Anasazi culture may be, it is not the only example of a major cultural change that has been associated with a climatic change. Western civilization may have arisen in this way.

The domestication of animals and plants

Around 12,000 years ago the most recent ice age was drawing to a close (see the section "Ice ages of the past—and future?" on pages 61–69). The global climate was growing warmer and the great ice sheets and mountain glaciers were retreating. In the Zagros Mountains, where modern Iran, Iraq, Syria, and Turkey meet, people had lived until then in caves and hunted wild game, mainly sheep and goats. At about that time sheep became the more important source of their food and there is archaeological evidence that they were starting to keep flocks of them; sheep were being domesticated. The map on page 47 shows the location of the

Zagros Mountains and the Taurus and Anti-Taurus Mountains of Turkey. Shading indicates the mountains and the map shows the position of some modern cities.

As the climate continued to grow warmer and the glaciers in the Zagros Mountains retreated to higher elevations, plant life advanced to higher levels. The newcomers included grasses that produce edible seeds—the ancestors of modern wheat and barley. People moved out of their caves and took to living in permanent dwellings in the foothills.

To the west and south of the mountains, on the plain lying between the rivers Tigris to the north and Euphrates in the south in modern Iraq, people began cultivating wheat and barley, and as well as sheep they tended goats and pigs and kept dogs. Agriculture had commenced. This region is approximately crescent-shaped and it is sometimes called the Fertile Crescent. It is also known by its Greek name, Mesopotamia, from *mesos*, meaning "middle," and *potamos*, meaning "river"—the land "between the rivers."

Temperature and rainfall continued to rise gradually, and between about 5000 B.C.E. and 3000 B.C.E. the climate in Europe was up to 3.6°F (2°C) warmer than it is now. Cultivation spread to the Nile valley and to the Indus valley in northwestern India. Then the global temperature fell and climates became drier in Arabia, Afghanistan, Egypt, and central Asia. There was less pasture for game and fewer plants to gather for food. Farming is hard work, but it guaranteed the food supply in the great river valleys where there was still enough water flowing down from the mountains to sustain the crops and livestock. People moved into the valleys and had to be accommodated. Cities were built and some scientists have suggested

The Zagros and Taurus Mountains and the Fertile Crescent

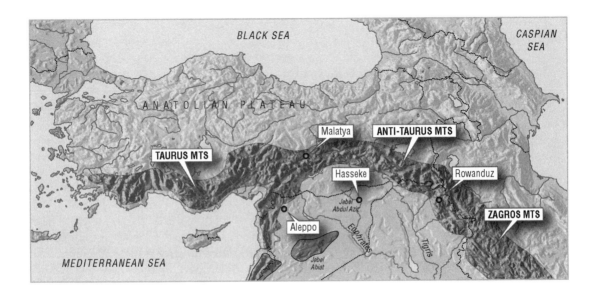

that these desert refugees became the slaves on whom the great civilizations depended for labor.

Whether or not that is what happened, there seems little doubt that the first great cities were built at a time when the climate was becoming cooler and drier. Depressions that move generally from west to east and bring rain to middle latitudes shifted to a more northerly track. This was a climatic change, and in responding to it the Mesopotamians and Egyptians built the cities and invented the urban way of life that are the foundations of modern western civilization.

Indus Valley civilization

Climate change can bring an end to civilizations, as well as triggering their birth. The most spectacular example of this is found in the Indus Valley, in Pakistan. From about 2500 B.C.E. until about 1700 B.C.E. a civilization flourished there. People grew wheat, barley, peas, sesame, dates, melons, and possibly cotton. Traces of cotton that were found there by archaeologists are the earliest known from anywhere in the world. There were elephants, rhinoceroses, cattle, and water buffalo. The elephant probably was domesticated and its ivory was used. People had dogs and cats, perhaps as house pets, and they may have had pigs, camels, horses, and asses.

The Indus Valley civilization was centered on two cities, Mohenjo-daro in the south and Harappa in the north, together with more than 100 towns and villages. Mohenjo-daro and Harappa were large cities, each covering an area of approximately one square mile (2.59 km^2) and about three miles (4.8 km) in circumference. The map shows their approximate locations. At its peak the Indus Valley, or Harappan, civilization covered an area greater than Mesopotamia and the Nile valley combined. Its influence extended from close to Delhi almost to the Arabian Sea 300 miles (480 km) west of Karachi and to Ludhiana in the northeast. Trade was extensive. Gold, silver, copper, lapis lazuli, and turquoise were imported.

After about 1900 B.C.E., however, urban life began to break down, gradually at first but rapidly from around 1700 B.C.E. The climate was becoming drier, but with occasional monsoon downpours that flooded Mohenjo-daro several times. Around 1500 B.C.E. Mohenjo-daro was destroyed by invading Aryan people. They settled in the Indus Valley but remained close to the rivers. Eventually they also left. There was still some water there as late as 330–323 B.C.E., when Alexander the Great crossed the region, but the lands that once raised sufficient crops to feed that vast civilization are today part of the arid, inhospitable Thar Desert.

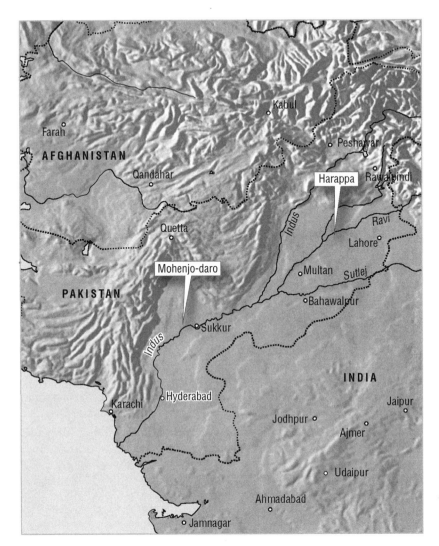

Mohenjo-daro and Harappa, cradles of the Indus Valley civilization

Out of the steppes of Central Asia

Central Asia is a vast region of grasslands called *steppe*. Traditionally, its inhabitants were nomadic pastoralists, driving their herds and flocks from one seasonal pasture to another. Many Mongolians still live a seminomadic life. Drought is a common occurrence in the dry climate. It makes farming unreliable, but only occasionally does it seriously injure the nomads.

Droughts in Central and Western Asia around 300 C.E. forced people known as the Hunni, or Huns, out of their homelands. They moved westward in search of food and water, but when they reached the River Danube they encountered the Roman Empire. Skilled horsemen and fierce and fearless warriors, they fought the Romans and established an empire of their own in southeastern and central Europe. Their most famous emperor was Attila (died 453)—often called Attila the Hun and known in his own day as the Scourge of God. From 434 until his death, Attila ruled the area from the Alps and Baltic to the Caspian. He died in his sleep and the empire was divided among his many sons, after which it ceased to be politically important. Drought drove another Mongolian invasion in 800.

The Mongol Empire

In the 13th century the Mongolians eventually established what may have been the biggest empire the world has ever seen. The story began during a prolonged period when the climate was moist. Traces of earlier shorelines show that sea level in the Caspian Sea was much higher then than it is now, and that it was rising. The steppe pastures grew dense and rich under the increased rainfall and warmer weather associated with it. The people flourished and the population increased, but around 1200 there was a fairly sudden change. It seems likely that the Central Asian climate came to be dominated by weather systems that drew cold, dry air southward from the Arctic. China had been suffering from cold, dry weather for some time, and this climate may have continued to spread westward until it brought the Little Ice Age (see the section "The Little Ice Age," on pages 87–93) to western Europe.

As the climate became drier and the pastures sparser, the tribes were crowded into smaller areas and their leaders fought for supremacy. In 1206 one of the tribal warlords was elected to rule a group of Mongols whose tribes had been so devastated by war that their members were effectively tribeless. His name was Temujin. We know him as Genghis Khan (c. 1167–1227). A brilliant administrator as well as military strategist, he was able to organize the demoralized peoples into a formidable group. They defeated the rival Tatar people, who lived to the south of Lake Baikal, and then he drew the remaining tribes into a federation.

Together, they began expanding the territory they controlled. They captured Beijing in 1215, and by the time Genghis died their empire stretched from the Caspian to the China Seas. Further campaigns added more territory. They occupied the steppe grasslands of southern Russia, where they formed an empire within the empire, known as the Golden Horde, and by 1300 the Mongol Empire extended westward to the Danube and from Lithuania to the Himalayas. Kublai Khan (1215–94), grandson of Genghis, was one of the greatest of all emperors of China, and another descendant of Genghis, Babur (Zahir ud-Din Mohammed, 1483–1530), conquered India and became its first Mogul emperor. It was not until the 18th century that the final remnants of the Mongol Empire disappeared.

Khmer Empire

Southern Asia also felt the effect of a climate change that pushed climatic zones southward. This change established a semipermanent area of high pressure (an anticyclone) over Thailand, Cambodia, Laos, and Vietnam. The climate became drier, and this may have helped the emergence of a civilization in what had been dense tropical forest. Khmer is the name of the Cambodian people and their language. The Khmer civilization reached its peak around 1200 C.E. After 1300 the climate became wetter again and the region reverted to forest.

The empire was founded in the sixth century, became divided in the eighth century, and was reunited by King Jayavarman II early in the ninth century. His successor, King Yasovarman I, established the capital at Angkor between 889 and 900. Suryavarman II built the temple complex at Angkor Wat, although it was not completed until after his death in about 1150. King Jayavarman VII built the temple at Angkor Thom in about 1200. Dedicated to Vishnu, Angkor Wat is the largest collection of religious buildings in the world. In 1992 the United Nations Educational, Scientific and Cultural Organization (UNESCO) designated Angkor a World Heritage site and added it to the List of World Heritage in Danger.

The Khmer Empire was based on a highly productive agricultural system, growing rice on irrigated land, and a well-organized bureaucracy. It was not peaceful, however. There were repeated wars with neighboring peoples and in 1177 the Cham people from Vietnam sacked Angkor. The Khmer Empire declined after around 1350. In 1434 the capital was transferred to Phnom Penh and the returning forest slowly engulfed Angkor.

While there can be no doubt that many major historical events have been influenced by climate, it is a mistake to think they were wholly determined by them. "Climatic determinism" is the over-simple idea that climate and changes in it can provide a complete explanation for the rise and fall of empires. History is much more complex than that. Events happen because of many factors, of which climatic change is sometimes one.

Nevertheless, in those cases where climate was a factor, it is also a mistake to omit or ignore it. Would the Anasazi people have abandoned their homes and dispersed if drought had not repeatedly destroyed their crops? Would cities have been built in Mesopotamia had it not been for an influx of population from adjoining regions that were turning into deserts? Would Genghis Khan have led the Mongol invasions of Europe if deteriorating pastures had not provided the opportunity for him to unite the previously warring tribes and the necessity of finding food for them? We cannot know, but it seems unlikely. When the climate changes dramatically, people have no choice but to respond, and those responses occasionally alter the course of history.

MILUTIN MILANKOVITCH AND HIS ASTRONOMICAL CYCLES

Milutin Milankovitch was born on May 28, 1879, in the village of Dalj, on the Croatian side of the border between Croatia and Serbia, near the Croatian town of Osijek. At that time Serbia was an independent nation and Croatia was part of Austria-Hungary. He studied at the Vienna Institute of Technology and in 1904 he was awarded a doctorate in technical science. Dr. Milankovitch worked for a time as the chief engineer for a construction company, but in 1909 he accepted an offer to teach applied mathematics at the University of Belgrade. He remained in this post for the rest of his life, except for the period from 1914 until 1918, when he was a prisoner of war, captured while serving in the Serbian army. His captivity was very civilized. The Austro-Hungarian authorities allowed him to continue his researches in the library of the Hungarian Academy of Science in Budapest. Milankovitch died in 1958.

Mathematicians specialize, and Milankovitch was especially interested in the way that the amount of solar radiation striking the surface of the Earth varies with the seasons and the latitude. We experience seasons because the Earth's axis of rotation is tilted (see the section "General circulation of the atmosphere" on pages 10–17) and the amount of solar radiation we receive varies through the year, because the Earth's orbit is not quite circular. It describes an ellipse. An ellipse is a geometric figure that has two foci; a circle has only one focus, at its center. If an orbiting body follows an elliptical path, it orbits about one of these foci, neither of which lies at the center of the ellipse. Consequently, the body is closer to the focus during one part of its orbit and farther away during another part. In the diagram illustrating this, F_1 and F_2 are the two foci and C is the geometric center of the figure.

Eccentricity

A circle may be big or small, but it is always a circle. Ellipses, on the other hand, vary in shape as well as size—they are more elliptical or less so. When the ellipse represents the path of an orbiting body, the extent to which the ellipse is stretched is known as the *eccentricity* of the orbit.

Eccentricity can be measured. The two foci and the center of an ellipse all lie along the major axis—the longest straight line that will fit inside the ellipse. Suppose, in the drawing, that the body is orbiting focus

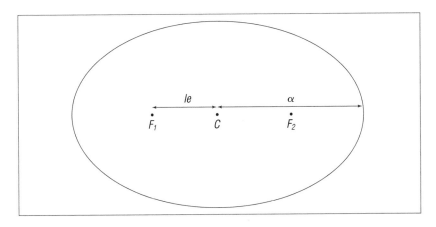

Eccentricity

F_1. The distance from F_1 to the center (C) is called the *linear eccentricity*, denoted by *le*. F_1 lies at the center of one half of the major axis. The length of this line is symbolized by α (the Greek letter alpha). Eccentricity (e) is then given by: $e = le/\alpha$. This must always be less than 1, because α is invariably larger than *le*. If the orbit is perfectly circular, so that F_1 lies at C, *le* will equal zero and $e = 0$. At present the eccentricity of Earth's orbit is 0.017, which is almost circular.

Earth reaches *perihelion*—the point in its orbit when it is closest to the Sun—in January and *aphelion*—the point farthest from the Sun—in July. This means that the Sun shines more intensely on the Earth in January than it does in July, but the difference is very small. With an eccentricity of 0.017, the distance between Earth and the Sun is only 3 percent greater at aphelion than it is at perihelion. This is the difference between approximately 95,687,000 miles (153,960,000 km) and 90,113,000 miles (144,991,000 km). It means we receive 7 percent more sunshine in January than we do in July. This hardly seems sufficient to affect global climate, although it means winters in the Northern Hemisphere are milder and summers in the Southern Hemisphere warmer than they would be if the orbit were perfectly circular.

Over a period of about 100,000 years, however, the eccentricity of the Earth's orbit changes from 0.001 to 0.054 and back again. When the eccentricity is almost circular (0.001) there will be almost no difference in the intensity of solar radiation falling on the Earth as a whole through the year, but an eccentricity of 0.054 is enough to make a significant climatic difference.

Planetary orbits are highly predictable. The gravitational fields of other bodies affect them, but these can be calculated. The mathematics is complicated, but Milankovitch was a mathematician, and he worked out the way the eccentricity of the orbit had changed over several hundred thousand years.

Obliquity

The rotational axis of the Earth is tilted from the vertical, but the angle of tilt—called the *obliquity*—also varies. This affects the way sunlight strikes the Earth. At present, the angle between the rotational axis and the plane of the ecliptic is about 23.45°, but over a period of about 42,000 years the obliquity changes from 22.1° to 24.5° and back again.

Changing obliquity. The greater the obliquity, the greater the intensity of solar radiation over polar regions.

The change is significant because it is the Earth's obliquity that produces our seasons in the first place. If the rotational axis were perpendicular to the plane of the ecliptic (obliquity = 0°) there would be no seasons. As the diagram shows, increasing the obliquity has the effect of increasing

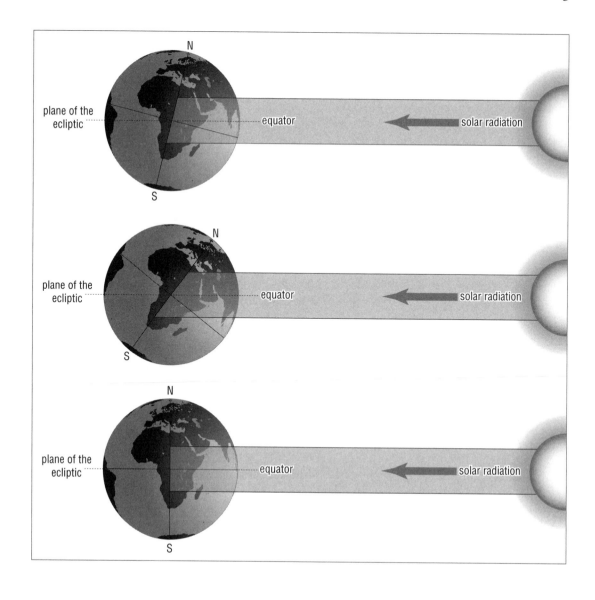

the amount of solar radiation falling over high latitudes in summer. Consequently, summers are warmer, but winters are cooler. In other words, the seasons become more extreme. Milankovitch also studied the cycle of changing obliquity and its effects.

The axial wobble

There is a third, more subtle cycle that takes place over about 25,800 years. It concerns the way the Earth's rotational axis wobbles. This is not the same thing as the way its obliquity changes—the two motions are at right angles to each other.

Earth behaves like a spinning top, and a spinning top has certain properties. As long as it maintains a high enough angular velocity, or rotational speed, and it experiences no outside force, the top is stable. It will remain upright, spinning on its pointed end. If something nudges it, however, the top will begin to wobble. If you imagine its rotational axis extended upward from the top, this will mark out a cone.

This is a property of gyroscopes, and the top is a gyroscope. You can see the effect more clearly with a toy gyroscope. It happens because the mass of the spinning gyroscope or top is concentrated around the edge, or equator. Earth also has more mass around its equator, so it is not quite spherical. The bulge is due to the gravitational attraction of the Moon and Sun and it means that the Earth behaves like a gyroscope.

Gyroscopes experience *precession*. This means that if a force is applied to a gyroscope, the gyroscope will move not in the direction of the applied force, but at right angles to it in the direction of rotation. Gravitational forces exerted by the Moon and Sun—the same forces that produce the tides—act at right angles to the rotational axis and the Earth responds like a gyroscope. It moves at right angles to the applied force and this makes it wobble like a top.

Hipparchus and the precession of the equinoxes

The axial wobble was another effect Milankovitch studied, but he was not the first person to notice it. That person was the Greek astronomer and mathematician Hipparchus (c. 190 B.C.E.–c. 120 B.C.E.). Hipparchus was the greatest of all Greek astronomers, and some of the discoveries he made and the deductions he made from them are still important today—the axial wobble is one of them. He also calculated the length of the year as 365.25 days, diminishing by 0.003 day each year, and the lunar period as 29 days, 12 hours, 44 minutes, and 2.5 seconds—which is one second too short.

Hipparchus was born in Nicaea, now called Iznik, in northwestern Turkey, and he established his observatory on the island of Rhodes, in the southeastern Aegean Sea. His research centered on measuring the size and distance of the Sun and Moon. In order to achieve this he was obliged to study the rotation and orbit of the Earth.

At the equinoxes the Sun rises exactly in the east and sets exactly in the west. There were no reliable clocks in the time of Hipparchus, so astronomers could not determine when day and night were of equal length, but they could identify the points of the compass and so they could recognize the equinoxes and use them as a basis for the calendar.

As the Sun crosses the horizon at dawn on the equinox its position marks the point where the ecliptic—the path of the Earth's orbit—intersects the *celestial equator*. Imagine a line drawn from the center of the Earth to the Earth's geographic equator and then extended to the very edge of the visible universe. Then turn the Earth so that the end of this line describes a circle around the "inside edge" of the universe. That line is the celestial equator and the sphere it encloses is the *celestial sphere*.

Astronomers measure the position of the Sun when it intersects the celestial equator by reference to the stars. Their positions remain constant—they are sometimes known as the "fixed stars"—and the Sun's position can be referred to the patterns of stars known as *constellations*. Unfortunately, this presents a difficulty: in daytime the stars are invisible. Hipparchus solved the problem by waiting for a lunar eclipse, when the stars are visible and the position of the Sun is known. A lunar eclipse happens when the Moon, Earth, and Sun are in a straight line, with Earth in the middle. Earth's shadow then falls on the Moon, and therefore the center of the shadow—in fact the center of the Moon's disk, which remains visible because some sunlight is refracted by the Earth's atmosphere—is at a point on the celestial sphere directly opposite the position of the Sun.

In about 130 B.C.E. Hipparchus measured the intersection at the equinox and compared his results with old records made by earlier astronomers. He concluded that over a period of 169 years the intersection had moved by two degrees. He called this the *precession of the equinoxes*.

In Hipparchus's day, at the spring equinox the Sun intersected the celestial equator in the constellation of Aries. By the time of Christ intersection occurred in Pisces. Today it is moving into the constellation of Aquarius. In other words, Earth's orbital position at the equinoxes is changing. Each year Earth is a little to the west of the position it occupied the previous year. This is the effect of precession. Hipparchus calculated the rate of precession as 45 or 46 seconds of arc a year. In fact, the rate is 50.26 seconds per year, so Hipparchus was very nearly correct.

Precession has another effect. Nowadays, we can find north on a clear night in the Northern Hemisphere by locating Polaris, the North Star or Pole Star, which stands vertically above the North Pole. Changes in obliquity mean that this has not always worked in the past and will not always work in the future, because the Earth's axis does not always point to Polaris. Around 3000 B.C.E., for example, the axis pointed to the star Thuban in the constellation of Draco, so that was the Pole Star. Hipparchus was unable to use this method of finding north, however, because in his lifetime there was no star directly above the North Pole.

The significance of precession

Our ordinary, everyday calendar is based on a year that is measured from equinox to equinox and solstice to solstice. This is called the *tropical year* and it contains an average of 365.242 *solar days*. A solar day is the time the Earth takes to complete one rotation. Its average length is 86,400 seconds (= 24 hours). Measure the year from one perihelion to the next, however, and the length is slightly different: 365.259 mean solar days. This is about 25.13 minutes longer. It means that the equinoxes return more quickly than do successive perihelia. The difference is one solar day every 57.3 years. This is the precession of the equinoxes.

Why should it matter? At present, Earth is at perihelion in January and at aphelion in July. This timing moderates temperatures, warming the Northern Hemisphere in its winter and cooling the Southern Hemisphere in its summer. As the dates of the equinoxes return faster than Earth's arrival at perihelion and aphelion, however, this effect changes. Ten thousand years from now the dates will be the reverse of those of today. Earth will then be at perihelion in July and at aphelion in January. This timing will cool the Northern Hemisphere in its winter and warm the Southern Hemisphere in its summer. The seasonal temperatures will be more extreme than they are now.

When the cycles coincide

Each of these three cycles—of eccentricity, axial tilt, and "axial wobble" or precession of the equinoxes—has a very small effect by itself. (The diagram illustrates all three.) What would happen, however, if all three cycles were to coincide? Suppose that when the precession of the equinoxes places Earth farthest from the Sun during the Northern Hemisphere winter, the Earth's orbit is also at its greatest obliquity, so that the distance between Earth and the Sun is at a maximum. The two effects would reinforce each other, bringing very cold winters to the Northern Hemisphere. Suppose that the axial tilt was also at a maximum at this time. In midwinter, the Northern Hemisphere would be tilted farther away from

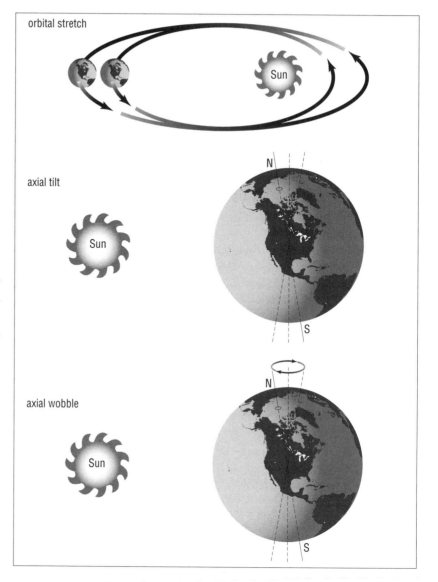

The three Milankovitch cycles. Three cyclical variations in the orbit and rotation of the Earth that trigger the onset and ending of glaciations. Orbital stretch is a change in the eccentricity of the Earth's orbit. Axial tilt is the variation in the angle at which the north-south axis of the Earth is tilted with respect to the vertical. Axial wobble is the way the Earth's axis slowly turns around the vertical.

the Sun than it is now. This would reduce still further the amount of solar radiation it received.

This concentration on what happens in the Northern Hemisphere is relevant to the climatic consequences. There is much more land in the Northern Hemisphere than there is in the Southern Hemisphere. Its lower specific heat capacity means that in winter land loses heat much faster than the ocean does (see the explanation of specific heat capacity on pages 30–31). If land receives less solar radiation in winter, before the winter ends it will have cooled to a lower temperature than the ocean would have done under similar circumstances.

The Milankovitch cycles

Milankovitch calculated the timing of each of these cycles over hundreds of thousands of years—they are known today as the *Milankovitch cycles*—and worked out when they coincided. This allowed him to calculate the changes in the amount of solar radiation reaching the Earth—more precisely, the radiation falling in summer from latitude 5°N to 75°N—and he represented this fluctuation as a curve on a graph. He found there were nine occasions when the time of the Earth's minimum exposure to solar radiation coincided with dates for the onset of ice ages that had been calculated by the German mineralogist Albrecht Penck (1858–1945). Milankovitch published his conclusions in 1920.

Adhemar and Croll

Milankovitch was not the first person to wonder whether the onset and ending of ice ages might be linked to astronomical cycles. In *Les Revolutions de la Mer* (1842) the French mathematician Alphonse Joseph Adhemar (1797–1862) observed that because of the eccentricity of the Earth's orbit and the obliquity of its axis, Antarctica received about 170 fewer hours of solar radiation each year than the Arctic. That, he proposed, is why it is the colder pole (he was wrong; see the sidebar "Why the Arctic is warmer than the Antarctic" on pages 25–26). Adhemar also calculated that changes in the obliquity of the axis might be linked to the onset of an ice age every 26,000 years.

His calculations aroused little interest, but the idea of a link between astronomy and climate persisted, and in 1864 James Croll (1821–90) published another interpretation. Croll, a self-educated Scottish climatologist and geologist, argued that the onset of ice ages is triggered by the coincidence of maximum eccentricity and the precession of the equinoxes. He worked at the Edinburgh office of the Geological Survey of Scotland and developed his climatological theory in his spare time, but after he retired he was able to devote much more time to it. In 1885 he published his last book on the subject, *Discussions on Climate and Cosmology.*

Like most scientists, Milankovitch was building on the work of those who had gone before. His arguments and calculations were very persuasive and his conclusions convincing—up to a point. The trouble was that the magnitude of the change in solar radiation the Earth receives varies by such a small amount that it seemed impossible it could have any great climatic effect. So climate scientists remained skeptical for a long time and the popularity of the Milankovitch theory has varied.

It received support in 1976, when studies of the oxygen isotope ratios in sediment cores taken from the seabed (see the section "Revealing the past" on page 37) showed that climate changes had occurred when the theory said they should. In 1999 another study of sediment cores confirmed this, finding that climate changes occurred over a cycle of 100,000 years with a longer cycle, of 413,000 years, superimposed on it.

Unfortunately, these discoveries do not quite prove that Milankovitch was correct. According to his theory, the effect of the 100,000-year cycle should appear only indirectly, as an influence that modulates the cycle of the precession of the equinoxes. Nor has anyone explained how such a small astronomical cause can produce such a large climatic consequence as an ice age, although scientists now suspect that changes triggered by the Milankovitch cycles may affect living organisms. By altering the size of plant and microbial populations, the cycles might alter the amount of carbon dioxide in the atmosphere. Changing the amount of carbon dioxide would then amplify the astronomical effect through the greenhouse effect. So the debate continues, but despite remaining doubts among some scientists, most paleoclimatologists now accept that the link between the Milankovitch cycles and climate change is real.

Milankovitch on Mars

The cycles that Milankovitch proposed are much more clearly evident on Mars than on Earth. This is because Mars is closer to the outer giant planets and has no large moon. Consequently, its orbital eccentricity varies from 0.00 (circular orbit) to 0.13—more than twice that of Earth—over the course of 95,000–99,000 years. Obliquity changes even more dramatically, from about 13° to 47°, over 120,000 years. The Martian equinoxes also precess, returning to an initial position over a period of about 51,000 years. These cycles coincide with major climate changes on Mars, measured as the rate at which ice forms and vaporizes around the Martian North Pole.

Milutin Milankovitch devoted his entire professional life to elucidating this link between the Earth's rotation and orbit and major climate changes. It was a formidable task—performed before there were even pocket calculators, far less computers, to help with the math! His theory could not be confirmed in his own lifetime, and even now we cannot say that it is proven beyond all possible doubt. Nevertheless, there is a considerable body of evidence to support it and scientists are beginning to understand how the link works. It shows that the climates of Earth and Mars change for entirely natural reasons due to forces outside the planets themselves.

ICE AGES OF THE PAST— AND FUTURE?

The 18th and 19th centuries were a time when scientists were busy classifying things. People nowadays are sometimes rather contemptuous of this activity. They call it "stamp collecting" and do not consider it "proper" science, because, in their view, simply naming and arranging things does little to explain the processes that were involved in their formation. This dismissiveness is unfortunate and misguided. We need names and systems of classification to bring order to the world around us. Without that order, studying natural phenomena is almost impossible.

Zoologists and botanists were classifying plants and geologists were classifying rocks. It was not long before they discovered that dotted over much of northern Europe, Asia, and North America there are deposits of gravel and large boulders that are quite unlike the surrounding and underlying rocks. These were called *erratics*. They were similar to rocks that were found hundreds of miles away, and at first no one could imagine what forces could have carried them so far.

Early in the 19th century, some scientists began suggesting that glaciers might have transported the erratics. This was a radical idea. There is no doubt that a glacier consists of enough ice to push a boulder or shovel gravel ahead of itself, but where were these glaciers? There were none anywhere near the erratics. Nevertheless, boulders and gravel are found at the base and to the sides of many glaciers; these deposits are called *moraines*. So the idea was attractive, even though it implied that the glaciers had once extended much farther than they do now and that glaciers flow, like very slow-moving rivers.

Louis Agassiz and the Great Ice Age

The debate was at its height when one of the most talented scientists of his generation turned his attention to it. Louis Agassiz (see the sidebar "Louis Agassiz and the Great Ice Age" on page 62) had already made a reputation based on his studies of fossil fish. In *Recherches sur les poissons fossiles* (Studies of fossil fishes) he classified more than 1,700 species.

Agassiz was born in Switzerland of French parents and was very familiar with Swiss glaciers. He was also in search of attractive places to

Louis Agassiz and the Great Ice Age

Jean-Louis-Rodolphe Agassiz (1807–73) was born at Motier, Switzerland. He attended schools at Bienne, near Bern, and Lausanne, and he studied at the universities of Zürich, Heidelberg, Munich, and Erlangen. He specialized in the classification of fishes, and in 1831 he moved to Paris where he continued his studies, classifying fossil fishes at the Natural History Museum. He was then appointed professor of natural history at the University of Neuchâtel, Switzerland.

In 1836 he turned his attention to the study of glaciers. Boulders made from rocks quite different from the underlying bedrock lay scattered on the plain of eastern France and in the Jura Mountains, on the border between France and Switzerland. Some geologists thought these boulders, called *erratics*, might have been pushed into their present positions by glaciers. If this idea was correct, it meant glaciers must flow like rivers and that at some time in the past they must have extended much farther than they do now. In 1836 and 1837 Agassiz and some friends observed grooves and scouring in rocks on either side of the Aar Glacier, in Switzerland, that might have been made by rocks dragged across them by movements of the glacier ice. In 1839 they found that a hut built 12 years earlier at a known position on the glacier had moved about one mile (1.6 km) and they drove a straight line of stakes into the ice across the glacier. When they returned in 1841 they found the line was U-shaped, indicating that ice at the center of the glacier had moved more than the ice at the sides.

Agassiz concluded that a great sheet of ice, similar to the Greenland ice sheet, had covered all of Switzerland and those parts of Europe where erratics were found in the geologically recent past—that is to say, within the last few million years. He published his conclusions in his book *Études sur les glaciers* (Studies of glaciers, 1840).

In 1846 Agassiz visited the United States to continue his studies and also to deliver a series of lectures. He remained in the United States and was appointed professor of zoology at Harvard University in 1848. He became an American citizen, and in 1915 he was elected to the Hall of Fame for Great Americans.

Agassiz found that North America had also been covered by ice. This discovery showed there had been a time when most of both Europe and North America had lain beneath vast ice sheets. He called this period the *Great Ice Age*.

spend his vacations, so in 1836 and 1837 he spent his summer vacations with a group of friends on the Aar Glacier, where he proved that glaciers flow.

Later he visited other parts of Europe, including Scotland, where he found further evidence of past glacial action. His observations over the next few years convinced him that glaciers had once extended over all those parts of Europe where erratics were found. He published his findings in 1840. They attracted a great deal of interest and in 1846 King Friedrich Wilhelm IV of Prussia awarded him a grant to visit the United States. There, Agassiz found similar evidence of past glaciation and concluded that a vast ice sheet had once covered a large part of North America and northern Europe. He called this time the *Great Ice Age*.

Glacials, interglacials, and geologic time

As well as classifying rocks, geologists were also dividing the history of the Earth into episodes they called *eras*, *periods*, and *epochs*. The table "Geologic Time Scale" below lists the present divisions of geologic time—the history of the Earth—with the approximate dates when they began.

The Great Ice Age occurred recently, so the period of time that encompassed it was called the "most new" epoch, but using the Greek words *pleistos* (most) and *kainos* (new) to make the word *Pleistocene*. The Great Ice Age has ended, however, so the time since then required a different name. It is called the "entirely new," or *Holocene* epoch—*holos* means

GEOLOGIC TIME SCALE

Eon	Era	Sub-era	Period	Epoch	Start (Ma)*
Phanerozoic	Cenozoic	Quaternary	Pleistogene	Holocene	0.01
				Pleistocene	1.64
		Tertiary	Neogene	Pliocene	5.2
				Miocene	23.3
			Paleogene	Oligocene	35.4
				Eocene	56.5
				Paleocene	65
	Mesozoic		Cretaceous		145.6
			Jurassic		208
			Triassic		245
	Paleozoic	Upper Paleozoic	Permian		290
			Carboniferous		362.5
			Devonian		408.5
		Lower Paleozoic	Silurian		439
			Ordovician		510
			Cambrian		570
Proterozoic					2,500
Archean					4,000
Priscoan					4,600

*Ma means millions of years ago.

(The Proterozoic, Archean, and Priscoan eons are sometimes known informally as the precambrian.)

"whole" or "entire." The Holocene is also known as the *Recent* and the *post-glacial* epoch. As the ice sheets retreated at the end of the ice age, melting ice caused sea levels to rise. Evidence of this rise was first found in the late 19th century along the coasts of New England and Belgium. The rise was called the *Flandrian transgression* and when the Holocene is studied as an *interglacial* episode it is often known as the *Flandrian*, a name that is mainly used in Europe. So the time in which we are now living can be called the Holocene, Recent, post-glacial, or Flandrian.

An interglacial is a time of warmer climates that falls between two glacials, or ice ages. Louis Agassiz was correct in his interpretation of the erratic rocks. They were pushed to their present locations by glaciers. He was mistaken, however, in supposing there was a single ice age. The truth was even more dramatic. For about the last 3 million years, ice ages have been occurring at intervals of approximately 100,000 years and lasting from 50,000 years to 250,000 years. They began in the Pliocene epoch, before the commencement of the Pleistocene, and there have been at least seven; some scientists suggest there were 20. Between these glacial periods

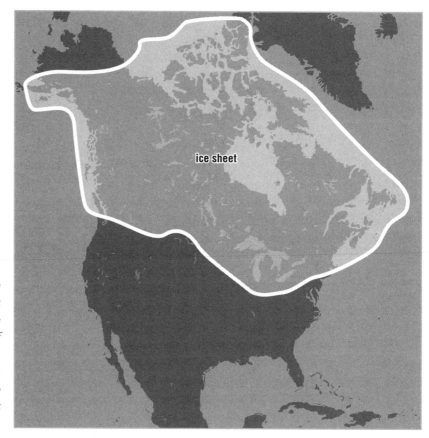

Laurentide ice sheet. The line shows the boundaries of the Laurentide ice sheet at the time of the last glacial maximum. about 20.000 years ago. The sea was frozen to the north and northeast of the ice sheet.

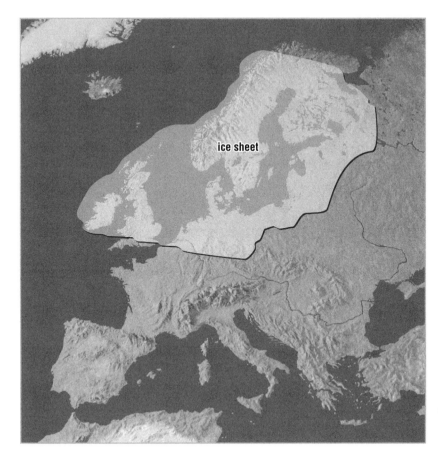

ice sheet

Fennoscandian ice sheet. The ice sheet that covered northern Europe from the North Cape to the Dnieper during the last ice age.

there have been warmer interglacials, each of which has lasted between 8,000 and 12,000 years. In other words, the global climate has swung repeatedly between glacial periods, when ice sheets covered a substantial part of the world, and interglacials, when the ice retreated. The maps show the extent of the Laurentide ice sheet over North America and the Fennoscandian ice sheet over Europe around 20,000 years ago during the coldest part—known as the *last glacial maximum*—of the most recent (Wisconsinian) glacial.

Each glacial and interglacial is known from evidence found in North America, Great Britain, Northwest Europe, and also the European Alps, eastern Europe, and Russia. The table "Pleistocene glacials and interglacials" on page 66 lists them, with their approximate dates and their North American, British, and northwest European names. The dates are derived mainly from studies of oxygen isotopes (see the section "Revealing the past" on page 37), but only the more recent ones can be dated by this method. Consequently, with increasing distance in time the dates become less precise.

PLEISTOCENE GLACIALS AND INTERGLACIALS

Approximate date ('000 years BP)	N. America	Great Britain	N.W. Europe
10–present	Holocene	Holocene (Flandrian)	Holocene (Flandrian)
75–10	Wisconsinian	Devensian	Weichselian
120–75	Sangamonian	Ipswichian	Eeemian
170–120	Illinoian	Wolstonian	Saalian
230–170	Yarmouthian	Hoxnian	Holsteinian
480–230	Kansan	Anglian	Elsterian
600–480	Aftonian	Cromerian	Cromerian complex
800–600	Nebraskan	Beestonian	Bavel complex
740–800		Pastonian	
900–800		Pre-Pastonian	Menapian
1,000–900		Bramertonian	Waalian
1,800–1,000		Baventian	Eburonian
1,800		Antian	Tiglian
1,900		Thurnian	
2,000		Ludhamian	
2,300		Pre-Ludhamian	Pretiglian

BP means "before present" (present is taken to be 1950). Names in italic refer to interglacials. Other names refer to glacials (ice ages). Dates become increasingly uncertain for the older glacials and interglacials, and prior to about 2 million years ago evidence for these episodes has not been found in North America; in the case of the Thurnian glacial and Ludhamian interglacial the only evidence is from a borehole at Ludham, in eastern England.

As their investigations continued and geologists became more familiar with the subtle, telltale signs of glacial action on rocks, earlier ice ages were discovered. Those of the Pleistocene are only the most recent. Ice ages were less frequent in earlier times, but several have been identified. The first occurred about 2.5 billion years ago, near the start of the Proterozoic eon. There were several more ice ages starting around 850 million years ago, in the late Proterozoic; one that lasted up to 20–25 million years in the Ordovician period; and another about 300 million years ago around the transition from the Carboniferous to the Permian periods. A more recent ice age began about 100 million years ago, during the Cretaceous period. Antarctica began to be covered in ice about 25 million years ago. The ice expanded around 12 million years ago and that is also when ice first appeared at the North Pole. The Antarctic ice reached its present extent about 5 million years ago, although dwarf trees were still growing in Antarctica as recently as 4 million years ago.

How glaciers begin and move

Glaciers are sometimes described as rivers of ice. This is misleading, because the glaciers associated with ice ages and with the Greenland and Antarctic ice caps are not like rivers, although they flow.

A glacier begins as a fall of winter snow that fails to melt the following summer. This snow is called *firn* and its edge, beyond which the winter snow does melt in summer, is the *firn line*. More snow falls the following winter, to become a new layer of firn, and its weight compresses the snow beneath it until the snow turns into solid ice.

Although it does not melt in summer, some snow and ice are lost. When the Sun shines strongly, ice can vaporize without melting first. This is called *sublimation*. The wind can also remove loose, powdery snow. This type of loss is called *ablation*. If there is a *zone of accumulation*, where the winter snowfall exceeds losses by sublimation and ablation, then a glacier will form.

Obviously, it will form first on high ground, where the temperature is lowest. After years or decades of accumulation, the weight of the glacier will start the ice at the base sliding downhill. The upper layer of ice is solid and brittle, but the pressure from above makes the ice near the base slightly plastic, so it will bend and slide over the underlying rock surface. That is when the glacier begins to flow. As the base of the glacier moves, the brittle surface ice breaks up into sections with deep crevasses between them. The surface of a glacier is extremely rough and uneven—and not in the least like the surface of a river.

The glacier may flow between hills by breaking and grinding away the softer rock to form a U-shaped valley, in which case it is known as a *valley glacier*; or it may spread to cover low-lying ground and become an ice sheet. The glacier ends at a *zone of ablation*, where the annual loss of ice by sublimation, melting, and ablation balance the quantity of ice being pushed forward.

Rocks, gravel, and other material that is pushed forward by the glacier stop moving when they reach the zone of ablation. That is where the debris accumulates to become a moraine— known as a *terminal moraine* if it lies ahead of the tip, or *snout*, of a glacier. Material thrust to the side forms a *lateral moraine*. Geologists and geomorphologists—scientists who study the way landscapes form—use the presence of moraines to determine the extent of glaciers that disappeared long ago.

Snowball Earth

Once ice sheets start to grow they can advance rapidly. The white surface of the snow reflects sunlight and, more importantly, heat from the Sun (see the section "How bright is the Earth?" on pages 113–120). This prevents the land from warming. The next winter, more snow falls and extends the ice-covered area, and low summer temperatures prevent it from melting.

What matters is the cool summer, when the temperature does not rise sufficiently to melt the ice. It makes no difference how cold the winters are.

There is a very controversial theory that on four occasions between 750 million and 580 million years ago the entire Earth was covered by ice. Geologists had known since the 1960s of glacial deposits that were similar to those of the Pleistocene, but Proterozoic in age. These deposits are found on every continent, and it seemed as though there had been a time when there were glaciers at sea level near the equator. In the 1980s, Joe Kirschvink, a scientist at the California Institute of Technology, suggested how this could have happened. He called that frozen world "Snowball Earth."

The geography of the world was different then. A large supercontinent had recently broken apart due to movements of the Earth's crust, so the dry land comprised a number of small continents, where no region was very far from the sea. Rainfall increased over land, and atmospheric carbon dioxide that dissolved in the rain reacted with silicon in the rocks and was washed into the sea. As more and more carbon dioxide was removed from the air in this way its atmospheric concentration fell dramatically. Global temperatures fell due to a reversed greenhouse effect (see the section "Greenhouse gases and the greenhouse effect" on pages 94–104) and large ice packs formed in polar regions. The ice then extended farther south, the white surface reflecting solar radiation and preventing the temperature from rising, until eventually the sea ice reached the equator. Average temperatures over the whole world fell to about –58°F (–50°C) and all of the oceans were frozen to a depth of more than half a mile (800 m).

Once the world was in this condition the climate was highly stable, but beneath the ice the solid Earth remained active. Heat from the interior of the Earth prevented the oceans from freezing completely, and volcanoes continued to erupt, releasing gases, including carbon dioxide. These entered the atmosphere.

The glacial climate was extremely dry. No rain fell, and without rain to dissolve it and bring it down to the surface, the carbon dioxide released by volcanoes gradually accumulated. It continued accumulating for about 10 million years. By that time the concentration reached about 10 percent of the lower atmosphere by volume. This was high enough to trigger a massive greenhouse effect. The atmosphere grew warmer and within a few centuries all the ice had melted.

While the Earth was covered in ice, its surface reflected solar radiation. Now, with the ice melting, the darker surface absorbed solar radiation—the effect that had contributed to the cooling was strongly reversed. Warming continued and the average temperature rose to more than 120°F (50°C).

The extremely high temperature caused large amounts of water to evaporate. It condensed and produced long and intense rainfall, and the rain washed the carbon dioxide from the air to the surface. George Williams, an Australian geologist at the University of Adelaide, found that all over Australia, and later all over the world, the ancient glacial deposits are covered by a layer of *cap dolostones*. Dolostone (mainly magnesium carbonate, $MgCO_3$) is a sedimentary rock formed when the calcium in limestone (calcium carbonate, $CaCO_3$) is replaced by magnesium. These particular dolostones that cap the glacial deposits appear to have formed from limestone that was precipitated over a very short period.

As the prolonged rain reduced the atmospheric concentration of carbon dioxide, the greenhouse effect diminished. Temperatures fell and gradually the climate stabilized.

The "Snowball Earth" hypothesis remains highly controversial. Other scientists maintain that the cap dolostones can be explained in other ways, and some climatologists have pointed out that if the world were ever to freeze over there is no way it could warm up again. Once ice covered all of the oceans the condition would be irreversible. Nevertheless, the scientists who propose the idea point to many lines of evidence they say support it.

Will there be more ice ages?

Snowball Earth, if it existed, ended many millions of years ago. No one suggests that the world could freeze over again to that extent, but most scientists agree that there will be more ice ages.

When Louis Agassiz proposed it, the Great Ice Age was believed to have been a single event that ended once and for all; it was confined to the Pleistocene epoch, and we now live under quite different conditions, in the Holocene. Then, as geologists unraveled more of the Earth's recent history, it became evident that there have been many ice ages. They have not come to an end, and the Holocene is no more than an interglacial.

Our present interglacial has already lasted for about 10,000 years. This is the average duration for an interglacial, so we should expect the next ice age to commence sometime soon—"soon" being within the next few thousand years.

The present eccentricity of Earth's orbit favors an interglacial, however, and the onset of ice ages seems to be linked to the 100,000-year orbital cycle (see the section "Milutin Milankovitch and his astronomical cycles" on pages 52–60). On the other hand, the obliquity of the Earth's axial tilt is decreasing, and the Tropics—the latitude in each hemisphere below which the Sun is directly overhead at noon on one day in the year—are retreating toward the equator at about 0.07 inch (1.7 mm) an hour. This change favors an ice age, as does the present timing of the equinoxes, because Earth presently reaches aphelion in July. A July aphelion depresses summer temperatures over the vast continents of the Northern Hemisphere, restricting the summer melting of snow.

Despite present concerns about a warming of the global climate, the fairly certain long-term prediction is of a return of the ice sheets. No one knows when they will start advancing, but there is likely to be a new ice age within the next few thousand years—and it could begin much sooner than that.

EDWARD WALTER MAUNDER AND THE UNRELIABLE SUN

In 1873 a young man called Edward Walter Maunder (1851–1928) left his job at a London bank and started work at the Royal Observatory, Greenwich, to the east of London. He had no formal qualification as an astronomer, but his new post was as a photographic and spectroscopic assistant. The Royal Observatory was a state institution, and its staff belonged to the civil service, admission to which was by public examination. Maunder passed the examination, so he was accepted into the service and posted to Greenwich.

He was given the task of photographing sunspots, then using the photographs to measure their sizes and plot their positions. Maunder was a keen observer and very meticulous. He calculated that the sunspots must be very large and that distant objects, although visible, must contain much fine detail that is invisible from Earth. He used this insight to suggest that the "canals" that many astronomers claimed to have seen on Mars were an optical illusion—a view that was unpopular at the time, but turned out to be correct. Maunder also suggested that the ancient Assyrian and Egyptian depictions of a winged god of the Sun in fact showed the outermost part of the solar atmosphere, known as the *corona*.

The 11-year sunspot cycle

As he worked away patiently with his examination of sunspots, Maunder found a pattern emerging. In 1843 the German astronomer Samuel Heinrich Schwabe (1789–1875) had discovered that the number of sunspots increases and decreases over a regular 11-year cycle. Maunder found that the solar latitudes in which sunspots emerge change in a regular way over the course of the sunspot cycle. The first ones appear some distance from the solar equator and later ones move gradually closer to the equator (see the sidebar).

Maunder did not spend all of his time photographing the Sun and studying the sunspots. He also searched the old records in the observatory library to discover what had already been learned about the sunspot cycle.

Years ago, the English astronomer William Herschel (1738–1822) had suspected there might be a link between the number of sunspots and the weather. In 1801 he attempted to link the number of sunspots each year to the price of grain. Grain prices rise when the weather is bad and the harvest poor and fall when the harvest is good.

Sunspots

The visible surface of the Sun, called the *photosphere*, is a layer of gas several hundreds of miles thick and with a temperature of about 9,900°F (5,500°C). From time to time, irregular dark patches are visible on the photosphere. These are *sunspots*. They are areas up to 31,070 miles (50,000 km) across where the temperature is about 2,700°F (1,500°C) cooler than their surroundings. Most sunspots have a dark center,

(*continues*)

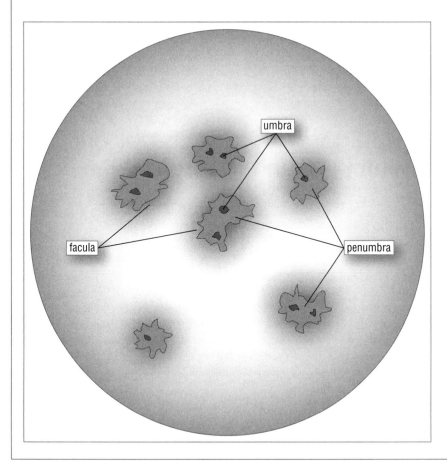

Sunspots

(*continued*)

called the *umbra*, surrounded by a paler *penumbra*. Each sunspot is surrounded by a *facula*. Faculae are very bright regions of the photosphere, where the temperature is higher than it is elsewhere—*facula* means "torch." The illustration shows the appearance of sunspots, although in order to do so clearly it greatly exaggerates their size.

Sunspots usually appear in clusters, each sunspot lasting for about two weeks, and the number of sunspots increases and decreases over a regular 11-year *sunspot cycle*. The cycle begins with a period of several weeks during which no sunspots are visible. Then they start to appear at latitudes 30°–40° in both hemispheres. Over the succeeding five years the sunspots appear and disappear continually, but their number increases steadily and they move closer to the solar equator. At the end of five years the number of sunspots reaches a maximum. After that the number declines over the next six years, but the sunspots continue to move closer to the equator. When they reach about latitude 7° the sunspots fade gradually. Then the cycle resumes, 11 years after the commencement of the preceding cycle.

Sunspots are caused by intense magnetic fields below the solar surface. These suppress the convection currents that carry hot gases to the top of the photosphere. The intensity of the stream of charged particles emitted by the Sun, known as the *solar wind*, is linked to the sunspot cycle. The solar wind intensifies as the number of sunspots increases. The intensity of the solar wind affects the intensity of both the cosmic radiation and ultraviolet radiation reaching the Earth.

The Spörer Minimum, Dalton Minimum, and Maunder Minimum

Then, in 1889, Maunder read an article by another German astronomer, Friedrich Wilhelm Gustav Spörer (1822–95). Spörer was also studying sunspots and he had discovered something very interesting. Astronomers had been observing and recording sunspot activity for centuries, but Spörer found that very few had been observed between approximately 1400 and 1520. This period came to be known as the *Spörer Minimum*. It was a time of very cold weather. People called it a "Little Ice Age." The Baltic Sea froze over completely in the winter of 1422–23. There were famines. Norse colonies in Greenland were abandoned because their crops failed and the sea froze over, preventing them from fishing. The colonists were starving and the survivors had no choice but to return to Scandinavia.

A similar, but less dramatic, "sunspot minimum" was just commencing at the time Maunder was studying the records. The *Dalton Minimum* lasted from about 1795 to 1820 and marked another period of cool weather, during which there was one year, 1813, that came to be known as a year without a summer.

What Maunder discovered, however, was a period lasting from 1645 to 1715 during which not a single sunspot was reported anywhere in the solar Northern Hemisphere and several periods lasting 10 years in which no sunspots were seen at all. Fewer sunspots were seen over the entire 70-year period than are seen now in a single average year. Auroras, or northern lights, were also rare. Nowadays, Scandinavians are treated to a display of them on most nights, yet during this period they were so uncommon that when one did appear people regarded it as an omen. In 1716 an aurora was seen in England and the Astronomer Royal, Edmond Halley (1656–1742), was so impressed he wrote a paper explaining it. It was the first he had ever seen. Auroras are caused by the interaction between particles of the solar wind and the atoms and molecules of atmospheric gases. When there are few sunspots the solar wind is weak and auroras are uncommon. Maunder described this first in an article he wrote in 1890 and again in another article published in 1922.

The *Maunder Minimum*, as it came to be known, was another period of cold weather. In London, the River Thames froze so firmly a fair was held on it. Mountain glaciers advanced. The area covered by sea ice increased. In some winters Iceland was completely surrounded by sea ice. Inuit people in kayaks were seen several times in the Orkney and Shetland Islands, to the north of the Scottish mainland, and on one occasion they turned up in the River Don, near Aberdeen. It was the coldest part of the Little Ice Age (see "The Little Ice Age" on pages 87–93). Maunder tried to persuade other scientists that he had discovered an important link between solar output and climate, but with little success. They thought he was relying too heavily on old records that were very probably inaccurate.

Tree rings and isotopes

We know now that the Maunder Minimum is real. Maunder's data were reliable and a period when there were very few sunspots did indeed coincide with a period of very cold weather. We know he was right because there is other evidence to support him, evidence that was not available in his own day.

The supporting evidence comes from studies of tree rings and ice cores (see "Climates of the Past" on pages 37–43). Tree rings are made from the cells surrounding the trunk that are produced as new growth every year. Their thickness reflects the growing conditions and so the climate can be inferred from the rings produced by a representative sample of trees of a number of species. They provide an indirect, or *proxy*, climate record.

Wood also contains the radioisotope carbon-14 (^{14}C). This is produced in the atmosphere by the bombardment of nitrogen atoms by cosmic radiation particles. Consequently, when the cosmic radiation intensifies more ^{14}C is produced, and the air contains less when cosmic radiation is weak. When, in the 1940s, the American chemist Willard Frank Libby (1908–80) discovered that the rate of radioactive decay of ^{14}C could be used to date biological material it was assumed that the proportion of ^{14}C in the atmosphere is constant. This allowed scientists to compile a "Libby standard" relationship between age and the ratio of ^{14}C to ^{12}C in the sample. It was only later that the standard was found to be incorrect, because its underlying assumption was false. The proportion of ^{14}C in the air is not constant. It changes, because the intensity of the cosmic radiation producing it changes. The dating calibration has now been corrected for this and earlier radiocarbon dates have been amended.

There was an advantage, however, to what might have seemed an embarrassing error. The error was discovered by comparing radiocarbon dates to tree-ring dates obtained from bristlecone pines (*Pinus longaeva*), which provide a continuous record over thousands of years. The comparison revealed variations in the proportion of atmospheric ^{14}C, and this, in turn, allowed scientists to infer the intensity of cosmic radiation.

Ice cores provide another record, because ^{14}C is one of a number of radioisotopes produced by cosmic-ray bombardment. There are also isotopes of nickel (^{59}Ni, with a half-life of 0.1 million years), calcium (^{41}Ca, half-life 0.11 million years), iron (^{60}Fe, half-life 0.3 million years), chlorine (^{36}Cl, half-life 0.31 million years), aluminum (^{26}Al, half-life 1 million years), and beryllium (^{10}Be, half-life 2.7 million years). Beryllium-10 is the isotope most widely used to measure past cosmic-ray intensity. Air containing these isotopes becomes trapped between snow grains, and some of them can be extracted from ice cores.

So the tree-ring climate record, together with written records, confirmed the period of cold weather. The radioisotopes confirmed the reduction in solar output. Together they showed that Maunder had been correct.

Despite the lack of recognition of his discovery, E. Walter Maunder was well known and widely respected for his other achievements. He became director of the Solar Division at the Royal Observatory, a Fellow of the Royal Astronomical Society, and he was editor of the *Journal of the British Astronomical Association*. He and his wife, Annie Scott Dill Russell (1868–1947), whom he met in 1891, when she arrived at the observatory to work as a "lady computer," collaborated in writing many popular articles on astronomy and the Sun.

More recently, many more sunspot minima have been found. The table lists some of them.

The link between sunspot minima and cold climatic episodes seems firmly established, as does the parallel link between sunspot maxima and warm periods. There is an even closer link between temperature and the length of the sunspot cycle. Although the sunspot cycle is usually described as having a period of 11 years, in fact this is an average around which the period varies. In 1890, for example, when the cycle was 11.7 years long, the average global temperature was 0.72°F (0.4°C) lower than usual, and in 1989, when the period was 9.8 years, the temperature was 0.45°F (0.25°C) warmer.

SUNSPOT MINIMA

Name	Dates	Remarks
Damon	1880–1930	Average global temperature 0.9°F (0.5°C) lower.
Dalton	1795–1825	Includes 1813, the "year without a summer."
Maunder	1645–1715	Average global temperature 1.8–3.6°F (1–2°C) lower.
Spörer	1400–1520	Little Ice Age
Wolf	1280–1340 B.C.E.	End of Pueblo and Hohokam American periods.
Greek	330	
Homeric	750	
Egyptian	1370	
Silver Lake	1870	
Noachan	2850	
Sumerian II	3290	
Sumerian I	3570	
Jericho	5190	
Sahelan	5950	

The inconstant Sun

Changes in the number of sunspots are related to the amount of energy being radiated by the Sun. On Earth, the most obvious effect is a reduction in the intensity of incoming radiation. This effect is real, but it is extremely small.

The radiation we receive from the Sun is known as the *solar constant.* This is measured as the amount of energy falling on one square meter perpendicular to the Sun's rays, at the outermost edge of the Earth's atmosphere. It is a minute fraction of the total energy radiated by the Sun. The Sun radiates in all directions, so you can picture its radiation expanding outward as a sphere with the Sun at the center. As the sphere expands, however, its surface becomes "stretched," like a drawing on a balloon when you inflate it, so that the radiation becomes less intense. The rate at which the intensity decreases is proportional to the square of the distance from the source. This is the famous "inverse square law" discovered by Isaac Newton, although he was concerned with gravitational force, not electromagnetic radiation. Earth is an average 93 million miles (149.5 million km) from the Sun, and when the Sun is high in the sky it is only 0.5° wide as seen by an observer on the ground. As the diagram shows, Earth receives only a very small amount of the light and heat of the Sun—never more than 1,367 watts per square meter. This is the solar constant.

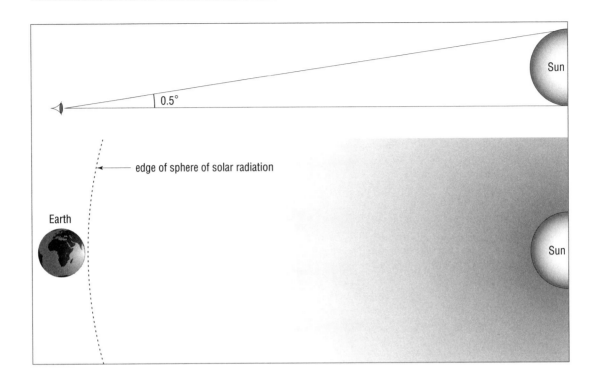

0.5°

Sun

edge of sphere of solar radiation

Earth

Sun

Solar constant. The Sun subtends an angle of 0.5° at the Earth's surface. Solar radiation is emitted in all directions, but the Earth is exposed to only a tiny fraction of the total.

During the course of the sunspot cycle, the solar constant varies by about 0.15 percent, depending on the number and size of the sunspots. The figure of 1,367 W m^{-2} that is usually given for the solar constant is in fact the maximum value. During a sunspot minimum it sometimes falls as low as 1,365 W m^{-2}. This is a very small variation that has no measurable effect on climate, partly because it is so small, but also because the atmosphere responds sluggishly to change. By the time the atmosphere has begun to warm or cool, the sunspot cycle has moved on, reversing the effect.

Long-term changes, of the kind that produced the Maunder Minimum and sunspot maxima, produce a much bigger variation in the solar constant, of 0.2–0.6 percent, and sustain it for a long time. This allows the atmosphere to respond fully.

Sunspots and cloud formation

Even so, it seems unlikely that so small a change, never amounting to as much as 1 percent, could produce such a big effect. The answer is that the climatic effect is not due to direct heating.

Solar astronomers believe that sunspots are magnetic disturbances. They occur in pairs, with magnetic field lines emerging from one sunspot and entering through its partner. The sunspot cycle is due to turbulence in the photosphere as the Sun rotates about the center of gravity of the solar system, a rotation that takes 11.1 years. When sunspots are present the stream of charged particles leaving the Sun—the solar wind—intensifies. The Sun also becomes brighter and emits more ultraviolet radiation.

Close to the Earth, the Sun's magnetic field and the solar wind combine to deflect the charged particles of cosmic radiation. Solar wind particles are trapped in the Earth's magnetic field and travel along field lines. These draw them down into the upper atmosphere over the magnetic poles and it is collisions between entering solar-wind particles and atmospheric gases that produce auroras.

Cosmic rays have much more energy. They penetrate the magnetic field and enter the atmosphere directly. Collisions between cosmic-ray particles and atmospheric atoms and molecules produce showers of other particles. These particles are charged and they appear to act very efficiently as freezing nuclei—particles onto which water vapor is deposited as ice crystals. Ice crystals then allow further deposition of ice and the process leads to the formation of clouds.

When the solar wind is weak, the amount of cosmic radiation entering the atmosphere increases, and the total amount of cloud increases. When the solar wind is strong, cloudiness decreases.

Cloud has a direct effect on the temperature at the surface and in the atmosphere, but it is complex and not fully understood. High-level clouds are thin and wispy. They allow most of the Sun's radiation to pass, but they trap infrared radiation from below, so they tend to warm the upper air. Clouds at a lower level are thicker and more reflective. They reflect incoming radiation and shade the surface, making it cooler, although this effect is partly offset by the release of latent heat as water vapor condenses. Cosmic rays appear to produce big, heavy, freezing nuclei that trigger the formation of dense, highly reflective cloud.

During sunspot minima the solar wind is very weak, and so Earth is exposed to more intense cosmic-ray bombardment. This triggers increased cloud formation, reducing the temperature at the surface. Increased cloudiness adds to the direct cooling effect that results from the reduction in the solar constant. It also appears that the climate is considerably more sensitive to changes in the intensity of solar radiation than to changes in concentrations of greenhouse gases.

The link persists

There is no doubt that prolonged sunspot maxima and minima coincide with periods of relatively warm and cool climate, and it may well be that the effect of changes in the solar wind on cloudiness provides the link. The correlation still continues. There was a sunspot minimum around 1900, a time when temperatures were generally low. The number of sunspots then increased, reaching a maximum during the late 1930s, a time of warm weather. Then sunspot activity and temperature decreased during the 1950s and 1960s and increased again from the 1970s, with two peaks in the middle 1980s, to another double maximum in the late 1990s, followed by two more maxima, one in 2000 and the other toward the end of 2001. Solar activity began decreasing toward the end of 2002. If the pattern continues, the current warm period may end at some time after 2010, and the 2020s may be relatively cool.

It is not surprising that changes in solar output, even very small ones, can wield a disproportionately large influence on climate. This does not mean, however, that the effect of greenhouse gases can be dismissed (see "Greenhouse gases and the greenhouse effect" on pages 94–104). Since the start of the 20th century, each warm and cool spell is very slightly warmer than the preceding one, so the global climate is becoming warmer. It does mean, however, that the warming is only partly due to the greenhouse effect and that a future reduction in solar output, which is probable, may significantly check the rate of warming.

THE MEDIEVAL OPTIMUM

Cahokia is an archaeological site covering 2,200 acres (890 hectares). It is located in southern Illinois, about eight miles (13 km) to the northeast of St. Louis, Missouri. One of its principal features is Monks Mound, a four-sided pyramid rising in four terraces to a height of 100 feet (30.5 m) and covering 12 acres (5 hectares). A temple once stood at the top. Monks Mound is the largest prehistoric earthwork anywhere in the Americas, and it is just one of about 120 mounds at Cahokia. In 1982, the United Nations Educational, Scientific and Cultural Organization (UNESCO) designated the area a World Heritage Site.

Estimates vary of the number of people who lived there. The city may have had 40,000 inhabitants or even more, although most historians believe that at its peak there were probably 10,000–20,000. However many there were, clearly the place was of major importance. No one knows what the citizens called themselves. "Cahokia" is the name of a subtribe of the Illini, the people who were living there when the first French traders arrived. By then the "Cahokians" had long gone, and no one knew anything about them. The city flourished around 1100 C.E. People grew corn in the surrounding area and hunted forest animals, especially deer. Oaks and cottonwoods dominated the forests that blanketed the river valleys.

Then, after about 1200, the landscape changed. Oaks disappeared, and a little later trees of all kinds declined and prairie plants grew in their place. Deer disappeared, and bison—prairie animals—took their place. Then, as the change continued, the tall grasses gave way to shorter grasses that demand less water. The climate was becoming drier.

Cahokia was not the only settlement in the area, although it was the biggest. As the crops began to fail, people abandoned the smaller villages and moved into larger ones, but then these communities also failed. Finally, around 1300, Cahokia itself was abandoned. When the French arrived they found only small, scattered settlements inhabited by a different people.

Weather across North America had become drier because the winds blew more often from the west. Westerly winds approaching from the Pacific lose their moisture as they rise to cross the Rocky Mountains, creating a rain shadow on the eastern side. As the frequency of the westerly winds increased, so the rain shadow extended deeper into the continental interior. Nowadays, in summer months when there are more westerly winds than usual, the rainfall is less than half the average in regions to the east of the mountains—in a "finger," with Cahokia close to its center.

Cold weather during the Dark Ages

The abandonment of Cahokia marked the end of a period when the climate was relatively warm and moist over all of the Northern Hemisphere. That warm period followed a period of cold weather lasting from the second half of the third century until the ninth century C.E. There was heavy snow over much of Europe in the winter of 763–64, and the intense cold killed many olive and fig trees. The winter of 859–60 was so cold that the ice was thick enough to bear the weight of horse-drawn wagons on the Adriatic Sea close to Venice. In some places the cold period lasted even longer. The winter of 1010–11 was so harsh that there was ice on the Bosporus, the narrow waterway linking the Sea of Marmara and the Black Sea, in northern Turkey, and even on the River Nile in Egypt.

During this cold episode, winter snow and ice also became more common in China, and lychee and mandarin orange trees were killed by frost. Then warmer conditions returned. According to records from the royal gardens at Kyoto, Japan, by the 12th century the cherry blossom was flowering two weeks later than it had flowered in the ninth century.

Norse colonies and explorations

In Europe and eastern North America, the good weather arrived fairly abruptly. Around 865 C.E. a Norwegian farmer called Folke Vilgerdson (or Floki Vilgerdason) arrived with his cattle in Iceland and attempted to start farming. It was a disaster. He saw a fjord fill with sea ice and watched his animals die during a harsh winter. He returned home to Norway and told everyone that the island was an impossible place, an "ice land," thereby giving it the name it still has. Less than a decade later, in 874, Ingólfur Arnarson, a chieftain from western Norway, landed close to the site of the present capital city, Reykjavík, and settled there with his family and dependents. By then, Iceland was habitable.

Norwegians were the first Europeans to colonize Iceland, but they were not the first to live there. Irish monks had visited Iceland as early as 790 and some may have been there still, living as hermits, when Arnarson's party landed.

By this time the peoples of northern Europe were able to make long sea voyages—without maps or compasses to guide them—and the Vikings were the bravest and most expert seafarers of all. It was then that the Norsemen—the Vikings—began raiding coastal communities throughout western Europe. These expeditions began around 790. In

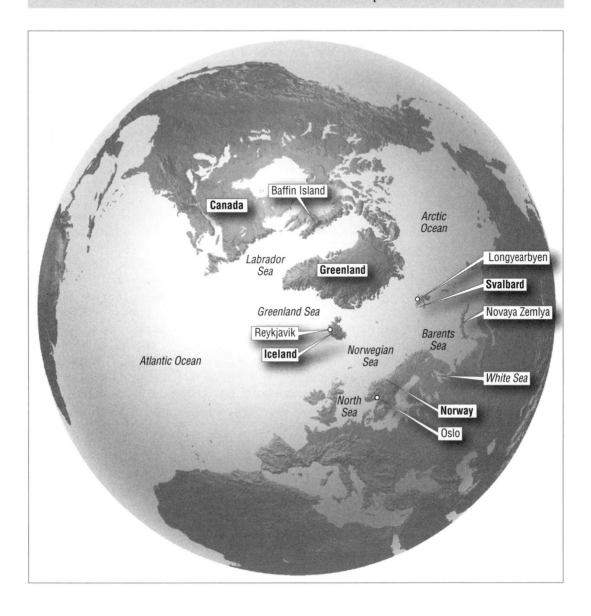

the centuries that followed, Viking ships sailed to the White Sea between Finland and Russia. Harald Hardråde, king of both Norway and England, is said to have taken a fleet of ships to explore the northern sea and visiting either Novaya Zemlya or Svalbard (it is not clear which) some time between 1040 and 1065. The Vikings visited Greenland and ultimately reached Canada somewhere to the north of Baffin Island, and also Newfoundland, far to the south. Interestingly, they called North America "Vinland," or "Wine-land," suggesting that soft fruits grew there—though not grapes—from which they obtained juice. The map shows the part of the world they explored.

The world explored by the Vikings

Erik the Red and settlements in Greenland

Around 980 or 982, Erik Thorvaldsson, nicknamed Erik the Red because of the color of his hair, discovered the eastern coast of Greenland. Erik lived in Iceland, but he had quarreled with his neighbors and the quarrel had deteriorated into a fight in which two men were killed. Erik was convicted of manslaughter and exiled for three years on pain of death. Having little choice, he set sail, heading west toward where his friend Gunnbjörn Úlfsson claimed to have sighted land. He settled near the present-day town of Qaqortoq (formerly Julianehaab) near the southern tip of the island he named "Greenland" in an attempt to entice others to follow him.

The name may have been meant as an enticement, but the oxygen isotope record (see "Revealing the past" on page 37) suggests that conditions were fairly good. Greenland in those days really was a "green land," at least along the coast. After three years there Erik returned to Norway, gathered would-be colonists, and sailed again in 986 with 25 ships, of which 14 arrived safely in Greenland. They founded two colonies, both of which flourished and grew. The Vesterbygd ("West Settlement") had about 75 farms and the Østerbygd ("East Settlement") had about 225. In about 1000 Leif Eriksson introduced Christianity and the first bishop was appointed in 1126.

An incident recorded in one of the histories of the colonization of Greenland, written more than 100 years after the event, indicates how much warmer the weather must have been then than it is today. Erik the Red had a cousin, Thorkel Farserk, who had arrived with Erik and was also one of the new Greenlanders. Thorkel invited his cousin to dinner, but then found that the sheep he intended to cook was on a nearby island in the fjord and no boat was available. So Thorkel swam to the island, a distance of more than 2 miles (3.2 km), caught the sheep, and swam back with it. This was a considerable feat, of course, but it tells us something more. If the temperature of the water had been lower than about 50°F (10°C), Thorkel could not have survived immersion for the time the journey must have taken. He would have succumbed to hypothermia and died. Today the water temperature in the fjords of southern Greenland seldom rises above 43°F (6°C) in the middle of summer, and it is usually several degrees lower. No swimmer could repeat Thorkel's feat nowadays.

Warm weather everywhere

The benign conditions were not confined to Greenland and Iceland, of course. During the early Middle Ages the climate was warmer over most of the Northern Hemisphere. A prolonged period of weather that is warmer than the weather before or after it is known as a *climatic optimum.* This period is the *medieval optimum.*

For about 200 years, beginning around 880, farmers were growing wheat around Trondheim, Norway, and they grew barley as far north as about 69.5°N. This is north of Narvik and well inside the Arctic Circle, far beyond the northern limit for present-day arable farming. Farms also expanded up the sides of the valleys during this period, moving onto land 330–660 feet (100–200 m) higher than any that had been cultivated earlier.

Farmers were plowing higher ground all over Europe. Remains of these old fields and long abandoned farming settlements can still be seen in parts of England, on what are now upland moors, more than 1,000 feet (300 m) above sea level. There are examples on Dartmoor and Bodmin Moor, in the southwest of England, for example, in Northumberland in the northeast, and elsewhere. Indeed, this expansion was causing problems. Sheep farmers relied on the upland grazing and in the 1280s there are records of complaints from them that the lowland farmers were plowing too much of the high ground and clearing away the pasture.

In recent years vineyards have become popular in southern England and they are now fairly common. They produce enough grapes to be viable, but modern Britain is not renowned for its fine wines. The late summer sunshine is barely strong enough for the grapes to produce a high enough sugar content to make good wine. Perhaps new grape varieties, cultural techniques, and somewhat warmer weather mean this will change in years to come, but if it does it will be a reversal to the situation that occurred in the Middle Ages. Then there were many vineyards, some as far north as 53°N, in Yorkshire. Some of those vineyards are sited in what are now frost hollows—depressions, such as valleys, where cold air collects on clear nights to produce late spring and early autumn frosts. Vines would be severely damaged or killed by frosts in such places nowadays. Clearly, the medieval growers were not troubled by early frosts that would harm the blossom or prevent the fruit from setting, or by late frosts that would damage the grapes before they had ripened. This suggests that average summer temperatures must have been 1.26–1.8°F (0.7–1.0°C) higher than the English average in the 20th century. Central Europe was even warmer. Temperatures there were 1.8–2.52°F (1.0–1.4°C) higher than the 20th century summer average. The industry was so successful, and the quality of the wine so good, that French wine producers sought a treaty to have the English trade stopped.

Thousands of miles away, in Kampuchea, the climate was also changing. It was already warm, of course, but all climatic changes are associated with alterations in the distribution of pressure and winds. The warm, dry weather of Europe was probably linked to a northward movement of the subtropical high-pressure belt, producing a summer anticyclone with a center extending from the Azores to northern Germany or Scandinavia. In Asia the effect was to produce a fairly permanent anticyclone over Thailand, Laos, and Kampuchea. This brought much drier weather. The tropical forest receded, allowing the Khmer empire, centered on Angkor, to flourish.

Sea levels and higher rainfall

The rise in temperatures was accompanied by a rise in sea level due partly to the expansion of the seas as the water temperature rose and partly to the melting of mountain glaciers. Measuring changes in sea level is complicated by the fact that the level of the land also changes. It can be lowered by coastal erosion and in places it is still rising as a result of removing the weight of the ice sheets of the most recent ice age (see "Is the sea rising?" on pages 158–163). In this case, however, there can be no doubt. Bruges (Brugge), Belgium, is now some distance from the coast, but in the Middle Ages it was an important Flemish port. That stretch of coastal plain, extending from modern Belgium (then Flanders) to the northern Netherlands, was repeatedly flooded in the 11th and 12th centuries. People moved inland when the sea inundated the land, then returned when the sea retreated. Eventually, though, many gave up and there was a major migration of people into Germany.

Norwich, in eastern England, is also an inland city, but then it was linked to the sea by a long fjord. A large area to the south of Kings Lynn, known as the fenlands, was then marsh, with narrow channels lined with reeds and willows. Ely, standing on top of a steep hill so it formed an island, was so completely isolated that in the 11th century its Anglo-Viking inhabitants were able to hold out for up to 10 years against the invading Normans. The map shows the location of these places.

Inland seas and rivers also contained more water. They are fed by rain, and rainfall was higher in the Middle Ages than it is now. The banks of the Caspian Sea were 26 feet (8 m) higher than their level in the 20th century. Several Sicilian rivers, including the Erminio and San Leonardo, were navigable in the 12th century. Today they are impassable, even for quite small vessels. The Ponte dell'Ammiraglio (Bridge of the Admiral) crossing the River Oreto at Palermo, Sicily, was built in 1113 to cross a river much wider than the one that exists today. The Sahara Desert received more rain than it does now and so did the semi-arid region of northwestern India.

Parts of North America were also wetter. From about 700 until 1200 forests were replacing prairie vegetation across much of the Middle West. Native American peoples in Iowa were regularly growing corn in an area that today receives barely enough rain for this crop.

Start of the deterioration

Then conditions started to deteriorate. Some time between 1200 and 1250 the Norwegian settlers in southern Greenland met Inuit people for the first time. Members of a culture that was widespread in eastern Canada, previously the Inuit had not ventured so far south. There is archaeological evidence to suggest that Inuit people belonging to a different culture had proved more successful at hunting, forcing them to move away from the region of Qaanaaq (Thule) where they had lived until then. At the same time, however, the sea ice was advancing southward and game—seals and walrus—were becoming scarcer. The climate was growing colder.

The Inuit and Norsemen traded peacefully, but around 1350 a ship from Østerbygd visited Vesterbygd and found the settlement deserted, with sheep wandering freely. Everyone had died, perhaps from plague, and the settlement remained abandoned. Østerbygd continued, but it was in decline. Skeletons that have been examined show that in the early years of the settlement the average height of adult men was 5 feet 10 inches (1.78 m), but by the early 1400s it was only 5 feet 5 inches (1.65 m). This is a clear sign of deteriorating diet. Food was often scarce.

There was a regular trading route by sea between Greenland and Iceland. Ships sailed along the 65th parallel. Around 1340, however, the route was shifted to the south because of the increasing amount of sea ice. In

Belgium, the Netherlands, and eastern England, where sea levels rose during the medieval warm period.

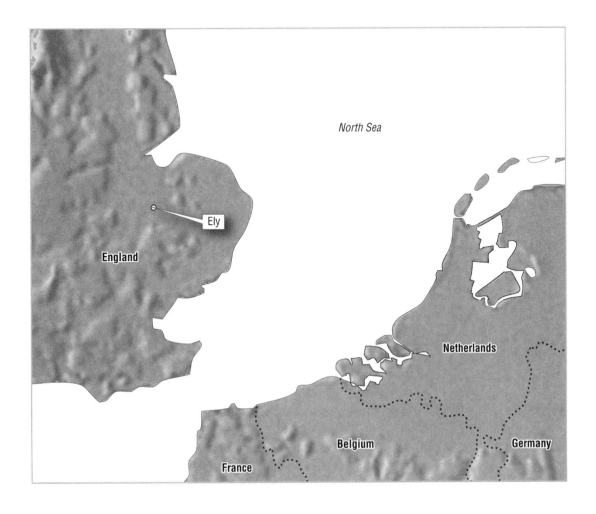

1369 one of the ships involved in the trade was wrecked and after that there were no more regular sailings. Around 1500 all contact between Greenland and Norway was lost. Traders visited Greenland occasionally in the years that followed, but in 1540 a ship from Hamburg was blown off course and landed near Østerbygd. The Germans found one body but no living inhabitants. The Norse colonization of Greenland had ended and it was not until 1720 that permanent posts were established there again, by the Danish–Norwegian government.

Conditions were also harsh in Iceland. According to tax records, in 1095 the population was 77,500, but it was reduced to about 72,000 by 1311. Icelanders were also going hungry—like the Greenlanders, they were becoming shorter in stature. Sea ice often surrounded the island for months at a time, destroying the shellfish and making sea fishing impossible because boats could not put to sea. The same ice brought polar bears as far south as Iceland, however, and they provided meat and furs. Polar bear skins were used to carpet churches. Sometimes the spring and summer were so cold the grass failed to grow. Farmers were unable to make enough hay and thousands of sheep died.

Europe and North America were becoming colder and southern Asia was becoming wetter. The Khmer empire fell, and around 1300 the forest reclaimed the region around Angkor.

The medieval optimum had ended.

THE LITTLE ICE AGE

When icicles hang by the wall,
And Dick, the shepherd, blows his nail,
And Tom bears logs into the hall,
And milk comes frozen home in pail,
When blood is nipp'd and ways be foul,
Then nightly sings the staring owl,
Tu-who;

(*Love's Labour's Lost*, Act V, Scene ii)

Nowadays in England, milk does not freeze between the time it leaves the cow and arrives at the farmhouse, even in the coldest winter. Yet when William Shakespeare (1564–1616) wrote these lines he must have been describing conditions that were very familiar to his London audience. This was not a joke and it was not an exaggeration. English winters were much colder than they are today. Shakespeare lived during the Little Ice Age.

By 1600 the generally cold conditions had been continuing for a long time. The first intimations of what was to come emerged around the year 1200. That is when it became obvious that the ice was extending southward. It surrounded Iceland and broke the trading links between Norway, Iceland, and the Norse settlements in Greenland. It helped drive Inuit people south from the northern tip of Greenland.

Increasingly severe storms

Further south, though, colder weather was not the first sign of the climatic deterioration. No one would have noticed the slight fall in average temperatures. What they would have noticed was the marked increase in ferocious storms, especially storms at sea. During the 13th century there were at least four occasions when storm surges flooded the North Sea coasts of Germany and the Netherlands, killing around 100,000 people each time. Crop damage by two floods, in 1240 and 1362, destroyed more than half of the agricultural income of Schleswig, in northern Germany.

Floods did more than damage property. They destroyed land entirely, so it ceased to exist. Heligoland is a small island about 30 miles (50 km) from the coast of Schleswig-Holstein, Germany, with a present population of 1,650. In 800 C.E. the coastline was about 120 miles (193 km) long. By 1300, storms had reduced this to about 45 miles (72 km) and by 1649 to eight miles (13 km). Today the area of the island is only about 0.4 square mile (1 km²). On the opposite side of the North Sea in eastern England, repeated storms eventually washed away entirely the ports of Ravenspur (also called Ravensburgh), Yorkshire, and Dunwich, Suffolk.

The storms reached a peak in the 13th century, but although they became less frequent in succeeding centuries they were still capable of inflicting appalling damage.

Wet summers, poor harvests, and famines

Storms at sea were accompanied by very wet weather on land. In England, 1200 was a year of continuous spring rain and severe flooding. The following year was similar, and the winter of 1201–02 was so cold that ale (a type of beer) froze solid inside houses and cellars and was sold by weight.

Summers were stormy and winters cold, but there were also long droughts. In 1212 the weather was so dry that there was a huge fire in London and in 1214 there was so little water in the River Thames that women and children could wade across it. There were good years, with fine summer weather and abundant harvests, but increasingly these became the exception. Winters were often cold, with heavy snow, and the rest of the year wet. There was famine in England in 1258, and a much more severe famine began in 1313 and lasted until the late summer of 1317.

The famine of 1313–17 affected the whole of western Europe and was most severe in 1315, when harvests failed everywhere. Countless people died, and there were also huge losses of sheep and cattle due to disease outbreaks as well as starvation. In the summer of 1315 the wet weather resulted from the distribution of pressure. Large high-pressure areas were stationary over Greenland and Iceland in the north and the Azores in the south, with low-pressure areas between them. This pressure pattern produced easterly and northeasterly winds across northern Europe, bringing cold, moist air from the Arctic and dry air from eastern Europe and Asia. Throughout the remainder of the 14th century the weather became even more extreme. There were prolonged spells of very cold weather, but also droughts, most notably in 1343, 1344, 1345, 1353, 1354, 1361, and 1362.

Diseases favored by wet weather

People were often hungry, even if food shortages did not amount to famine, and the cool, wet conditions favored the development of fungi and bacteria that caused disease. In the course of the 14th century the average life expectancy in England fell from about 48 to 38 years. This was due only partly to hunger. There was also disease.

From time to time entire villages succumbed to ergotism, caused by the ergot fungus (*Claviceps purpurea*). Ergot grows on the grains of rye, turning them dark purple, and it was easy for infected grain to contaminate the food supply on which a whole community depended. Ergot produces toxins that survive milling, so the ergot can poison flour. When consumed, it causes convulsions, hallucinations, burning sensations, and gangrene in the fingers and toes that in those days was sometimes fatal. The disease was usually known as St. Anthony's fire, because many of its victims were cared for by a religious order dedicated to St. Anthony.

Even more serious, of course, was bubonic plague—the "Black Death." The plague, known at the time as the Great Pestilence or Great Mortality—the name "Black Death" was first used in 1823—reached the town of Feodosiya (then called Kaffa), in the Crimea, Ukraine, in 1346. It spread rapidly across Europe, reaching southern England in 1348, and by 1350 it was infecting people throughout Scotland. Throughout Europe up to one-third of the entire population died.

Agriculture retreating from marginal land

Whole villages were abandoned, but plague was not the only reason. All over northern and central Europe people had been deserting villages throughout the first half of the 14th century. Crops had been failing, partly because of the bad weather but also because of soil deterioration and shortage of seed, and famine had driven the surviving villagers away. Only a minority—probably less than one-fifth—of the abandoned settlements failed due to plague or the fear of plague.

Little by little, the changing climate was making it impossible to cultivate the high ground and land in high latitudes that had been plowed during the medieval optimum. In Norway the rural population drifted southward and toward the coast. The plague had a very uneven effect in Norway. In some places it killed up to 90 percent of the population, but others were barely affected. There, as elsewhere in Europe, however, the disease left many lowland farms abandoned and farmers were able to move onto them from the more marginal land. The disease facilitated the migration from the northern and upland areas where the crops had been failing.

Further south, North Africa was also becoming drier by the middle of the 14th century. The climate had been much wetter since the 11th century. The Sahara Desert did not extend farther north than about latitude 27°N, and even in the uninhabited part of the desert, travelers often encountered herds of wild cattle, but the pasture was disappearing. Pollen recovered from the region around Lake Chad show that plants typical of a monsoon climate began to become rarer from around 1300 and had disappeared by 1500.

The climatic deterioration continued fairly slowly until the middle of the 16th century. From 1500 until 1550, winters were much like those of the first half of the 20th century, but the summers were cooler and wetter.

Glaciers begin advancing

After 1550, the climate grew markedly colder. Glaciers began advancing and in late May or early June 1595 (there is some uncertainty about the precise date), the Giétroz Glacier in Switzerland entered the River Danse, damming it and causing a flood when the dam broke that submerged the town of Bagnes, killing 70 people. As recently as 1926 there was a house in Bagnes that still had a beam bearing the inscription: "Maurice Olliet had this house built in 1595, the year Bagnes was flooded by the Giérotz glacier." Bagnes suffered badly, but the small hamlet of Ander Eggen was totally demolished by the advancing ice in 1595. The area where it had been was turned into a wasteland that came to be known simply as "Gletschera" (glacier). The Giérotz Glacier blocked the river again in 1774 and it advanced again in 1815, reaching its maximum length in 1818.

Glaciers were advancing throughout the Alps. They reached their greatest lengths between 1550 and 1850 and many communities suffered. During the early years of the 17th century the glaciers near Chamonix, France, caused floods that destroyed La Rosière, Bonnenuit, and Le Châtelard, three hamlets that had been there for several centuries. There is a possible record of Le Châtelard in 1289 and it was certainly paying taxes to a nearby priory from 1384. In 1562 one of the inhabitants of Le Châtelard refused to pay his taxes, causing a furious and violent dispute that was fully documented. La Rosière appears in tax records from 1390.

Scandinavian glaciers began to advance somewhat later than those of the Alps. Some time between 1694 and 1705, the Drangajökull and Vatnajökull ice sheets in Iceland advanced so far that they destroyed farms that had existed at least since 1200. Norwegian glaciers began advancing around the same time, destroying the forests that lay in their paths. The trunks of trees that were uncovered in the 1940s, as the glaciers retreated, have been dated. They were killed some time between 1500 and 1700. North American glaciers also advanced at this time, so that they extended much farther in the 16th and 17th centuries than they do now.

Alpine glaciers reached their maximum extent around 1850, and then, as the climate began to grow warmer, their condition sometimes caused panic. The Chamonix glaciers had pushed huge masses of rock—*terminal moraines*—ahead of them, and this rock overhung inhabited valleys. In September 1852 hot winds and heavy rain started to melt the ice holding the rocks together. Pierre Devouassaz, a peasant living nearby at the time, said he and everyone else had to hide in the cellars as the rocks and water came cascading down, flooding villages and washing away roads.

Cold winters in the lowlands

Away from the mountains, most winters were very cold. Olive trees in the south of France were killed by frost during the latter part of the 16th century and there were seven winters when the River Rhône froze solid.

Further north, in Flanders (now Belgium), the bitterly cold winters of the middle 16th century stimulated the introduction of a new style in landscape painting. Pieter Brueghel the Elder (*c.* 1525–69) painted "Hunters in the snow" in February 1565, depicting the first winter in which the countryside remained covered in snow for an extended time. In other paintings completed around the same time, Brueghel revealed the vulnerability of the poor to the harsh winter weather that was becoming increasingly common.

There was a slight recovery during the 16th century, but temperatures plummeted toward the end of the century. The coldest part of the Little Ice Age occurred between about 1690 and 1710—the Maunder Minimum (see "Edmund Walter Maunder and the unreliable Sun" on pages 70–78). During this period, some of the small lochs in the Highlands of Scotland had ice around them throughout the year and there was permanent snow on the tops of the Cairngorm Mountains. This suggests that temperatures were 2.7–3.6°F (1.5–2.0°C) lower than the 20th-century average.

European settlers establishing colonies in North America suffered from the severity of the winters. Many people—Native Americans as well as settlers—died from cold during the winter of 1607–8 and there was severe frost at Jamestown, Virginia.

Frost fairs

Shakespeare's description of icicles and frozen milk was clearly accurate, and there may have been occasions when he could walk across the River Thames. It froze over more than 20 times between the winters of 1564–65 and 1813–14. Admittedly, the river was more prone to freezing then. Since that time the tributaries flowing through London have been channeled through pipes, and some of the bridges have been rebuilt, allowing the tides to flow upstream more freely and vigorously, breaking any ice that starts to form. Fairs were held on the ice, people skated and played games, the wealthy crossed the river in their carriages, and boats were trapped until the ice melted. People were accustomed to the river freezing and so it would have caused little commercial inconvenience and some traders would have made money from their stalls at the "frost fairs."

Dutch canals also froze. This was more serious because, as well as being important commercial thoroughfares, they drained surplus water from low-lying land. Winters in the Netherlands were especially severe between 1670 and 1700 and again around 1800.

Distribution of pressure

Winter conditions in Europe resulted from the distribution of pressure, and this often produced conditions in North America that were different from those in Europe. Sometimes there was a hard winter in Europe, but a mild one in North America. This happened when high pressure with two centers over northern Greenland and Iceland extended southward as a broad ridge of polar air that covered all of western Europe. At the same time, there was low pressure over western Russia and also over Labrador and high pressure over the central Atlantic at about 30°N. The cold air over Europe brought extreme conditions. Ice on the Thames was thick enough to bear the weight of coaches, there was deep snow in southern France, the Swiss lakes froze, and there was sea ice around the shores of the Adriatic. Ice along the English south coast was sometimes thick enough to bear the weight of a man. The high pressure over the central Atlantic brought warmer air to most of North America, where the winter was mild, but possibly rather dry. This describes the winter of 1683–84 but is typical of many others.

Other winters brought extreme cold to North America. When the polar air extended no farther south than northern Greenland, pressure was low over Labrador and Iceland, and high over southwestern Europe and Scandinavia, Iceland would have a mild winter, but it would be very cold in North America. This is the pattern that occurred in the winter of 1684–85, for example, when harbors were closed by ice along the eastern coast of the United States, and vast crowds of people walked, skated, and played on the ice in Boston Harbor. Northern Europe also experienced a harsh winter, several Swiss lakes froze, and the Thames froze over several times, although the ice may not have been very thick.

Winters were harsh, but the summers were also cool, resulting in many harvest failures. The growing season in England was probably about five weeks shorter around 1700 than it was in the 20th century, and in the coldest years, when the average summer temperatures were about 3.6°F (2°C) cooler than those of today, it was two months or more shorter.

Harvest failures caused famines, but they also had another, stranger effect. By the middle of the 18th century, Norway had one of the biggest fleets of merchant ships in the world. The boom in shipbuilding began between about 1680 and 1720 and appears to have been driven by the owners of farms near to the coast. As their crop yields declined, they started to sell timber from their land in order to sustain their incomes.

They needed ships to transport the timber to overseas markets, and so they opened shipyards and had them built.

Slow recovery and the origin of the "traditional" Christmas scene

The world began to recover during the 18th century, but the recovery was hesitant. The winter of 1708–9 was mild in Ireland and Scotland, but the sea froze along the Flemish coast and people crossed the Baltic on foot. In 1716 the Thames froze so solidly that the tide raised the ice by 13 feet (4 m) without disturbing the fair being held on it. The 1720s and 1730s, on the other hand, brought some of the mildest winters of the century, although the summer of 1725 was the coolest ever recorded. Cold winters returned in the 1740s. The average temperature over the whole of 1740 in England was 44°F (6.8°C), the coldest ever recorded.

There were warm spells, but every so often the icy weather returned. Christmas is usually associated with snow. Christmas cards often depict snow-covered landscapes and contrast the cold outdoors with the warmth of a log fire seen through a window. This is the "traditional" Christmas scene, although nowadays a white Christmas is extremely rare in Britain. We owe the image mainly to Charles Dickens (1812–70). His early childhood, from 1812 until 1819, coincided with the coldest winters England had seen since the late 17th century. Christmases really were white, and that is how Dickens remembered them and how he described them in his hugely popular Christmas stories. This also explains why Christmas cards so often show people dressed in the styles of the early 19th century and traveling by stagecoach.

The glacial retreat began around 1860 in the Alps and Scandinavia, and it has continued at a fairly steady rate since then. That is when the recovery from the Little Ice Age became firmly established. There were still cold winters, with substantial amounts of ice on the Thames in 1894–95, and in 1924 people could walk across the narrow strait from Malmö, Sweden, to Copenhagen, Denmark, and people even drove cars on the ice. The winter of 1962–63 was as cold as some of those when there were frost fairs, but the industrial heating water discharged into the Thames, combined with the changes in the engineered water flow, prevented the river from freezing. It is unlikely to freeze in winter again.

By the early 20th century the recovery was more evident. The 1880s and 1890s had been extremely cold, but temperatures rose fairly steadily from about 1900 until 1940. There was a slight cooling from 1940 until the late 1970s, but the Little Ice Age had ended and before long people began worrying about a new phenomenon—the "greenhouse effect."

GREENHOUSE GASES AND THE GREENHOUSE EFFECT

By day, the temperature on the surface of the Moon rises above 212°F (100°C). At night it falls to about –274°F (–170°C). The Moon orbits Earth and so it is the same distance from the Sun as we are and receives the same amount of sunshine, yet it experiences much greater extremes of temperature. The difference between the terrestrial and lunar climates is due to the fact that Earth has an atmosphere and oceans and the Moon does not. In contrast, the planet Venus is closer to the Sun than Earth is, so it receives more intense solar radiation, but it also has a much thicker atmosphere than Earth, consisting mainly of carbon dioxide. The surface pressure on Venus is 92 times that on Earth and the surface temperature averages 867°F (464°C). Lead melts at 621.5°F (327.5°C), so Venus enjoys a hot climate!

Air and water distribute heat over the Earth's surface. This damps down extremes of temperature (see "General circulation of the atmosphere" on pages 10–17 and "Transport of heat by the oceans" on pages 18–27), but it is only part of the explanation. The atmosphere insulates the Earth. It keeps us warm, rather like a blanket.

A blanket keeps us warm by conducting heat very poorly. Body warmth raises the temperature of the blanket fibers and of the billions of tiny pockets of air trapped among them, and the blanket then retains the warmth. Lose the blanket on a cold night and you will soon feel the drop in temperature. On a hot night you might kick off the blanket in order to cool down. The Moon has no blanket.

Blankets cannot be made from just anything. Certain materials are effective and others are not. Similarly, the presence of an atmosphere is not enough by itself. It depends on the chemical composition of the atmosphere. If the air consisted of nothing but nitrogen and oxygen, for example, life would be very unpleasant—if it were possible at all.

Effective temperature

It is possible to calculate what the temperature should be at the Earth's surface. The solar constant (explained in "Edmund Walter Maunder and the unreliable Sun" on pages 70–78) is the amount of energy Earth receives from the Sun measured over a unit area at the top of the atmosphere. It arrives mainly as short-wave radiation. Adjust this for the total area exposed to solar radiation, deduct the amount that is reflected by

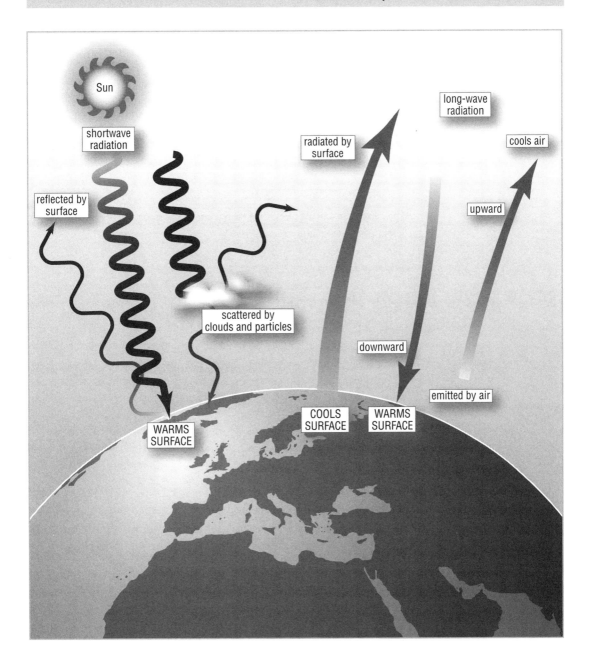

clouds, atmospheric particles, and the surface, and what remains is the amount that can be absorbed by the surface. Deduct the amount of long-wave radiation that is emitted from the surface back into space, and the remainder is the energy that warms the air above the surface. The calculation has revealed what the average air temperature should be at ground level over the entire planet. This is known as the *effective*

The greenhouse effect

temperature. It is about 1.4°F (−17°C). Obviously, the equatorial belt is warmer and the polar regions are cooler, but this should be the average temperature.

If this were the case, Earth would be locked in a perpetual ice age. Clearly it is not, and the actual average global temperature is 59°F (15°C). This is 57.6°F (32°C) warmer than the effective temperature. The difference is due to the absorption of long-wave radiation in the atmosphere. It is absorbed not by the principal atmospheric gases—nitrogen and oxygen—but by water vapor and a number of minor constituents of the atmosphere. The absorbed radiation warms the air. Once warmed, the air also emits radiation in all directions. Some travels into space and some travels back to the surface. The diagram illustrates the mechanism.

Radiation emission and absorption

Once the surface of the Earth becomes warmer than the interplanetary space surrounding it, its surface begins to emit radiation at a wavelength that is proportional to its temperature (see "Radiation from the Sun and from the Earth" on pages 128–134). Earth emits radiation in the infrared waveband, at wavelengths of approximately 3–30 μm ("μm" are micrometers, equal to millionths of a meter). Its radiation is most intense at about 10 μm. As the diagram on page 97 shows, water vapor absorbs radiation at wavelengths of 5.3–7.7 μm and above 20 μm. Carbon dioxide absorbs at 13.1–16.9 μm. Ozone absorbs at 9.4–9.8 μm. Between them, these gases would absorb all of the outgoing radiation if it were not for a "window," between 8.5 μm and 13.0 μm. There is no atmospheric gas that absorbs radiation at these wavelengths.

When molecules of water vapor, carbon dioxide, ozone, or one of a small number of other gases absorb outgoing infrared radiation they also begin to radiate and, because they are airborne, they radiate in every direction. Some of their radiation is directed upward, out of the atmosphere altogether. Some is directed to the sides, where it encounters other molecules and warms them, so they also start to emit radiation. Some is directed downward, to the surface, where it is absorbed. As this radiation bounces back and forth its wavelength changes. Whenever radiation at 8.5–13.0 μm moves upward, it escapes through the window and leaves the atmosphere. Eventually all of the radiation from the Earth's surface leaves Earth, but its departure is delayed.

During the day, the surface of the Earth absorbs solar radiation and grows warmer. It also radiates its heat away, but it continues absorbing heat faster than it loses it. Consequently, its temperature, and that of the air above it, rises, reaching a peak in the middle of the afternoon. As the Sun sinks lower in the sky the intensity of the sunshine decreases. The Earth's surface absorbs a decreasing amount of heat, but it continues to radiate its own heat. This continues through the night and the temperature falls as the Earth emits more radiation than it absorbs. The following morning the Sun rises, its radiation intensifies, and the balance shifts. The diagram shows how this daily cycle produces a period from about 9 A.M. to about 4 P.M. during which there is an energy surplus allowing the surface to grow steadily warmer. From 4 P.M. to 9 A.M. there is an energy deficit at the surface, so it becomes cooler. These times represent an average. Between the spring and fall equinoxes (in March and September, respectively, in the Northern Hemisphere), there are more hours of daylight than there are of darkness and so the surface absorbs more heat than it loses, with the positive heat balance peaking in the middle of summer. The opposite situation obtains between the fall and spring equinoxes, when there are more hours of darkness than of daylight and the surface loses heat.

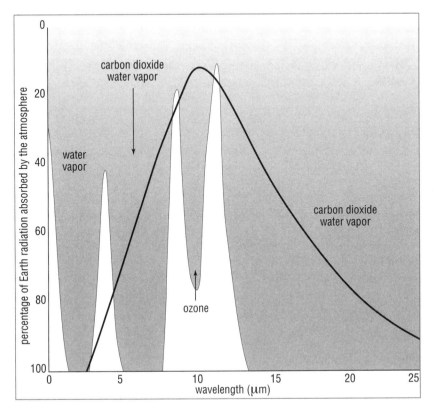

Absorption of radiation by greenhouse gases. The radiation curve shows the radiation emitted from the Earth's surface, peaking at about 10 μm wavelength. The shaded areas show the percentage of this radiation that is absorbed by particular gases at particular wavelengths.

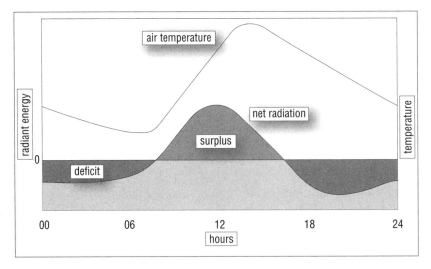

Radiation and temperature during the day

Jean-Baptiste Fourier, John Tyndall, and the greenhouse effect

The absorption of outgoing radiation that warms the Earth is usually likened to the effect of a greenhouse rather than a blanket. It is called the *greenhouse effect*, a name it acquired in 1822, when Jean-Baptiste Joseph Fourier (1768–1830) first used that metaphor.

Fourier was a French mathematician and physicist who made many important contributions to science and had an interesting and exciting life. A supporter of the French Revolution, he was later arrested and narrowly escaped the guillotine, but went on to serve Napoleon, accompanying him on his campaign in Egypt. Later, Napoleon made Fourier a baron and then a count. He was professor of analysis at the Ecole Polytechnique, a highly prestigious college in Paris, and he received many scientific honors.

Fourier believed that the conduction of heat could be described mathematically. He developed this idea over many years, finally publishing his account of it in 1822, in *Théorie analytique de la chaleur* (*Analytical theory of heat*, published in English in 1827). This became one of the most influential scientific books of the century. In it, Fourier suggested that the atmosphere allows the rays of the Sun to pass through it unimpeded, but retains the rays from the ground—in his own words "comme une serre" ("like a greenhouse").

The name is not very apt, because although the glass of a greenhouse is transparent to shortwave solar radiation but partly opaque to infrared radiation, the greenhouse really works by preventing cold air from entering.

Nevertheless, it has been called the greenhouse effect ever since and the gases responsible for it are called *greenhouse gases*.

Fourier did not suppose that the greenhouse effect was due to particular atmospheric gases, rather than a property of the atmosphere as a whole, so he had no reason to speculate about what would happen if the concentration of those gases were to change. The Irish physicist John Tyndall (1820–93) may have been the first scientist to do that.

Tyndall studied radiant heat—infrared radiation. He discovered that while oxygen, nitrogen, and hydrogen are completely transparent to infrared radiation, water vapor, carbon dioxide, and ozone are fairly opaque to it. They trap infrared radiation, and Tyndall said that without water vapor in the atmosphere, the surface of the Earth would be permanently frozen. Then he went on to speculate about the possible climatic consequences of altering the chemical composition of the air. It was a hint at the feasibility of climate change induced by human activities, but John Tyndall was a man of many interests and he never pursued the idea.

Svante Arrhenius

The scientist who did pursue the idea was the Swedish physical chemist Svante Arrhenius (see the sidebar). He considered the effect only of carbon dioxide, because he realized that the rapid industrialization of Europe, North America, and later of the whole world was based on the burning of coal. Combustion is a process that oxidizes carbon to carbon dioxide with the release of heat. Consequently, Arrhenius saw that the atmospheric concentration of carbon dioxide would inevitably increase over the coming century.

This was not the question he set out to answer, however. There was much debate at the time among members of the Stockholm Physics Society about the cause of ice ages. Arrhenius thought that changes in the atmospheric concentration of carbon dioxide might be the trigger. This was remarkably perceptive, despite being incorrect. Scientists now link the onset and ending of ice ages with changes in the Earth's orbit and rotation (see "Milutin Milankovitch and his astronomical cycles" on pages 52–60). Over a much longer period, however, they do believe carbon dioxide may have played an important role in the regulation of the global climate.

The faint Sun paradox and the Gaia hypothesis

This is because of the "faint Sun paradox." Stars slowly grow hotter as they age. This means that in the distant past the Sun was cooler than it is today.

Svante Arrhenius

Svante August Arrhenius (1859–1927), a Swedish physical chemist, was the first scientist to calculate the influence of atmospheric carbon dioxide on the air temperature. He published the results in 1896, in a paper, "On the Influence of Carbonic Acid in the Air upon the Temperature of the Ground" (*Philosophical Magazine*, vol. 41, pp. 237–71).

Arrhenius was born on a country estate outside Uppsala, but in 1860 the family moved into the city. He was educated at school in Uppsala and at Uppsala University. His doctoral thesis, on electrical conductivity, was awarded the lowest grade, but later earned its author the 1903 Nobel Prize in chemistry. Arrhenius spent all of his working life in Sweden, as a lecturer and later professor of physics at the Stockholms Högskola (from 1960 the University of Stockholm), and from 1905 until shortly before his death he was director of the Nobel Institute for Physical Chemistry.

For his study of the atmosphere, Arrhenius calculated the effect on air temperature of changing the concentration of carbon dioxide to 67 percent, 150 percent, 200 percent, and 300 percent of its value in the 1890s. He then applied these changes to 13 belts of latitude, from 70°N to 60°S, for the four seasons of the year, and also calculated the annual mean temperature for each latitudinal belt. He concluded that doubling the concentration of carbon dioxide would increase the surface temperature by 8.91°F (6.95°C) at the equator and by 10.89°F (6.05°C) at 60° N.

Svante Arrhenius was a happy, contented man, with many friends. His interests were wide and he was a popular lecturer and author. He wrote about toxicology, immunology, and astronomy. Arrhenius was the first to propose that life on Earth had arrived in the form of spores that had drifted through space, and he was keenly interested in the possibility of life on Mars. His popularity meant he was constantly in demand and his punishing work schedule may have weakened his health, contributing to his relatively early death at the age of 68.

About 3.5 billion years ago, when the first single-celled living organisms appeared on Earth, the Sun was about 25 percent cooler than it is now. Despite this, the planet was not encased in ice. The reason scientists have for believing this is that there are sedimentary rocks that have been dated at about 3.8 billion years old. These rocks began as sediments that accumulated on the bed of lakes or the sea. Sediments consist of mineral particles that are detached from rocks on land, mainly by wind and rain, and are transported to the coast by rivers. In other words, the existence of sedimentary rocks proves that there was liquid water on the planet at that time. The oceans were not frozen and the land was not buried beneath ice sheets.

Neither was the temperature so high that the seas boiled. We know this must be so because living organisms find the chemical compounds they need in solution. Consequently, the first cells must have lived in liquid water.

Probably the average global temperature was not much different from that of today. The paradox is that temperatures were much the same as they are today, yet the solar radiation warming the Earth was much fainter. The solution to the paradox involves greenhouse gases—principally carbon dioxide. There must have been so much more carbon dioxide in the air then than there is now that the greenhouse effect was sufficient to maintain the relatively high temperature.

Since that time the Sun has grown hotter but, with the possible exception of the "Snowball Earth" and "Greenhouse Earth" episodes (see the sidebar), the temperature has remained within limits that are suitable for living organisms. This has been achieved by a steady reduction in the atmospheric concentration of carbon dioxide. Reducing the amount of carbon dioxide in the air has had a negative greenhouse effect that offset the increasing solar output and prevented the temperature from rising.

The reduction in carbon dioxide was a natural physical and chemical process, but one that was accelerated greatly by living organisms. Carbon dioxide is soluble in water. It dissolves in cloud droplets, forming carbonic acid (H_2CO_3): $CO_2 + H_2O \rightarrow H_2CO_3$. Carbonic acid is carried to the sea, where some of it sinks to the bottom as sediment that is eventually buried in the form of carbonate (carbon-containing) rocks (see "The carbon cycle" on pages 105–112). The amount of buried carbon present in carbonate rocks implies a rate of burial that is faster than would be possible by purely physical and chemical means, however. Living organisms clearly

Snowball Earth and Greenhouse Earth

In various parts of the world there are rocks that geologists have identified as glacial deposits. These were placed in position between 500 million and 1 billion years ago and they are found all over the world. Their origin remains a puzzle, but some scientists believe they were deposited at times when the entire planet, except for the highest mountains, was covered by ice. Professor Joseph Kirschvink of the California Institute of Technology has coined the term "Snowball Earth" to describe the world at those times.

The Snowball Earth condition occurred four times between 750 million and 580 million years ago. The global average temperature was then about –58°F (–50°C) and all of the oceans were frozen to a depth of more than 0.6 mile (1 km). They did not freeze completely because heat from below the Earth's crust was continually being released.

The arrangement of land masses at that time was such that rainfall was very heavy over land. The rain washed carbon dioxide from the air and it was carried to the seas. Gradually the atmospheric con-

centration of carbon dioxide decreased and the temperature fell. Once ice had spread to cover the entire ocean surface, no liquid water was exposed to the air and evaporation and precipitation ceased.

Volcanoes continued to erupt, however, releasing carbon dioxide into the air, where it accumulated because there was no precipitation to remove it. After about 10 million years, the concentration was so high that it triggered a massive greenhouse effect. Within a few centuries all the ice had melted, but temperatures continued rising, eventually to about 120°F (50°C). This was the "Greenhouse Earth" condition.

The high temperature produced a very high rate of evaporation. Clouds formed, precipitation became intense, and the rain washed enough of the carbon dioxide from the air for the climate to stabilize.

The Snowball Earth–Greenhouse Earth hypothesis is controversial. Many climatologists reject it and others have calculated that although the climate became very cold, ice did not cover all of the ocean surface—the condition was more like a "Slushball Earth."

The Gaia hypothesis

While working as a consultant to NASA (the National Aeronautics and Space Administration) during the preparations for the Viking program to place two landers on the surface of Mars, James Lovelock, philosopher Dian Hitchcock, and others discussed how it might be possible to detect whether a planet supports life. Extraterrestrial life is likely to be utterly different from any kind of life on Earth, so how would we recognize it? They reasoned that any living organism must absorb certain substances (nutrients and a source of chemical energy) obtained from its environment and excrete metabolic waste products into its environment. These activities would alter the chemical composition of the environment. Such alterations should be detectable because the composition of the environment would then be different from the equilibrium it would reach if it were subject only to physical and chemical laws.

The idea that living organisms inevitably alter their environment led to the realization that, having altered it, their activities—respiration, feeding, excretion—inevitably maintain it in its altered state. This is the state that is congenial to them, and so it follows that conditions on a planet that supports life are significantly altered and managed by the living organisms to their own advantage. In fact, life takes over the running of the planet.

This can be seen clearly in the case of Earth, where in the absence of life the atmosphere would contain very little nitrogen and methane if it also contained oxygen, because both nitrogen and methane would be oxidized and disappear. With the help of energy supplied by lightning, nitrogen would form soluble nitrates and be washed to the surface in rain, and methane would be converted to carbon dioxide and water. Their presence indicates that

these gases are constantly being returned to the air, and because no inorganic chemical reactions are capable of this, biological processes are most likely responsible—and, of course, they are. Venus and Mars, in contrast, have atmospheres that are in chemical equilibrium, and their compositions are easily explained. Living organisms also regulate the temperature of the lower atmosphere by adding or removing carbon dioxide and the salinity of the oceans by adding or removing salt.

Lovelock discussed this idea with a friend, the novelist William Golding, who suggested that the new concept be called "Gaia." In Greek mythology Gaia (or Ge) represents the Earth. Lovelock's proposal has since become known as the Gaia hypothesis. (A hypothesis is a proposed explanation for certain phenomena that awaits testing by experiment.)

There are two versions, called "weak" and "strong." The weak version holds that the cycles through which elements move are driven mainly by the action of living organisms. These cycles involve carbon, nitrogen, phosphorus, sulfur, iodine, and other elements, which move between the rocks of the solid Earth, the atmosphere, and the oceans. The strong version takes this further and holds that the Earth is itself a living organism.

Bioremediation, in which bacteria are used to clean up pollution, and the suggestion that the addition of iron to ocean water might stimulate marine algae (phytoplankton) to remove more carbon dioxide from the air and thus modify the climate, are both "Gaian" ideas. The hypothesis has also proved very fruitful in directing scientific thought toward the possibility of biological explanations for phenomena. Nevertheless, it remains controversial, and many scientists find it unacceptably vague or reject it outright.

accelerated it and in doing so they maintained climatic conditions that were favorable for themselves. This idea forms the basis of the "Gaia hypothesis" developed by James Lovelock (see the sidebar).

Before Arrhenius could commence his calculations, he needed to know the extent to which carbon dioxide absorbs infrared radiation. This had recently been measured by the American astronomer and physicist Samuel Pierpont Langley (1834–1906). Using Langley's measurements, Arrhenius calculated the thermal effect of altering the atmospheric concentration of carbon dioxide by different amounts in 13 belts of latitude for each of the four seasons of the year, and the average annual effect for each belt. It was a prodigious task, involving many thousands of calculations that he performed with pencil and paper, long before there were electronic calculators to help, far less the powerful computers climate scientists use today.

Svante Arrhenius believed it would take a very long time for the industrial combustion of coal to produce any significant climatic effect. He also believed the process would be limited by the availability of coal. Once the coal was exhausted—or, more accurately, once so much of it had been mined that it was uneconomic to mine the low-quality, inaccessible deposits that remained—carbon-dioxide production would cease and the warming would come to an end.

The enhanced greenhouse effect and global warming potentials

The change that Arrhenius studied is additional to the greenhouse effect that had regulated the global climate throughout the history of the planet. It is an *enhanced greenhouse effect* that is caused by a number of greenhouse gases in addition to carbon dioxide.

Water vapor is the most powerful of all greenhouse gases, but it is never included in the list of greenhouse gases because its concentration varies greatly from place to place and hour to hour and is considered to be outside our control. Other greenhouse gases are present in much smaller amounts than carbon dioxide, but their relative rarity is partially offset by their much higher absorptive capacities. These are rated as *global warming potentials* (GWP) by comparison with the absorptive capacity of carbon dioxide. Carbon dioxide is given a GWP of 1 and those of the other gases are calculated as multiples of it. The table lists the GWPs of the principal greenhouse gases.

Methane (CH_4) is released by the bacterial decomposition of celluloses in the digestive systems of ruminant animals such as cattle, sheep, and goats, and of termites—the bacteria make it possible for termites to digest wood. Methane-releasing bacteria also inhabit airless mud and flooded rice paddies. Natural gas consists mainly of methane, and leaks from gas pipes also release methane into the air.

Nitrous oxide (N_2O) is released into the air from soils in tropical rain forests and dry savanna grasslands, and from the oceans. It is also released during the industrial manufacture of fertilizers, nitric acid, and nylon, and in the exhausts of automobiles fitted with three-way catalytic converters.

GLOBAL WARMING POTENTIALS FOR PRINCIPAL GREENHOUSE GASES	
Gas	GWP
Carbon dioxide	1
Methane	21
Nitrous oxide	310
CFC-11	3,400
CFC-12	7,100
Perfluorocarbons	7,400
Hydrofluorocarbons	140–11,700
Sulfur hexafluoride	23,900
Trifluoromethyl sulfur pentafluoride	18,000

CFC-11 (CCl_3F) and CFC-12 (CCl_2F_2) are the principal chlorofluorocarbon (CFC), or freon, compounds. They were formerly used as aerosol propellants, working fluids in refrigerators, freezers, and air conditioning systems, in fire extinguishers, and in the manufacture of foam plastics. Because of their effect on the ozone layer, the manufacture and use of CFCs is now banned in most countries and is being rapidly phased out in the others.

Perfluorocarbons (CF_4 and C_2F_6) are used medically to support injured lungs. The compounds are completely nontoxic and have a high affinity for oxygen, so lungs can be filled with the liquid to support the tissues. Sulfur hexafluoride (SF_6) and trifluoromethyl sulfur pentafluoride (SF_5CF_3), made by reacting perfluorocarbons and sulfur hexafluoride, are used industrially. Hydrofluorocarbons (principally $CHCl_2F$, CH_3CClF_2, and CH_3CCl_2F) are used as substitutes for CFCs.

THE CARBON CYCLE

Carbon is present in the atmosphere mainly as carbon dioxide (CO_2). It entered the atmosphere in the first place from volcanic eruptions. Beneath a volcano, hot rock, called *magma*, is held trapped under great pressure in a *magma chamber.* When the pressure overcomes the resistance of the rocks capping the magma chamber, the magma is released and the volcano erupts. Once the pressure is removed, the hot rock expands and certain of its ingredients, called *volatiles*, vaporize. The volatiles include carbon dioxide. During the early history of the Earth there was more volcanic activity than there is today, and there was no photosynthesis to remove carbon. That is how carbon dioxide came to accumulate in the atmosphere. Volcanoes are much less active today, but they continue to erupt, and each time a volcano erupts, more carbon dioxide enters the air.

All living cells contain carbon. Green plants trap CO_2, separate the carbon and oxygen, and combine the carbon with hydrogen derived from water to manufacture sugars. The process is called *photosynthesis* (see the sidebar) and it releases oxygen as a waste product. It was photosynthesis by cyanobacteria (formerly known as *blue-green algae*) hundreds of millions of years ago that removed carbon dioxide from the atmosphere and released oxygen, eventually changing the composition of the atmosphere to the one we have today, containing 20.95 percent oxygen, but very little CO_2.

Animals obtain the carbon they need by eating plants. Carnivorous and insectivorous animals feed on herbivorous animals, so they also obtain their carbon from plants, but indirectly.

Respiration

Carbohydrate foods—fats, sugars, and starches—are used to supply the energy needed to power the processes that allow living things to function. Even when we are lying down quite still, our bodies require energy. The minimum amount they need is known as the *basal metabolic rate* (BMR), and it is measured in a person who has slept for at least eight hours and is lying motionless and who has not eaten for at least 12 hours—because digestion uses energy. The BMR for an adult person is 1,200–1,800 kcal day^{-1} (5–7.5 MJ day^{-1}), although it varies widely between individuals.

There are two processes that release energy from carbohydrates. The first, and least efficient, is *anaerobic respiration*. This takes place under airless conditions and only some single-celled organisms use it. *Fermentation*, used by yeasts, is a type of anaerobic respiration. The other process is *aerobic respiration*. It requires the presence of oxygen. All plants and animals use aerobic respiration, which should not be confused with *breathing*—passing air or water across lung or gill membranes in order to absorb oxygen from it into the bloodstream. Respiration, both anaerobic and aerobic, takes place as a sequence of chemical reactions and they have a similar purpose. This is to release energy that is used to attach a phosphate group of atoms to a molecule of adenosine diphosphate (ADP), thereby converting it to adenosine triphosphate (ATP). ATP is transported through the organism, and when it arrives at a location where there is a deficit of energy, the phosphate group is detached (ATP → ADP), releasing the energy that was used to attach it. All living organisms transport and use energy by this ADP ↔ ATP reaction.

Photosynthesis

The process by which certain bacteria and all cyanobacteria and green plants use energy derived from sunlight (*photo-*) to construct (*synthesize*) sugars from carbon dioxide (CO_2) and water (H_2O) is known as *photosynthesis*. The overall sequence of reactions can be summarized as:

$$6CO_2 + 6H_2O + \text{light energy} \rightarrow C_6H_{12}O_6 + 6O_2 \uparrow$$

The arrow pointing upward indicates that oxygen (O_2) is released as a gas; $C_6H_{12}O_6$ is glucose, a simple sugar.

Photosynthesis proceeds in two stages. One, dependent on light energy, is called the *light-dependent* or *light* stage. The other is the *light-independent* or *dark* stage. These are shown in a simplified form in the diagram.

During the light stage, *chlorophyll*, a chemical compound present in the cells of photosynthesizing bacteria, including cyanobacteria, and in bodies called *chloroplasts* in plant cells, absorbs light energy. An electron escapes from the chlorophyll molecule, is captured by an adjacent molecule, and then passes from one molecule to another along an *electron-transport chain*, eventually being used to split water molecules:

$$H_2O \rightarrow H^+ + OH^-$$

The hydroxyl (OH^-) donates its extra electron to the chlorophyll, neutralizing it, and hydroxyls then combine to form water, with the release of oxygen:

$$4OH \rightarrow 2H_2O + O_2 \uparrow$$

Free hydrogen atoms attach themselves to molecules of nicotinamide adenine dinucleotide phosphate (NADP), converting it to NADPH. This completes the light-dependent stage.

NADPH loses its H during the light-independent stage, and the NADP returns to the light-dependent stage.

The light-independent stage begins when a CO_2 molecule attaches to a molecule of ribulose biphosphate (RuBP) in the presence of the enzyme RuBP carboxylase (rubisco). The carbon from the CO_2 then enters a series of reactions that end with the synthesis of glyceraldehyde phosphate, a three-carbon sugar (a sugar with three carbon atoms in each of its molecules) that is used to make other compounds such as glucose, and the reconstruction of RuBP. RuBP is then ready to enter a further sequence. This cycle of reactions was discovered by the American biochemist Melvin Calvin (1911–97) and is known as the *Calvin cycle*.

Respiration is a process in which carbon is oxidized. In aerobic respiration the oxygen is obtained from the air or from oxygen that is dissolved in water. Anaerobic respiration, including fermentation, obtains oxygen from oxygen-containing compounds. The oxidation of carbon produces carbon dioxide, and this is the waste product from all forms of respiration. Aerobic respiration, for example, on which we depend, can be summarized as:

$$C_6H_{12}O_6 + 6O_2 \rightarrow 6CO_2 + 6H_2O$$

The CO_2 returns to the air or dissolves in water. All of the carbon dioxide that is removed from the atmosphere by photosynthesis eventually returns to it through respiration.

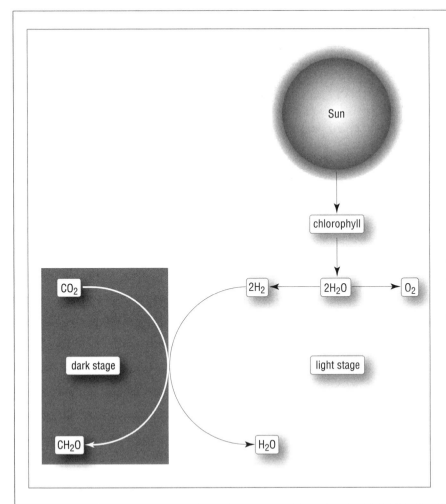

Photosynthesis. The series of chemical reactions by which plants use the energy of sunlight to manufacture sugars has two stages. Water is broken down into hydrogen and oxygen in the light stage. and in the dark stage carbon from carbon dioxide is used to make sugars.

The carbon reservoirs

The carbon is engaged in a cycle, but although photosynthesis and respiration make up the biggest part of that cycle, they are not the whole of it. Quantities in the carbon cycle are always given as the amount of carbon, not carbon dioxide, because it is carbon, not oxygen, which moves through the cycle. The diagram illustrates the carbon cycle in a simplified form.

The Earth contains about 1,100 million billion tons (10^{17} tonnes) of carbon. Almost all of it is contained in carbonate (carbon-containing) rocks such as limestone, and in fossil fuels. Chalk—a very common rock—is made from the calcium carbonate ($CaCO_3$) from the minute shells of marine organisms. Fossil fuels—peat, coal, petroleum, and natural gas—contain about 44 thousand billion tons (4×10^{12} tonnes) of carbon, representing the partially decomposed remains of once-living plants and animals. Methane hydrates contain about double that amount—88 thousand billion tons (8×10^{12} tonnes). This is methane that is held inside the crystal structure of ice. It is found in sedimentary rocks, mainly beneath the sea floor but also in some places on land. Rocks, fossil fuels, and methane hydrates comprise the *geological reservoir* of carbon.

Although the atmospheric concentration of carbon dioxide is only about 370 parts per million by volume—0.037 percent—and the air contains even less carbon monoxide and methane, the total amount of carbon in the atmosphere amounts to about 803 billion tons (730 billion tonnes). This is the *atmospheric reservoir* and the figure is an average for the year, because it changes with the seasons. During summer, plants are growing vigorously and photosynthesis draws carbon dioxide out of the air, so the

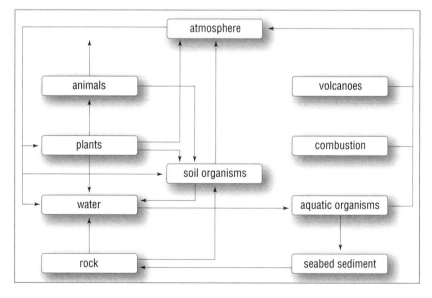

The carbon cycle. Carbon moves through the air and is absorbed by plants. Plants and animals pass carbon to soil organisms and seabed sediments and their respiration returns it to the air.

atmospheric reservoir is slightly reduced. In winter, photosynthesis slows or ceases, but respiration continues, so carbon dioxide is being added to the air faster than it is removed and the amount in the reservoir increases.

Much more carbon is held in the *ocean reservoir*. Carbon dioxide dissolves in water and so the oceans absorb it from the air. It is then called *dissolved inorganic carbon* (DIC). Aquatic microorganisms, plants, and animals also contain carbon in their tissues. Carbon in their waste products and the remains of dead organisms also dissolves in sea water. This constitutes *dissolved organic carbon* (DOC). Rivers carry both DIC and DOC to the sea. In all, the ocean reservoir holds about 41,800 billion tons (38,000 billion tonnes) of carbon.

There is also a *land reservoir*, composed of carbon that is held in the soil—as decomposing organic matter and as air enriched in carbon dioxide that is held in pore spaces between soil particles—and carbon contained in living soil organisms. Soils contain about 1,650 billion tons (1,500 billion tonnes) of carbon, and other living organisms—principally plants—contain 550 billion tons (500 billion tonnes).

The cycle—sources and sinks

There are two principal components of the natural carbon cycle, both of which are in balance over the year. Photosynthesis removes about 132 billion tons (120 billion tonnes) of carbon from the air each year, and respiration returns a similar amount. About 99 billion tons (90 billion tonnes) of carbon dissolves into the oceans each year and a similar amount comes out of solution and enters the air as carbon dioxide.

In addition to these large exchanges of carbon, there are also smaller ones. Not all the carbon released by the decomposition of land plants enters the air directly. About 440 million tons (400 million tonnes) are washed into rivers as DOC and transported to the ocean.

When carbonate rocks are exposed to air or water, they begin to release carbon. The process is called *weathering*, and it results from reactions between the carbonic acid in rain and the calcium carbonate in the rock. Weathering releases about 220 million tons (200 million tonnes) of carbon each year. Rivers carry the carbon that is released on land to the oceans. In the oceans, the decomposition of organic matter also releases carbon dioxide into solution. Together, weathering and the transport of DOC add 660 million tons (600 million tonnes) of carbon to the oceans each year and the decomposition of marine organic matter releases 220 million tons (200 million tonnes) of carbon. Of the 880 million tons (800 million tonnes) of carbon entering the oceans from DOC and weathering, 220 million tons (200 million tonnes) accumulates as sediment on the seafloor and eventually becomes carbonate rock. About 660 million tons (600 million tonnes) returns to the atmosphere. A little of the carbon held

		NATURAL CARBON CYCLE	
Sources	Annual amount (billion tons)	Sinks	Annual amount (billion tons)
Respiration	132	Photosynthesis	132
Oceans	99.66	Oceans	99
Volcanoes	0.11	Burial as rock	0.22
Weathering	0.22	Weathering	0.22
Decomposition		DOC from land	0.44
in oceans	0.22	Fossilization	0.33
Total	232.21		232.21

in the soil becomes trapped under airless conditions that arrest its decomposition. This is the start of the fossilization process that converts dead plant material into coal, and it begins with the formation of peat and the accumulation of airless mud in river estuaries and on some lake beds. This accounts for about 330 million tons (300 million tonnes) of carbon a year.

On average, volcanoes release less than 110 million tons (100 million tonnes) of carbon a year. This completes—and closes—the natural carbon cycle. Parts of the cycle that release carbon into the atmosphere are called *sources* and those parts of the cycle that remove carbon from the atmosphere are called *sinks*. The table lists the principal sources and sinks, and summarizes the amounts of carbon involved.

Carbonate lysocline and carbonate compensation depth

The fate of dissolved carbon depends on the temperature and pressure under which it is held. Carbon dioxide is more soluble at low temperatures and high pressures. The fizz in a can of soda is produced by carbon dioxide that is held in solution under pressure and usually chilled. Opening the can releases the pressure, and the carbon dioxide escapes into the air as a mass of tiny bubbles. Warm the can before opening it and the escaping carbon dioxide will eject a froth of liquid.

When carbon dioxide dissolves in water it forms a solution containing free hydrogen ions carrying positive charge (H^+), bicarbonate ions with negative charge (HCO_3^-), and carbonic acid (H_2CO_3). This makes the water acid. The reaction is reversible, so its products can change back into carbon dioxide and water.

$$H_2O + CO_2 \leftrightarrow H^+ + HCO_3^- + H_2CO_3$$

Many marine organisms use bicarbonate to convert calcium (Ca) present in sea water into the calcium carbonate ($CaCO_3$) of their shells.

$$Ca^{2+} + 2HCO_3^- \rightarrow CaCO_3 \downarrow + H_2O + CO_2$$

The downward-point arrow indicates that calcium carbonate is insoluble and when the organisms die, their shells sink to the sea floor. The carbon dioxide can then react with water once more to form bicarbonate and carbonic acid. The water remains acid. If the shells sink below a certain depth, however, they enter a region where the low temperature and high pressure mean that the water contains more dissolved carbon dioxide in the form of carbonic acid. The calcium carbonate then dissolves. This produces bicarbonate, increasing the alkalinity of the water.

$$CaCO_3 + H_2CO_3 \rightarrow Ca^{2+} + 2HCO_3^-$$

The depth at which calcium carbonate begins to dissolve is known as the *carbonate lysocline* and the depth at which the process is complete is the *carbonate compensation depth* (CCD). The carbonate lysocline is at an average depth of 11,484 feet (3,500 m) and the CCD is at 13,780–14,765 feet (4,200–4,500 m) in the Pacific Ocean and about 16,405 feet (5,000 m) in the Atlantic Ocean. This is the way carbonate sediments form, eventually to be changed into carbonate rocks, and it explains why this process does not occur in the deep ocean basins—the calcium carbonate dissolves before it reaches the ocean floor.

Perturbing the natural cycle

When the Industrial Revolution began, water was the principal source of power. Factories had to be sited close to a place where there was a sufficient fall of water to drive a water mill. When steam engines were introduced factories could be sited anywhere because they used coal as a fuel.

With that change, from water power to steam, the process of industrialization began releasing carbon that had been stored below ground as coal. This perturbed the natural carbon cycle. At first the effect was insignificant, but it accelerated during the 20th century. In 1880 the air contained about 280 parts per million (0.028 percent) of carbon dioxide by volume. Today it contains about 370 parts per million (0.037 percent), an increase of about 32 percent in little more than a century.

The burning of fossil fuels is now releasing approximately 7.15 billion tons (6.5 billion tonnes) of carbon a year. Cement manufacture also releases carbon dioxide—about 0.22 billion tons (0.2 billion tonnes) of carbon a year. This is because the process involves converting limestone into lime. Limestone is principally calcium carbonate ($CaCO_3$) and lime is calcium oxide (CaO). The limestone is *kilned*—heated strongly by burning fossil fuel—to drive off the carbon dioxide:

$$CaCO_3 + heat \rightarrow CaO + CO_2 \uparrow.$$

Together, these amount to an annual emission of about 7.37 billion tons (6.7 billion tonnes) of carbon. The rate of emissions is increasing. In the 1980s it averaged about 5.98 billion tons (5.44 billion tonnes) a year. The rate of emission does appear to be slowing, however, due to improvements in the efficiency with which fuel is used and to deliberate steps governments and industries have taken to reduce emissions.

Forest clearance, especially in the Tropics, also releases carbon, mainly through the burning of vegetation. Together with other changes in land use, this releases approximately 1.87 billion tons (1.7 billion tonnes) of carbon a year.

Total emissions therefore amount to about 9.24 billion tons (8.4 billion tonnes) a year.

Carbon dioxide fertilization and the missing carbon sink

Changes in land use also absorb carbon. New forests are being planted on a huge scale, for example, and the productivity of farmland is being improved. These changes remove carbon from the air. The overall effect is to remove about 2.09 billion tons (1.9 billion tonnes) of carbon a year.

Although we are emitting more carbon dioxide every year, the rate at which it accumulates in the atmosphere is not increasing. About 3.52 billion tons (3.2 billion tonnes) of carbon are added to the air each year and the rate has remained unchanged since the 1980s. No one knows why this is so, but the most likely explanation is that plants grow more vigorously when there is more carbon available to them for photosynthesis. This is called the *carbon dioxide fertilization effect.*

The figure of 2.09 billion tons (1.9 billion tonnes) for the amount of carbon that is being moved out of the atmosphere as a result of changes in land use is an estimate introduced in order to balance the carbon budget. When the amount of carbon being emitted is compared with the amount that is being absorbed by the oceans, this is the amount of carbon that remains unaccounted for. It is sometimes called the "missing carbon sink." Obviously the carbon must go somewhere, and the most likely explanation is that most of it is being removed from the air by the expansion of temperate forests throughout the Northern Hemisphere.

HOW BRIGHT IS THE EARTH?

On a clear night the full Moon is very bright. Moonlight casts sharp shadows and it is sometimes light enough to read a book. The Moon generates no light of its own, of course. We see it because the Sun shines on it. It looks white, but when the Apollo astronauts landed on it the surface they saw was not white, but gray. In fact, the Moon has a fairly dark surface.

The Moon shines more brightly when it is full than it does when we can see only one-half of it or less—even when allowance is made for the fact that we see a smaller area. This is because we see a full moon by sunlight that is reflected almost directly at us, and at any other phase of the Moon the sunlight is reflected at a much greater angle, as shown in the illustration on page 114. Lunar rocks and dust particles reflect more light directly back toward the source than they reflect to the side. Cloud droplets do the same. If you fly with clouds below the airplane and blue sky above, the clouds will appear very bright, but the brightest cloud appears immediately around the shadow of the aircraft.

Despite shining so brightly that sometimes it is palely visible during the day, the Moon is very much darker than Earth. If you could travel far enough into space to be able to see both the Earth and Moon together, you would find that even if you could enlarge the Moon until it was the size of Earth, Earth would still be much the brighter of the two. Occasionally, when the Moon is new, the whole of the Moon is faintly visible, with the narrow crescent brightly lit. The dimly lit part is made visible by earth-shine—sunlight that is reflected from the Earth.

Apart from the Moon, Venus is the brightest object in the night sky. It is often visible in the late evening and early morning, when the Sun is just below the horizon. We are able to see it when the sky is light because while the Sun is not directly visible, Venus is brighter than the sky itself.

Earth shines brightly because so much of its surface is covered by clouds. This shows clearly on satellite images of Earth and on the photographs taken by astronauts. The clouds are constantly changing, of course, but on average rather more than half of the surface is covered by cloud at any time. The table shows the average amount of cloud cover over each belt of latitude.

Albedo

The amount of diffuse light a surface reflects—its reflectivity—is known as the *albedo* of that surface. The word is derived from the Latin *albus*,

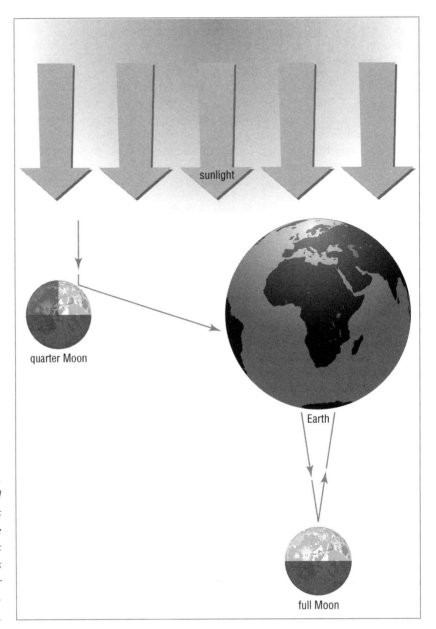

sunlight

quarter Moon

Earth

full Moon

Albedo. At full moon, sunlight is reflected directly at the Earth. This makes the Moon shine more brightly than it does when the sunlight is reflected at a greater angle, as it is at a quarter moon, for example.

which means "white." A value for the albedo of a surface is obtained by measuring the amount of light falling onto the surface—the incident light—and the amount of light being reflected by it, and comparing the two. The term describes only the diffuse light reflected from an uneven surface. A perfectly smooth mirror, reflecting all of the light falling upon it, does not have an albedo. The diagram shows the relationship between direct incident light and indirected reflected light.

AVERAGE CLOUD COVER (PERCENT)		
Latitude (degrees)	Northern Hemisphere	Southern Hemisphere
0–10	63	46
10–20	51	57
20–30	47	79
30–40	55	82
40–50	64	74
50–60	70	63
60–70	68	54
70–80	70	55
80–90	65	57
Total	59	63
Earth total	61	

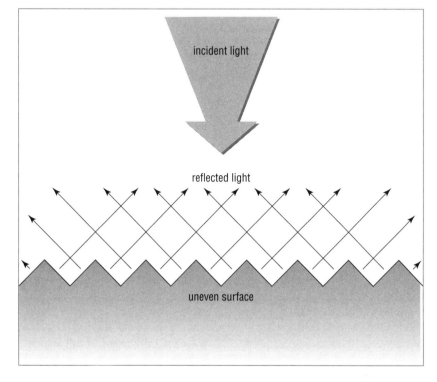

Incident light and reflected light

Albedo is always reported as the percentage of the incident light that it reflects. The percentage is usually expressed as a decimal fraction, where 100 percent is 1, for example, and 50 percent is 0.5. A body with an albedo of 1 would reflect all of the light falling on it, and a body with an albedo of 0 would reflect no light at all. The table lists the typical albedos for a number of surfaces and also the average albedo for the Earth as a whole and the albedos for the Moon, Mars, and Venus. The range for the albedo of Mars is due to the haze that usually covers the planet. The albedo in red light is about 0.30 and that in blue and ultraviolet light is 0.04. The albedo of Venus changes according to the angle at which light is reflected. The albedo of an open water surface varies greatly depending on the angle of the incident radiation. When the Sun is directly overhead, water is almost black, with an albedo of 0.02. When the Sun is on the horizon, most of its light is reflected and the albedo is 0.99. That is why people sailing in small boats are at a high risk of sunburn early in the morning and late in the afternoon.

ALBEDO	
Surface	Value
Fresh snow	0.75–0.95
Old snow	0.40–0.70
Cumuliform cloud	0.70–0.90
Stratiform cloud	0.59–0.84
Cirrostratus	0.44–0.50
Sea ice	0.30–0.40
Dry sand	0.35–0.45
Wet sand	0.20–0.30
Desert	0.25–0.30
Meadow	0.10–0.20
Field crops	0.15–0.25
Deciduous forest	0.10–0.20
Coniferous forest	0.05–0.15
Concrete	0.17–0.27
Black road	0.05–0.10
Open water	0.02–0.99
Earth	0.31
Moon	0.068
Mars	0.04–0.30
Venus	0.55–0.90

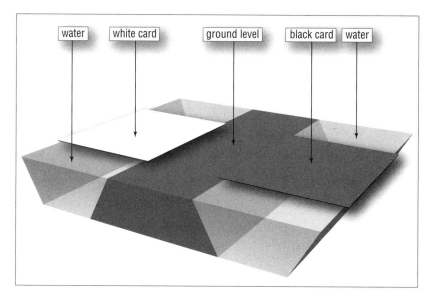

water | white card | ground level | black card | water

Measuring albedo

The table shows that, despite shining so brightly on clear nights, the Moon is a dark body, with an albedo of only 0.068—it reflects only 6.8 percent of the sunlight falling upon it. Venus, in contrast, reflects up to 90 percent. Venus is so bright because it is permanently enshrouded by light-colored cloud. Its surface is completely hidden. Many years ago this led some people to suppose that oceans and swamps, inhabited by strange beasts, covered most of the surface of Venus.

Albedo and temperature

Light that is not reflected is absorbed. We make use of this fact. In cold weather we often wear dark clothes, hoping they will absorb such heat as the Sun delivers, and in hot weather we wear light-colored clothes to reflect heat. Winter clothes are also thicker, of course, and we wear more layers of them, and summer clothes are thinner and we wear fewer layers. That is really why winter clothes are warm and summer clothes keep us cool, but the albedo of the clothes contributes to the effect. The difference is between approximately 0.10 for dark winter clothes and 0.90 for light summer clothes.

You can measure the difference more precisely by placing two containers of similar size—empty ice cream tubs are ideal—outdoors on a sunny day. Fill both containers with water at the same temperature and cover one container with a sheet of white card and the other with a sheet of black card. If you can bury both containers so their rims are at ground level, as shown in the diagram, your result will be more accurate. Leave them for about an hour and then measure the temperature of the water in each container, and you should find that the water beneath the black card is significantly warmer than the water beneath the white card.

Since the shade of the surface determines how much sunlight is absorbed, clearly albedo has an important influence on climate. Subtropical deserts would be even hotter than they are if they did not reflect more than 25 percent of the radiant heat falling on them. Antarctica and Greenland would be warmer if they were a darker color and absorbed more heat.

Positive feedback

While the albedo remains constant its climatic influence does not change, but on Earth the surface albedo sometimes changes over a large area and when this happens the process can become self-reinforcing. A change that triggers further change in the same direction is known as *positive feedback* and its consequences can be dramatic.

Suppose, for example, that ocean currents ceased to transport warm water into the Arctic Basin (see "Transport of heat by the oceans" on pages 18–27). The ocean would lose heat by radiation, its temperature would fall, and the area covered by winter sea ice would increase. Snow would fall on the sea ice. This would change the albedo from that of the dark ocean surface (average about 0.50) first to that of sea ice (0.30–0.40), but then to that of fresh snow (0.75–0.95). Increasing the proportion of reflected radiation would prevent the surface temperature from rising. Cold air would spread across North America and Europe. As it crossed the Atlantic it would be in contact with snow and ice, rather than water, so it would remain cold.

If this condition persisted for some years, a summer would come when not all of the winter snow melted over the sea ice and over land. The area covered by snow would increase, just a little at first, but the albedo of the region would increase slightly. Air above the permanent snow and adjacent to it would remain cold, and the following winter the permanent snow would spread a little farther. Temperatures would remain below freezing throughout the year, and as fresh snow continued to arrive, its weight would compress the underlying snow, forming ice. Ice sheets would form and start spreading outward.

In the 1970s, when average global temperatures were falling, some scientists feared that this type of positive feedback might plunge the world into a new ice age. The effect is so powerful that they calculated it would take no more than a few decades before the ice sheets were advancing rapidly. The albedo feedback process was called *snowblitz*. Nowadays, when scientists are concerned about a rise in global temperature rather than a new ice age, a snowblitz seems rather improbable, although this type of positive feedback may have changed climates in the remote past (see the sidebar "Snowball Earth and Greenhouse Earth" on page 101).

Ice-albedo feedback and climate warming

Positive feedback can work in either direction, however, and ice ages can end rapidly. Within no more than a century the ice sheets can be in full retreat, with temperatures rising rapidly everywhere. This rapid warming is due largely to ice-albedo positive feedback. Transposed to modern times, this is the albedo effect that climate scientists worry about most.

It could happen, for example, if the area covered by sea ice in winter were to decrease by a large amount. This would have no effect on sea level, because the ice is already part of the sea, but it would reduce the albedo and the sea would absorb more warmth. This would raise the temperature of the air over the sea.

When the plans were first made to exploit oil reserves on the North Slope of Alaska, it was obvious that the oil would need to be transported across the state to an ice-free port. A pipeline was the most practical way to achieve this, but there were fears of the adverse effects such a pipeline might have. Below the surface of the terrain the Trans-Alaska Pipeline would cross, there is a layer of permafrost—permanently frozen ground. Oil passing through the pipeline would be warm—the oil would not flow if it froze—and the warm pipeline might melt the permafrost. This would have three adverse effects. The first was industrial. As the ice melted, the ground above the permafrost would become soft and it would no longer support the weight of the pipeline. There was a risk the pipeline might fracture. The second risk was ecological. In summer, the layer above the permafrost—the *active layer*—thaws. This allows plants to grow. If the upper part of the permafrost were to melt, however, the active layer would deepen, turning the ground into a quagmire of mud. Vegetation would still colonize it, but animals, such as the caribou that feed in the area, would have difficulty. The third effect was climatological. Melting permafrost might release large amounts of greenhouse gases. The problem was solved by carrying the pipeline on supports, so it is held well clear of the ground—and migrating caribou are able to pass beneath it. Construction took a little more than three years, and the design has succeeded. Since the pipeline opened in June 1977, the permafrost has not melted.

These were genuine fears. Some people also feared that a fracture of the pipeline might spill oil over a large area. If this were to happen in winter, when the ground is covered by snow, a white surface would turn black, drastically reducing its albedo—perhaps from 0.90 to 0.10. The black oil would absorb solar radiation, melt the snow beneath it, and the warmth might extend downward until it melted the permafrost. This fear was unfounded. If the pipeline did fracture, spreading black oil across a snow-covered surface, the next snowstorm would bury the oil, restoring the high albedo.

Changing land use alters the albedo

Other changes do alter the surface albedo, however. Felling a broad-leaved, deciduous forest to provide farmland increases albedo, and converting a coniferous forest to meadow has an even larger effect. As albedo increases, more solar radiation is reflected and the surface temperature decreases. Changing forest to farmland has a cooling effect. Planting forests, on the other hand, may have a warming effect, because it reduces albedo, although the warming this caused would not be sufficient to offset the benefits of increasing the absorption of carbon dioxide by expanding the forest area.

The biggest change results from building roads and expanding urban areas. Grassland and farm crops have an albedo of 0.10–0.25. Concrete has an albedo of 0.17–0.27 and a black road of 0.05–0.10.

We can and do alter the albedo over substantial areas of the Earth's surface. Whether this is climatically significant is another matter, because the albedo also changes naturally. The albedo of the ocean changes during the course of a day from 0.99 around dawn to 0.02 at midday to 0.99 around dusk. In other words, more than 70 percent of the Earth's surface changes from white to black in the course of every day. If there is a storm at sea, the surface may be hidden by cloud, but around the center of the storm there may be cloud-free areas where the winds are strong enough to whip the sea into white-capped waves. Again, the albedo changes. If the storm happens in the middle of the day it changes from black to white. A large forest fire releases huge clouds of smoke. The smoke is pale in color because it contains particles of gray wood ash and a large amount of water droplets. This increases the albedo, possibly from about 0.20—a forest in full leaf—to 0.70—a gray cloud.

Albedo changes constantly, but the natural changes tend to cancel. The albedo of the ocean surface changes in a regular way through the day, so its average remains constant. Sea storms rise up and die down, and they do so at an average rate over the world as a whole. Even forest fires have only a temporary effect. Eventually they are extinguished.

Changes we make ourselves, by converting the land surface from one use to another, have a more permanent effect. The albedo does not revert in a few hours, days, or weeks. Consequently, we should bear in mind that when we plant forests or clear-fell them, allow overgrazing to reduce pasture (albedo 0.15) to desert (albedo 0.27), or build roads and cities on what was formerly natural countryside, we alter the color of the surface. When we alter the surface color, we alter the albedo, and on a large enough scale this might affect the climate.

CLOUDS AND PARTICLES

Gazing from the window of the airplane, you see the cloud tops shining brightly in the sunlight. Their albedo is high—they reflect most of the solar radiation that is falling on them. You can feel the effect at once as the airplane descends through the cloud and into the dull, damp weather below it. Above the cloud, in the bright sunshine, you felt the warmth of the sunshine on the window. Below the cloud the warmth has gone and when you walk down the steps onto the tarmac the air feels distinctly chilly. It seems obvious that clouds shade the surface and therefore reduce the temperature. Unfortunately, it is not quite that simple.

In the first place, clouds are not all the same. Perhaps there was a layer of cirriform cloud—cirrus or cirrostratus—high above the tops of the lower clouds. It took some time for the aircraft to climb through the lower clouds. The layer was deep and from the window the clouds themselves looked dense. Once you were inside the cloud, you could no longer see the ground, and until the aircraft broke through the top of the cloud, you could not see the blue sky above. A little while later the airplane climbed through the cirriform layer. This was a very different experience. As you approached the clouds, you could see blue sky through them. It took only a moment to pass through them and they appeared thin and wispy.

Some clouds are more reflective than others

These differences are real and significant. A deep layer of dense cloud is much more reflective than a thin layer of more diffuse cloud. Dense cloud forms at a lower level than diffuse cloud, so cloud albedo also changes according to the height of the cloud. The table shows just how large the difference is. The surface of undulating cloud tops that covers most of the sky—usually altostratus—is more than twice as reflective as the thin, wispy, cirriform clouds. Heaped up "cauliflower" clouds—cumulus—reflect more than three times the amount of sunlight that cirrus reflects.

Consequently, there is a large difference in the degree to which each type of cloud cools the ground beneath it. It is not enough to assume that cloud cover reduces surface temperature. It is also necessary to know the type of cloud.

It is also necessary to know the extent of the cloud cover—how much of the surface lies beneath cloud. Even this is not so simple as it may seem. Cloud cover is measured at surface weather stations using a mirror, with its surface divided into 10 or 16 squares. The observer places the mirror

CLOUD ALBEDO		
Cloud type	Height (thousands of feet)	Albedo
Stratus, stratocumulus	10	0.69
Altocumulus, altostratus, nimbostratus	20	0.48
Cirrus, cirrostratus, cirrocumulus	30	0.21
Cumulus, cumulonimbus	10–40	0.70

Cloud cover as seen from space and from the ground. The satellite records 50 percent of the sky covered by cloud. The ground observer, who can see to the sides of the clouds, reports 75 percent of the sky covered.

horizontally in the open, so it reflects the whole of the sky, then counts the number of squares that are covered by cloud. The resulting number is reported either as tenths or as eighths—known as *oktas*. Weather satellites also observe the amount of cloud cover, but because they look downward from high above the cloud, they see it differently. In the diagram, cloud obscures half of the ground surface. The satellite crossing overhead measures this four-okta cloud cover. An observer at the surface station sees

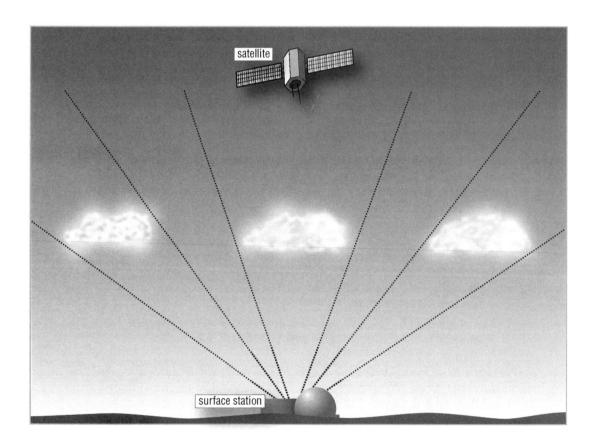

things differently, however. She sees clear sky between and to the sides of the clouds, but she sees any clouds that are not directly overhead partly from the side. This makes them seem larger, because she sees the base continuing around the side. Consequently, she reports 75 percent of the sky as cloud covered—six oktas.

Reflection and absorption

On a clear night the temperature drops rapidly as the ground surface loses by radiation the heat it absorbed during the day. Cloudy nights are much warmer. In spring and fall, meteorologists use their forecasts of cloudiness to predict whether there will be an overnight frost. Clouds that shade and therefore cool the surface by day prevent it from cooling by night.

Clouds reflect and absorb the heat that is radiated from the surface and they reradiate some of the heat they absorb. This is how they warm the air below the cloud. Incoming solar radiation is predominantly at short wavelengths, but outgoing terrestrial radiation is at long wavelengths (see "Radiation from the Sun and from the Earth" on pages 128–134). The difference in wavelength affects the way clouds reflect and absorb radiation.

Water droplets and ice crystals reflect shortwave radiation very efficiently. That is why clouds shine so brightly. They do not reflect all of the sunlight, of course. If they did, the ground below would be in total darkness. Some of the radiation passes through the cloud. As the radiation passes through the cloud, liquid droplets, ice crystals, and water vapor absorb a proportion of it. Water absorbs shortwave radiation very inefficiently. How much the water vapor and cloud particles absorb and reflect depends on the distance light must travel in passing through the cloud. This is known as the *optical thickness* of the cloud. The greater the optical thickness, the greater is the likelihood that radiation will strike a droplet, crystal, or molecule, and be reflected or absorbed by it. Clouds are believed to absorb between 1 percent and 10 percent of the radiation passing through them. Cirriform clouds absorb the least (about 1 percent) and cumulus and cumulonimbus absorb the most (10 percent). The average is about 5 percent.

Clouds are much less efficient at reflecting radiant heat—radiation at near-infrared wavelengths (see the sidebar "Solar spectrum" on page 133)—and much more efficient at absorbing it. The proportion of the outgoing radiation the cloud absorbs depends on its optical thickness. If the cloud is more than about 3,300 feet (1 km) thick, it will absorb all of the outgoing radiation.

This does not mean the heat remains forever locked inside the cloud. As soon as the cloud droplets and ice crystals absorb energy, they begin radiating it in all directions. Some of this radiation is directed downward and warms the lower parts of the cloud and the ground surface beneath the cloud. Some is directed upward and it collides with and transfers energy to particles at a higher level. These are colder, so although the additional energy raises their temperature, they nevertheless remain cooler than the particles below. The heat leaving the planet is proportional to the surface temperature (see the sidebar "Blackbody radiation" on page 129), and if a cloud covers the surface, the relevant temperature is that at the top of the cloud. If the top of a cloud is very cold it will radiate very little energy into space, regardless of the temperature lower down.

Low clouds that remain close to the surface temperature throughout their depth have an overall cooling effect on the atmosphere, because they radiate energy into space. Clouds with high tops, where the temperature is very low, have a warming effect, because little of the heat that they absorb is lost from the cloud top.

Clouds reflect incoming radiation. This has a cooling effect on the climate. They also absorb radiation, which has a warming effect. They absorb heat radiated from the surface. This has a cooling effect if the clouds are low and warm, but a warming effect if they extend to a great height. Clearly, their effects are complicated, but fortunately scientists have been able to cut through the confusion and simply measure what happens. They have used satellites to measure the amount of radiation falling on cloud-covered regions of the Earth and the amount leaving from the cloud tops. They found that over the world as a whole, clouds reduce the amount of radiation reaching the surface by 48 watts per square meter (W m^{-2}) and reduce the amount of radiation leaving the Earth by 31 W m^{-2}. The difference, of 17 W m^{-2}, is the amount by which clouds cool the Earth.

Clouds form by the condensation of water vapor. This releases latent heat (see the sidebar "Latent heat and dew point" on page 32), warming the surrounding air. Cloud formation therefore warms the air. This affects conditions inside the cloud itself, but it has no wider climatic effect. This is because before very long all the water that condenses to form the cloud evaporates once more, absorbing precisely the same amount of latent heat from the surrounding air that it released when it condensed.

Cloud condensation nuclei

Water vapor will not condense very readily unless there are small particles onto which it can form droplets. These particles were first identified by John Aitken (see the sidebar) and they are known as *Aitken nuclei* or *cloud condensation nuclei*. The air contains large quantities of them, especially over land.

Cloud condensation nuclei are of a particular size and the air contains particles of many other sizes. Some are solid and some liquid. The bigger ones are visible to the naked eye. You can see them floating in sunbeams. Most are too small to see, however.

John Aitken and cloud condensation nuclei

John Aitken (1839–1919), a Scottish physicist and engineer, was born and died at Falkirk, Scotland. His health was poor, and he was never fit enough to hold an official position. Instead, he worked from a laboratory at his home, where he built his own apparatus. He was a member of the Royal Society of Edinburgh, and many of his discoveries were first described in articles in its journals.

Aitken became interested in dust and discovered that water vapor will not condense to form cloud droplets unless particles of a suitable size, between 0.005 μm and 0.1 μm, are present. These particles are now called *cloud condensation nuclei*. The smallest of them, less than 0.4 μm across, are called *Aitken nuclei*. He determined to measure the amount of dust present in the air, and to this end he designed and built a dust counter, now known as the *Aitken nuclei counter*.

This comprises a chamber with a pump, containing a graduated disk and sodden filter paper. The filter paper ensures that the air inside the chamber is always close to saturation. A sample of air is drawn into the chamber, and then the pump withdraws air, causing the air inside to expand rapidly. The air cools as it expands, and as its temperature falls below the dew point temperature, water vapor condenses. Some of the resulting droplets fall onto the graduated disk, where they can be counted with the help of a small microscope. Each droplet is assumed to contain one cloud condensation nucleus, so Aitken was able to estimate the number of particles in a unit volume of air. He found that there are usually about 820–980 nuclei in each cubic inch of air (5–6 million per liter) over land and about 164 in^{-3} (1 million l^{-1}) over the ocean.

Atmospheric aerosols

Airborne particles are known collectively as *aerosols*. Large particles fall to the surface fairly quickly, usually within minutes. Small ones fall so slowly that they remain airborne for longer, but even they seldom remain in the air for more than a matter of hours. They are constantly replenished, however, and while they remain in the air they both scatter and absorb radiation.

Aerosols include mineral grains blown into the air by desert dust storms and by plowing dry soils, volcanic ash, smoke, and salt crystals left in the air when drops of sea spray evaporate. Some gases released from factory chimneys and from burning fossil fuels react in the air to form a variety of solid particles. There are also aerosols of biological origin, such as pollen grains, fungal and bacterial spores, and dimethyl chloride released by marine algae. Terpenes, which are chemicals released by plants, especially coniferous trees, form the particles that produce a blue haze, for example over the Smoky Mountains, in Tennessee.

Whether particular particles will scatter or absorb radiation depends on their size and color. Black smoke particles absorb radiation, for example, sulfate particles reflect it, and mineral dust may do either, depending on its composition. It also depends on the amount of particulate matter present. Particles are removed from the air by *fallout, impaction, rainout,* and *washout.* Fallout is the removal of particles by gravity. As the term suggests, they fall to the surface. Impaction removes particles that collide with surfaces and adhere to them. Rainout removes particles onto which water vapor condenses to form droplets that fall as precipitation. Washout removes particles that are gathered by raindrops and snowflakes as they fall through the air.

The concentration of aerosols varies widely. A period without rain allows them to accumulate, often sufficiently to reduce visibility. A shower then washes them to the surface. This is why the sunshine seems so much brighter after a shower and distant objects are more sharply delineated. Nevertheless, the quantity of aerosols is surprisingly large. On average, air over land contains approximately 2.5–65.5 million per cubic inch (150,000–4 million cm^{-3}).

Effect on radiation

The extent to which they affect radiation also depends on the time of day. As the diagram shows, when the Sun is high in the sky its radiation travels a shorter distance through the atmosphere than it does when it is low, and consequently it encounters and reacts with a smaller number of aerosol particles.

Scientists still have much to learn about the way aerosols affect radiation and, through that, the climate. In its 2001 scientific report, the Intergovernmental Panel on Climate Change (IPCC) estimated the present effects of five types of aerosol: sulfate; unburned hydrocarbons from fossil fuels; black smoke; particles from forest, bush, grass, and other vegetation fires; and gases and ash ejected during volcanic eruptions. The IPCC concludes that all of these have an overall cooling effect on climate, with the exception of black smoke, which has a warming effect. It is a small effect, however, ranging from a warming effect of about 0.2 watts per square meter (W m^{-2}) for black smoke to a cooling effect of up to about 1.0 W m^{-2}.

Aerosols and clouds

Aerosols also have an indirect effect on radiation, because certain of them act as cloud condensation nuclei (CCN). Adding aerosols by burning vegetation or fossil fuels increases the concentration of CCN and this can alter the characteristic of clouds.

Satellite observations have found that clouds in areas close to where fossil fuels and vegetation are being burned are more reflective—have a

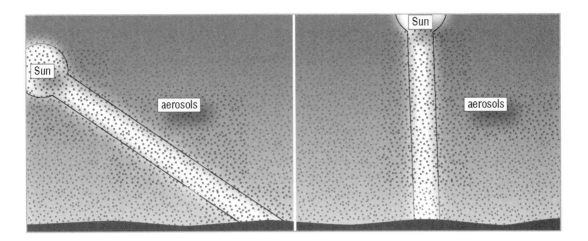

higher albedo—than those farther away. This is because the clouds are enriched in sulfate particles from burning fuels containing sulfur, and in aerosols from smoke, ash, and other substances derived from burning plant material. Since they reflect more sunlight, these clouds have a greater cooling effect than other clouds.

They also tend to last longer. Adding more CCN increases the rate at which water vapor condenses, producing a much denser cloud comprising much smaller droplets. The increasing droplet density is responsible for the raised albedo—light is more likely to encounter a droplet—but the smaller droplets reduce the likelihood that the cloud will deliver rain. In warm clouds, where the temperature is above freezing throughout, raindrops form by the collision and coalescence of cloud droplets, and the process begins with droplets that grow large enough to start falling. They then gather smaller droplets, like the drops that run down a windowpane. Increasing the CCN concentration limits the size cloud droplets, can reach, greatly reducing the number that grow big enough to start falling. Air pollution caused by sulfur dioxide, the gas that changes to sulfate aerosols by reactions in the air, and by forest, bush, and grass fires, increases cloudiness but decreases rainfall.

Clouds and aerosols have a powerful effect on the global climate, but it is an extremely complicated one. They reflect incoming radiation, which cools the Earth's surface, but they also absorb radiation, which warms the surface.

Aerosols and Sun angle. When the Sun is low in the sky (left) its radiation passes through a greater thickness of atmosphere than it does when it is high (right). The longer travel distance means the radiation encounters more aerosols.

RADIATION FROM THE SUN AND FROM THE EARTH

There are three ways for heat to travel from one place to another. The most immediate is *conduction*. When you hold a warm object in your hand, heat passes from the object to your hand, making its surface temperature rise. This is conduction. It requires that two bodies at different temperatures be placed in direct contact with each other. *Convection* works by gravity, and heat can be transferred by this means only through fluids. Contact with a warm surface raises the temperature at the base of a mass of fluid. The warmed fluid expands, reducing its density, and cooler, denser fluid sinks beneath it, pushing it upward and then being warmed in its turn. This is how heat is transferred from one region of the atmosphere to another.

Neither of these mechanisms allows heat to travel from the Sun to the Earth, because the two bodies are not in direct physical contact and there is no fluid medium separating them. The warmth we receive from the Sun arrives as radiant heat, which is a form of *electromagnetic radiation*. Unlike conduction and convection, radiation requires no medium through which to travel. It traverses empty space.

Electromagnetic radiation

Electromagnetic radiation is one of the fundamental forms of energy. It is associated with oscillating electric and magnetic fields—hence the name—at right angles to each other and to the direction in which the radiation is traveling. It can be regarded as pure energy traveling either in waves or as a stream of particles, called *photons*. Although the two descriptions sound contradictory, in fact they are not. All types of electromagnetic radiation travel at the same speed, whether it is pictured as an advancing wave or as a stream of photons. In a vacuum it travels at 2.9979×10^8 meters per second—186,629 miles per second (299,790 km s^{-1}). This is known as the "speed of light," light being a particular waveband of electromagnetic radiation. Electromagnetic radiation travels more slowly through a medium, such as air or water.

All bodies that are hotter than their surroundings emit electromagnetic radiation. The Sun is hotter than the space surrounding it and that is why it radiates heat and light. The amount of energy the body radiates is related to its temperature by physical laws that describe the behavior of *blackbodies* (see the sidebar).

It is the temperature at the surface of the body, where it makes contact with its surroundings, that determines the amount of energy the body radiates and the intensity of its radiation. Deep in the interior of the Sun the temperature is about 27,000,000°F (15,000,000°C). This temperature does not affect solar radiation, however, because the temperature at the visible surface of the Sun—the photosphere—is about 10,800°F (6,000°C). This is the temperature at which the Sun emits blackbody radiation.

Blackbody radiation

All hot objects radiate heat. You can feel the heat when you stretch out your hands toward the hot coals of a fire or a hot central-heating radiator. This is a universal physical law. Any body that is at a temperature higher than the temperature of its surroundings will radiate heat.

A body that absorbs all of the electromagnetic radiation falling upon it and then radiates the energy it has absorbed at the maximum rate possible is known as a *blackbody*. This is because any body that absorbed *all* of the radiation falling upon it would reflect no light at all and would therefore be perfectly black, so a blackbody would be visible only by virtue of its own radiation. The concept is theoretical, because in the real world there can be no such thing as a body that reflects no radiation at all (except a black hole).

All forms of electromagnetic radiation travel at the speed of light. Changing the amount of energy the radiation possesses cannot alter its speed. Instead, it alters its wavelength, which is the distance between one wave crest or trough and the next. As the amount of energy increases, the wave-

length decreases—the crests and troughs move closer together.

The amount of energy a blackbody radiates depends on its temperature. More precisely, the amount of energy radiated is proportional to the fourth power of the temperature. This is expressed as:

$$E = \sigma T^4$$

where E is the amount of radiation integrated over all wavelengths in the spectrum, T is the temperature in kelvins, and σ (Greek sigma) is the Stefan–Boltzmann constant. The relationship between radiant energy and temperature was discovered in 1879 and developed further in 1884 by the Austrian physicists Josef Stefan (1835–93) and his former student Ludwig Eduard Boltzmann (1844–1906), and it is known as the *Stefan– Boltzmann law*.

The wavelength of the radiation varies inversely with the temperature—the higher the temperature the shorter is the wavelength. This relationship was discovered in 1896 by the German physicist Wilhelm Wien (1864–1928) and is known as *Wien's law*. It is expressed as:

(continues)

(continued)

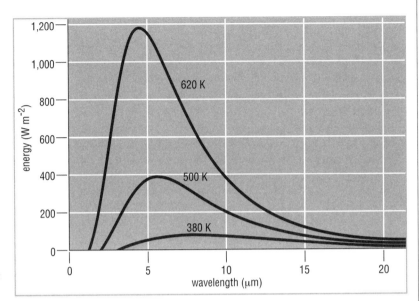

Blackbody radiation. The graph relates the energy emitted by radiation at different wavelengths.

$$\Lambda_{max} = C/T$$

where Λ^{max} is the wavelength of the maximum emission (Λ is Greek lambda), T is the temperature in kelvins, and C is Wien's constant. This is 2,897 μm, so the equation becomes:

$$\Lambda^{max} = 2,897/T \ \mu m.$$

The graph shows the relationship between temperature, the wavelength of the radiation emit-ted, and the energy (in watts per square meter) of that radiation.

This relationship between temperature and wavelength explains why the color of certain materials changes as their temperature rises. A red fire does not radiate as much heat as a white-hot one.

The spectrum and the rainbow

Light is a form of electromagnetic radiation, and when white light passes through a prism it separates into a range of colors—violet, indigo, blue, green, yellow, orange, and red. These are the colors of a rainbow and they are made in the same way, because raindrops act as prisms. When light crosses from one medium, such as air, to another, such as water, its speed and direction change. The light bends. This is called *refraction*. Light striking a raindrop is refracted as it enters the drop, crossing from air to water. It then strikes the rear of the drop and is reflected. As it leaves the drop it is refracted for a second time. The degree by which radiation is refracted varies according to the wavelength. White light is composed of radiation with a number of wavelengths, and each of these is refracted by a different amount. That is how the white light comes to be separated into its constituent wavelengths. We see each wavelength as a different color. Red light emerges from a raindrop at an angle of approximately 42° to the incident sunlight; violet light emerges at 40°; and the other colors emerge at angles between 40° and 42°. When raindrops are refracting and reflecting light in this way, if you stand with your back to the Sun you will see a band of red light at 42° to the sunlight in every direction and bands of the other colors at other angles down to 40°. Consequently, the red light will form an arch with the other colors below it and violet on the inside. The diagram illustrates what happens.

Although every raindrop breaks light into all of its colors, we see only one color from a particular raindrop. If light of one color reaches our eyes, the other colors will either pass above us or disappear onto the ground before they reach us. There are so many raindrops, however, that enough light of each color reaches us for the complete rainbow to be visible.

Sometimes a secondary rainbow is visible above the primary bow and with the colors reversed. This happens when light is reflected twice inside the raindrops. The double reflection results in the red light being at the bottom of the bow and the violet light at the top.

The bands of colors produced by a prism are called a *spectrum*. They demonstrate that white sunlight comprises radiation at a number of wavelengths. We see the light as white when all the wavelengths reach our eyes together. When the colors of light are mixed together they form white.

Rainbow

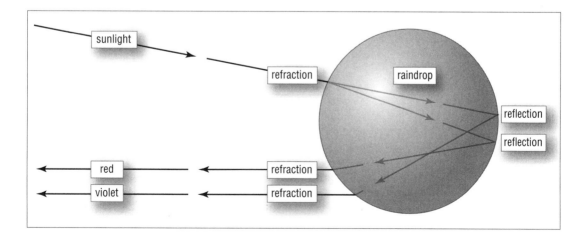

The complete electromagnetic spectrum

Blackbody radiation is not confined to a particular wavelength or even *waveband*—a range of wavelengths. The amount of energy a blackbody radiates is proportional to its temperature, and its temperature determines the wavelength at which it radiates most intensely, but to either side of this peak the radiation tails off toward longer and shorter wavelengths.

Visible light forms only a part of the electromagnetic spectrum, but it is the region at which the Sun radiates most intensely, in the 0.4–0.7 μm waveband. Our eyes are sensitive to radiation in this waveband, but they cannot detect radiation at wavelengths shorter than 0.380 μm (violet) or longer than 0.765 μm (red). The Sun radiates across a much wider spectrum than this, however, and therefore most of its radiation is invisible (see the sidebar).

Earth also acts as a blackbody. Its surface is much cooler than that of the Sun and so it emits much less energy and radiates at much longer wavelengths. The spectrum of terrestrial radiation peaks at 9–15 μm. When the spectra of the Sun and Earth are shown graphically, as in the illustration, it is clear that their radiation peaks are widely separated. The peak of the solar spectrum lies in the waveband of visible light—in fact, between yellow and green light, at 0.577–0.597 μm. Earth's spectrum peaks in the infrared waveband—called "infrared" because it lies beyond the wavelength of red light (0.765 μm).

Solar wind, cosmic rays, and radioactive decay

Solar radiation is the principal source of energy driving the atmospheric processes that produce the global climate, but it is not the only one. Earth is also exposed to the *solar wind*. This is a stream of particles that constantly move outward from the outermost region of the Sun's atmosphere, called the *corona*, traveling at 155–500 miles per second (250–800 km s^{-1}). The particles comprising the solar wind are charged and consist mainly of protons (+) and electrons (–). The wind is directed by the Sun's magnetic field and its intensity varies with the number of sunspots (see "Edmund Walter Maunder and the unreliable Sun" on pages 70–78). Solar-wind particles are captured by the Earth's magnetic field and travel along field lines. These descend over the North and South Pole, and that is where the particles also descend, encountering atoms and molecules of atmospheric gases as they do so. Those encounters release the photons of light that are visible as the auroras. The solar wind does not affect climate directly, but it does interact with *cosmic radiation*.

The solar spectrum

Light, radiant heat, gamma rays, X rays, microwaves, and radio waves are all forms of electromagnetic radiation. This radiation travels as waves or particles called *photons* moving at the speed of light. The various forms differ in their wavelengths, which is the distance between one wave crest and the next. The shorter the wavelength, the more energy the radiation has. A range of wavelengths is called a *spectrum*. The Sun emits electromagnetic radiation at all wavelengths, so its spectrum is wide. The diagram shows the electromagnetic spectrum.

Gamma rays are the most energetic form of radiation, with wavelengths between 10^{-10} μm and 10^{-14} μm (a micron, μm, is one-millionth of a meter, or about 0.00004 inch; 10^{-10} is 0.0000000001). Next come *X rays*, with wavelengths of 10^{-5}–10^{-3} μm. The Sun emits gamma and X radiation, but all of it is absorbed high in the Earth's atmosphere and none reaches the surface. *Ultraviolet* (UV) radiation is at wavelengths of 0.004–4 μm; the shorter wavelengths, below 0.2 μm, are absorbed in the atmosphere but longer wavelengths reach the surface.

Visible light has wavelengths of 0.4–0.7 μm, *infrared* radiation 0.8 μm–1 mm, and *microwaves* 1 mm–30 cm. Then come *radio waves* with wavelengths up to 100 km (62.5 miles).

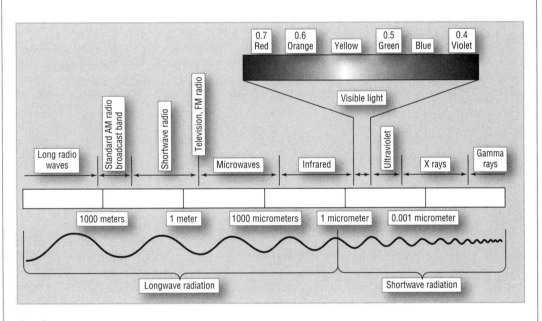

The electromagnetic spectrum

Cosmic radiation comprises the nuclei of the most abundant elements. Protons—hydrogen nuclei—are the most plentiful. In addition to nuclei there are electrons, positrons, neutrinos, and gamma-ray photons. All of these have very high energies. Unlike solar-wind particles, they pass through the Earth's magnetic field and enter the atmosphere, where they collide with the nuclei of nitrogen and oxygen atoms. These collisions

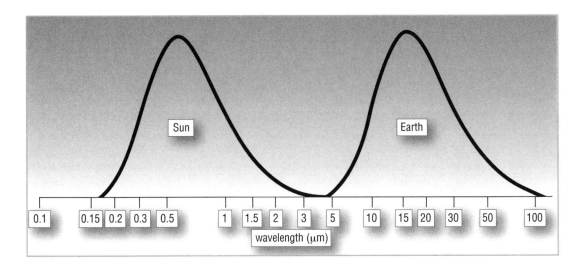

Solar and terrestrial radiation   produce *secondary cosmic rays*, comprising altered atomic nuclei, particles resulting from the fragmentation (*spallation*) of nuclei, and a range of elementary particles including gamma-ray photons. These particles trigger cloud formation and so cosmic radiation does affect the climate.

Earth also generates energy by the radioactive decay of elements, principally uranium, thorium, and potassium, below the surface. The interior of the Earth may still retain some heat from the time of its formation and may generate heat through the continuing accumulation of metals in the core, but radioactive decay is the principal source of terrestrial heat.

The internal heat of the Earth drives the movement of tectonic plates and the raising of mountain ranges, slowly but steadily altering the surface geography and topography, and it causes volcanic eruptions. The distribution of the continents and the size and orientation of mountain ranges affect the formation and movement of air masses, so there is a sense in which internal heat influences climates over long timescales. Volcanic eruptions have a more immediate effect, by injecting gases and particles into the atmosphere.

Energy to move air masses, evaporate water, and generate all the features of the world's climates is supplied by the radiation we receive from the Sun. This energy is then reradiated from the Earth's surface and so returns to space. In addition to solar and terrestrial radiation, the global climate is also affected by cosmic radiation, the intensity of which is influenced by the intensity of the solar wind. Finally, radioactive decay releases the energy that causes continents to move, oceans to grow wider and narrower, mountain chains to rise, and volcanoes to erupt, all of which have climate effects.

THE RADIATION BALANCE

Earth receives energy from the Sun in the form of solar radiation. It then radiates the energy it has received back into space in the form of terrestrial radiation (see "Radiation from the Sun and from the Earth" on pages 128–134). The two are in balance—the amount of outgoing energy from the Earth is equal to the amount of incoming energy from the Sun. If this were not so, the Earth would grow steadily hotter or colder. The global climate does change over time, of course, and at present many people are worried that it may be growing warmer, but these are small changes that cancel out over long periods. In general, the energy budget of the Earth is in balance. The surface absorbs energy and the atmosphere loses energy.

It is a complicated balance, however. Although it is true to say that the Earth absorbs and radiates equal amounts of energy, this is a huge over-simplification of what actually happens.

Neither solar energy nor terrestrial radiation is distributed evenly. Equatorial regions enjoy a much warmer climate than do the polar regions, because they receive more solar energy. In latitudes lower than 40°, however, the surface absorbs more energy in the course of the year than the atmosphere loses. In latitudes higher than 40°, the opposite is the case. There the atmosphere loses more energy than the surface absorbs. Nevertheless, the equatorial regions are not becoming hotter and the Arctic and Antarctic are not growing colder. This is because heat is transferred from the warmer areas to the cooler areas, of course, and this transfer has to be factored into the global energy budget. If it is omitted, the budget will balance only if we assume that the equator is 25°F (14°C) warmer than in fact it is and that the North and South Poles are 45°F (25°C) colder.

Heat is transferred by the movement of air (see "General circulation of the atmosphere" on pages 10–17) and by ocean currents (see "Transport of heat by the oceans" on pages 18–27). Horizontal heat transfer is called *advection*, and it must also balance. The amount of warmth that moves into high latitudes must be equal to the amount the land and ocean lose by radiation in the same latitudes. If this were not so, some parts of the Earth would grow steadily warmer or cooler. Moving toward the equator from the North or South Pole, the amount of heat arriving by advection increases steadily until it reaches the latitude, about 40°, where the amount of radiant heat being absorbed is large enough to inhibit advection from lower latitudes. The amount of heat moving by advection reaches zero at the equator. This is shown in the diagram on page 136, where the amount of energy is given in megawatts (millions of watts) per square meter (MW m^{-2}). The diagram also illustrates the fact that the Northern and Southern Hemispheres are independent of each other and that energy does not cross from one to the other.

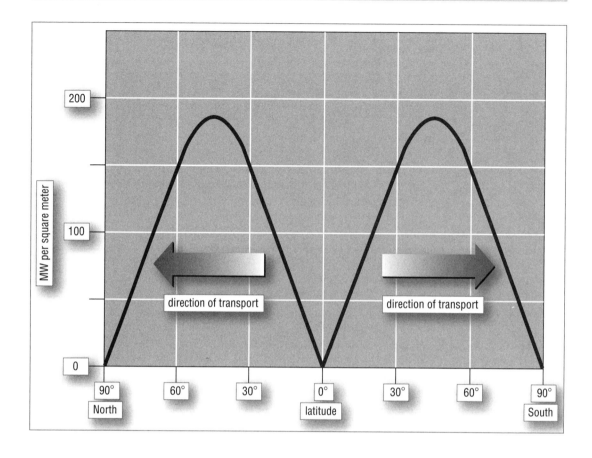

Transfer of heat by advection

Latent heat and the Bowen ratio

The absorption and release of latent heat (see the sidebar "Latent heat and dew point" on page 32) also transfer energy from one part of the Earth to another through the movement of clouds. When water evaporates over the ocean, absorbing latent heat, and condenses when it crosses the coast, releasing latent heat, energy has been transported from the ocean to the land.

This is an important component of the overall movement of heat. Latent heat does not affect the temperature—the heat is hidden, which is what the term means—and so the transfer of energy by this process is measured as the ratio of sensible heat—heat that changes the temperature and therefore can be measured with a thermometer—to latent heat. This is known as the *Bowen ratio*. It is expressed as: $\beta = H/LE$, where β is the Bowen ratio, H is the sensible heat, L is the latent heat of vaporization, and E is the rate of evaporation. If β is greater than 1, more energy is being released into the air as heat than is being absorbed by evaporation or the sublimation of ice. In places with a dry climate, β is greater than 1 and in deserts it can reach 10. In places with wet climates β is less than 1 and in tropical rain forests it can be as low as 0.1. The global average over the year is $\beta = 0.6$.

On Mars, where the climate is extremely dry, convection transports only sensible heat. Warm air rises and cool air subsides, so the effect is to transport heat upward, keeping the surface cool by removing heat from it. Earth is very different because of the large amount of water on the surface. Over the world as a whole, most of the air that rises by convection is close to saturation. Moisture condenses above the surface, and descending air is dry. Convection therefore transports water vapor upward or, to put it another way, it transports latent heat that is taken from the surface when water vaporizes and released into the air above the surface through condensation and cloud formation.

Diurnal and seasonal changes

The budget is complicated still further by the Earth's rotation and by its tilted axis. Obviously, the surface absorbs no solar energy at night, when it is dark. There is a very large variation in energy gain and loss over the 24-hour cycle. In the tropics this can amount to a net gain of about 1,000 W m^{-2} at noon and a net loss of about 70 W m^{-2} at midnight.

As the illustration shows, the Earth's axial tilt produces the seasons by turning first one hemisphere and then the other to face the Sun. The

How axial tilt produces the seasons. Because the rotation axis of the Earth is tilted in respect to the plane of its solar orbit, in June the Northern Hemisphere receives more solar radiation than the Southern Hemisphere and in December the situation is reversed. This produces the seasons.

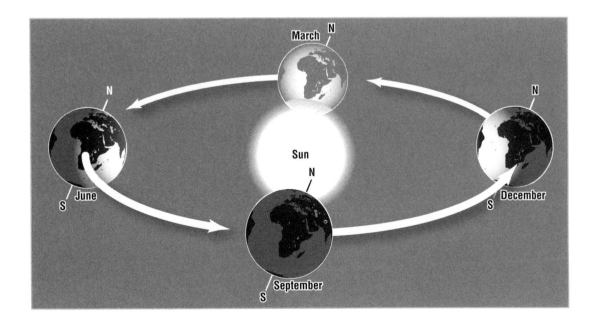

effect is to increase the number of hours of daylight in summer and decrease them in winter. During the summer, therefore, the surface gains heat for longer than it loses it and in winter it loses heat for longer than it gains it. That is why summers are warmer than winters. At the North and South Poles, where the Sun remains below the horizon for six months of the year, the surface continues to lose heat at about 70 W m^{-2}. In Antarctica, however, the temperature falls by about 1°F (0.5°C) per day during the autumn, but reaches its lowest value at the March equinox, after which it falls very little. Antarctica is the only part of the world where this happens. The continent is said to have a *coreless winter*. It is the large difference in the amount of energy being gained at each latitude that produces the vigorous weather systems that are characteristic of climates in middle and high latitudes.

Despite the complications and regional variations, the total amount of energy falling onto the surface of the Earth can be measured. The movement of that energy, as it is reflected, absorbed, and scattered can be traced. The energy leaving the Earth, by reflection and infrared radiation, can also be measured. Not surprisingly, the two sides of the balance sheet produce the same total. The Earth's energy budget is in balance.

Incoming radiation and the ozone layer

Solar radiation enters the atmosphere. About 18 percent of the incoming shortwave radiation is absorbed by ozone near the top of the stratosphere and in the troposphere by clouds, water vapor, and aerosols. Absorption by oxygen (O_2) and ozone (O_3) produces the ozone layer by the reactions:

$$O_2 + photon \rightarrow O + O$$
$$O_2 + O + M \rightarrow O_3 + M$$
$$O_3 + photon \rightarrow O_2 + O$$
$$O_3 + O \rightarrow 2O_2$$

M is a molecule of any substance, but usually nitrogen. This sequence of reactions absorbs ultraviolet radiation and when governments acted to halt and reverse the depletion of the ozone layer it was because of fears that exposure to ultraviolet radiation is harmful to human health. The reactions also have a climatic effect. Incoming energy that is absorbed high in the stratosphere is energy that does not reach the surface. Effectively, the oxygen–ozone reactions reduce the amount of solar radiation. If the ozone layer is depleted so that it is less effective as an ultraviolet filter, more

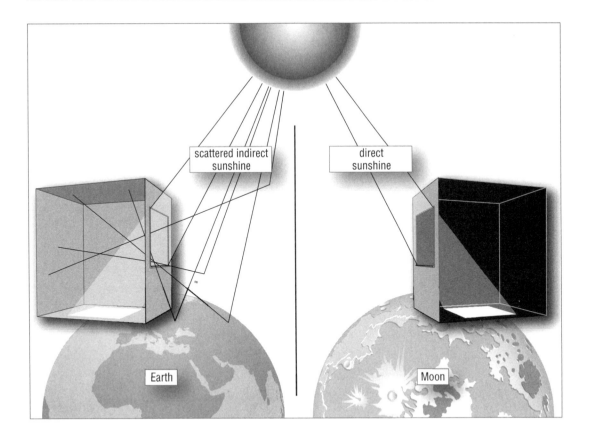

energy will penetrate the troposphere, where it has a climatic warming effect. The effect is quite small, but it exists.

Effect of scattering

Clouds, the air, aerosols, and the surface reflect about 35 percent of the incoming radiation back into space. Although the Earth has an overall albedo of about 0.31, a large part of its brightness is due to clouds. Pictures of Earth taken from space show that the clouds and polar ice sheets are brilliantly white, but that the remainder of the surface is fairly dark.

Sunlight is also scattered by air molecules and aerosols, some of it back into space, so that much of the sunlight we receive arrives in a very diffuse form. Scattering sends light in all directions. It allows light to penetrate inside a room, for example. On the Moon, which has no atmosphere, all of the sunlight is direct. Shadows are always very sharp and if there were buildings with windows, the lights would have to remain switched on even in the middle of the day because, as the drawing shows, light would not reach into every part of the room. Away from area illuminated by the direct sunlight the room would be in total darkness. It is also this scattering of light by the Earth's atmosphere that gives a clear sky its blue color, produces red dawns and sunsets, and that makes a dust-laden

Why the sky is blue

As sunlight passes through the atmosphere, it strikes air molecules. These collisions scatter the radiation, but the way it is scattered depends on the size of the particles compared with the wavelength of the radiation. Lord Rayleigh (1842–1919), the English physicist (born John William Strutt), discovered that shortwave radiation is scattered most efficiently if the particles are much smaller than the wavelength of the light. This is called *Rayleigh scattering*. Air molecules average 0.0004 μm across and the wavelength of light is most intense at about 0.5 μm.

The shortest wavelengths are scattered first. Violet and indigo wavelengths are scattered and absorbed high in the atmosphere, so they do not contribute to the color of the sky. Blue is scattered next. It is light at close to the peak intensity, so there is more blue light in the solar spectrum than there is light of any other color. Rayleigh scattering sends blue light in all directions, but more is scattered forward than back or to the sides. Diffuse blue light reaches our eyes from all sky directions and gives the lower layers of the sky its blue color.

Larger particles also scatter light, but they scatter all wavelengths equally. This was discovered in 1908 by the German physicist Gustav Mie (1868–1957) and is called *Mie scattering*. Because they scatter all wavelengths, these particles make the sky appear white. The sky is white when the air carries a large amount of dust, and a blue sky is a deeper color after a shower of rain has washed dust to the surface. The sky is deeper blue in the middle of the day than it is in the early morning or late afternoon because, at these times of day, sunlight travels a greater distance through the air and more of it is affected by Mie scattering.

The sky often appears red or orange when the Sun is close to the horizon. This is because light must then travel through a much greater thickness of air than it does when the Sun is higher, and for a great deal of this distance the light is moving through the lowest part of the atmosphere, often close to ground level. It encounters water vapor, dust, salt crystals, and particles of many other types. These scatter all wavelengths equally, but air molecules continue to scatter blue light, so blue light is scattered more than the other colors and most of it is scattered out of the line of sight. This leaves the orange and red wavelengths predominant.

sky white (see the sidebar). The remaining incoming radiation is absorbed by the land and ocean surfaces.

Outgoing radiation

The Earth then radiates away the energy it has absorbed. The diagram summarizes the global energy budget. The numbers in the drawing refer to the percentages of the total energy budget. Those with a plus sign represent incoming solar energy and those with a minus sign represent outgoing terrestrial radiation. Other numbers indicate the movement of energy between the Earth and atmosphere. The table shows the budget in more detail.

The surface of land and sea receive 51 percent of the solar constant—the amount of solar energy that reaches the topmost layer of the atmosphere—25 percent as direct radiation and 26 percent as indirect radiation that has been scattered during its passage through the atmosphere. The surface reflects 4 percent of the incoming radiation directly back into space and emits 5 percent as long-wave (infrared) radiation, also directly into space. Infrared radiation from the surface also transfers 13 percent of the total to atmospheric water vapor, carbon dioxide, and cloud droplets, and the surface loses 24 percent as latent heat and 5 percent as sensible heat. The total outgoing radiation amounts to 51 percent of the solar constant.

Radiation budget. The numbers refer to the percentage of the total at each stage. Numbers that carry a + or − sign represent energy that reaches the Earth from the Sun (+) and that leaves as terrestrial radiation (−). The arrows indicate the direction of energy flow.

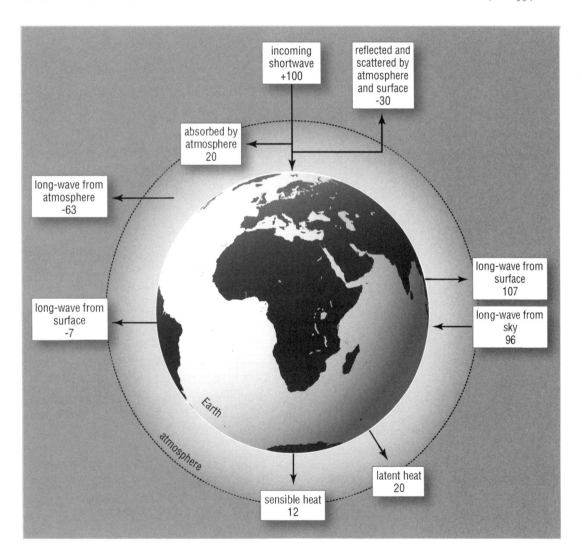

ENERGY BUDGET
(EARTH AND ATMOSPHERE)

Incoming	Percent of the total
Absorbed by ozone	3
Absorbed by water vapor and aerosols	13
Absorbed by clouds	2
Reflected by clouds	24
Reflected by air and aerosols	7
Reflected by surface	4
Subtotal	53
Absorbed by surface from the Sun	25
Absorbed by surface from air and clouds	22
Subtotal	47
Total incoming	100

Outgoing	
Shortwave from water vapor, carbon dioxide, and clouds	31
Shortwave from surface	4
Subtotal	35
Long-wave from surface	5
Long-wave from water vapor, carbon dioxide, and clouds	60
Subtotal	65
Total outgoing	100

The stability of the global climate depends on maintaining the balance between incoming and outgoing radiation. From time to time that balance has shifted and the shifts have brought major climatic changes. The onset and ending of ice ages are the most extreme changes, of course, but there have been many less dramatic periods of increased warmth and cold (see "Edward Walter Maunder and the Unreliable Sun," "The Medieval Optimum," and "The Little Ice Age" on pages 70–78, 79–86, and 87–93 respectively).

MEASURING CLIMATE CHANGE

Measuring the temperature is surprisingly difficult. We are used to having thermometers around the house and these are good enough for most purposes, but they have their limitations. There is a joke among physicists: "The person who has a thermometer knows the temperature; the person who has two thermometers is never quite sure."

Galileo (1564–1642) invented the first thermometer—called a *thermoscope*—in 1593. It is shown in the illustration. It was a gas thermometer and its principle is very simple. A sealed glass vessel contains colored water and air. A glass tube rises vertically from the vessel. The open lower end of the tube is immersed in the water and there is a closed bulb at the other end. As the air in the vessel expands and contracts with changes in temperature, it pushes water up the tube or allows it to fall to a lower level. The thermoscope was very sensitive to changes in temperature, but it was also affected by changes in air pressure and this made it very inaccurate. The French physicist Guillaume Amontons (1663–1705) improved on the design, but it was not until 1714 that the Polish-Dutch physicist Daniel Gabriel Fahrenheit (1686–1736) invented the mercury thermometer we still use today—and the scale to calibrate it.

Modern scientists use electronic thermometers, called *thermistors*. These measure changes in the resistance to an electric current that are produced by changes in temperature, and they are very accurate. Even so, making accurate measurements is not so easy as it may appear.

Siting the thermometer

No matter how accurate it may be, a thermometer will give very inaccurate readings if it is incorrectly sited. If a glass thermometer is placed in direct sunlight, for example, the mercury or alcohol in the bulb will absorb solar radiation and its temperature will rise for that reason. The thermometer will then display the temperature inside the bulb, but this will be quite different from the temperature of the surrounding air. This is why the air temperature must always be taken in the shade.

Even then, it may not be the typical air temperature that the thermometer measures. In the 18th century many people thought it was good enough to measure the temperature indoors, in a north-facing room without a fire. Later, when the fashion for gardening led to keeping thermometers outdoors, people thought they could obtain the most accurate

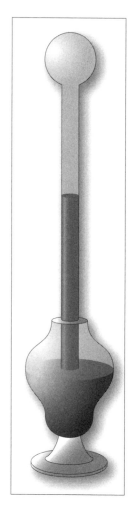

Air thermoscope. The thermoscope that was invented by Galileo. As air in the bulb at the top expands and contracts, colored water in the tube is pushed down or drawn up.

reading by placing the thermometer outdoors on a north-facing wall. In the Northern Hemisphere, placing the thermometer on a north-facing wall ensures that it is kept out of direct sunshine.

Toward the latter part of the 18th century, meteorologists began to notice that the air often felt warmer than the temperature shown by the thermometer, especially on fine days in spring. On investigation they found that the thermometer was measuring the temperature of the layer of air next to the north-facing wall. The temperature of this air was controlled by that of the wall itself and the wall was often colder than the air some distance away, out in the open. This was especially true in spring, when the wall was just beginning to warm up after the cold winter. Under these conditions the thermometer reading was too low. In summer the opposite happened. The warm wall raised the temperature of the air next to it and the thermometer reading was too high.

Various suggestions were made for ways to solve the problem, but it was not easy. Place the thermometer out in the open, well clear of any wall, and the wind might affect it. Place it low down or close to solid objects where it was out of the wind, and it could be affected by their thermal radiation. The solution was finally found by Thomas Stevenson (1818–87), head of a family firm that made lights and lenses for lighthouses and father of Robert Louis Stevenson (1850–94), the author of *Treasure Island, The Strange Case of Dr. Jekyll and Mr. Hyde, Kidnapped*, and several other popular stories. The *Stevenson screen*, shown in the drawing on page 141, is a box with a hinged front, painted white to reflect sunshine rather than absorbing it, with two thicknesses of louvered sides arranged so that the louvers form a V shape in cross section. There is an air space between the top of the box and the roof, and the floor is also ventilated to prevent it from warming due to radiation from the ground. The "screen" stands on legs that raise it so that the bulbs of its thermometers are about four feet (1.25 m) above the ground. This is the lowest height at which the thermometers record the temperature clear of the influence of the ground itself. The screen is protected against direct solar radiation, wind, and radiation from the ground and surrounding objects. Its thermometers can be guaranteed to register air temperature.

Need to standardize instruments and the way they are used

This raised yet another problem. Unless all observers are taking readings at the same hour, it is extremely difficult to compare their records, even if they are using standard equipment, properly sited. If one person is in the habit of noting the temperature immediately after breakfast, for example, and her neighbor prefers to do so after lunch, but neither troubles to record the

*Stevenson screen.
A Stevenson screen is
a container of standard
construction that is
used to house
the thermometers used
at a weather station.
The screen is painted
white, has double-
louvered sides, and is
sited in the open well
clear of the ground.*

time of day, merely noting the temperature, they will appear to record markedly different climates—despite living next door to each other.

Small variations in method can make a big difference. When weather stations changed from using alcohol maximum and minimum thermometers in a wooden housing to using thermistors in a plastic container, maximum temperatures apparently fell by about 0.7°F (0.4°C), minimum temperatures rose by approximately the same amount, and the daily temperature range decreased by 1.3°F (0.7°C). This was due entirely to the equipment being used.

Between 1940 and 1941, the sea-surface temperature appeared to rise by almost 0.9°F (0.5°C) and it was some time before the reason was discovered. Prior to the 20th century, sea-surface temperatures were measured by lowering a bucket over the side of a ship to obtain a water sample, and then taking its temperature. Early records were made using wooden buckets. Then some ships began to use canvas ones and by the latter part of the 19th century most ships were using canvas buckets. These sometimes produced different readings, because water cools more quickly in a canvas bucket. The bucket was hauled onto the deck and there was a short delay while the thermometer was placed in the water and registered the temperature. During this delay the water either cooled in the cold air or warmed in the hot sunshine. Provided the type of bucket was noted, however, the data could be corrected, and by the 20th century only canvas buckets were being used.

In 1940 and 1941, the technique changed, because during wartime it was too dangerous to show the lights that were needed when lowering a bucket over the side at night. Instead, the temperature was measured by thermometers fixed inside the engine intake, where water is taken in to cool the engines, but the meteorological centers using the data were not informed. When scientists came to compile a long-term record of sea-surface temperature, they had to correct the data by +0.234°F (+0.13°C) from 1856, when wooden buckets were used, and by +0.756°F (+0.42°C) in the early 20th century when canvas buckets were used, in order to bring them into line with modern readings.

The Central England temperature record

Not surprisingly, given the difficulties, there are very few reliable records of temperature that extend back over centuries—or even over most of the 19th century. Gordon Manley was one person who managed to compile such a record. It lists the average temperature over a substantial area of central England from 1659 until the present day (see the sidebar).

One of the problems Manley had to overcome arose from the change from the Julian to the Gregorian calendar that was made in England in 1752. By that time there was a difference of 11 days between the two calendars and so the British law implementing the change ordered that the day following September 2 should be September 14. There were riots, because people suspected they had been cheated. They demanded, "Give us back our 11 days!" It meant that before temperatures could be compared, dates prior to September 1752 had to be adjusted. This is not too difficult for daily records—you simply add 11 days to the date. It is more complicated for monthly records, because the start and end of the months have changed. Not only does this mean that records from before 1752 are based on measurements of a different interval from those made after 1752, it also means the English records are not compatible with records from other European countries, because most of them adopted the Gregorian calendar much earlier.

Measuring very small changes

Meteorologists record temperatures for purposes of weather forecasting. They need to be able to inform people of the temperature they may expect over the next few days, and in particular whether the temperature will present any hazards, such as gales, snow, ice, or frost. They also need to track the way the temperature changes from day to day, because this is part of the forecasting procedure. Meteorological records are precise, of course, but they are not intended primarily to help climatologists to track temperature changes over decades. They do not need to take account of changes in methods, provided that all observers make the same change at the same time. Nor do they need to record slow changes, such as the gradual encroachment of a city into the formerly rural area where a particular

Central England temperature record

It is impossible to detect any change in climate unless there is a record of past conditions against which recent trends can be checked. Such long-term records are extremely scarce. Many professional and amateur meteorologists have measured the temperature, pressure, and rainfall and have kept weather diaries, but their records are difficult to interpret. The observers were not using standard instruments, calibrated in the same way, they were not siting their instruments in the same types of location, and they were not taking readings at the same time of day— or always at the same time each day. Lack of standardization can introduce huge discrepancies.

Professor Gordon Manley, a British geographer and climatologist, compiled one of the best sets of long-term temperature records. It covers an area of central England bounded by Preston, Bristol, and London—the map shows the area. The record is of mean monthly temperatures from 1659 and a con-

tinuous record of mean daily temperatures from 1772 until the present. Professor Manley published the record as a paper, "Central England Temperatures: monthly means 1659 to 1973" (*Quarterly Journal of the Royal Meteorological Society,* vol. 100, pp. 389–405, 1974). Manley spent most of his working life at Bedford College, University of London, where he was professor of geography. He was also president of the Royal Meteorological Society.

Mean daily temperatures are calculated as the mean of the minimum and maximum temperatures for the 24-hour period. All temperatures are in degrees Celsius.

Since Professor Manley died, the record has been kept up to date at the Climate Data Monitoring section of the Hadley Centre of the United Kingdom Meteorological Office. That is where the Central England temperature record is held. It is not available to students or to the general public.

(continues)

(continued)

Central England climate record. The record of temperature from 1659 covers an area bounded by Bristol, Preston, and London.

weather station is located. A change of this kind occurs too slowly to affect the day-to-day comparisons of temperature.

Climate change occurs when there is a sustained rise or fall in the average temperature over the entire world. Detecting such a change is difficult, because it is gradual. Between 1860 and 2000 the average global temperature is believed to have risen by 0.72–1.44°F (0.4–0.8°C). This is an average rise of 0.005–0.01°F (0.003–0.006°C) each year. The temperature has not risen steadily, however. There was a fairly rapid rise between about 1905 and 1945, followed by a fall in temperature that continued until the late 1970s, and then a resumption of the rise. The change each year is well within the limits of natural variability. Cool and warm summers, cold and mild winters, vary by more than the change scientists are trying to detect.

Air temperature is measured in four different ways. Surface weather stations measure the temperature at surface level. Weather balloons measure the temperature above the surface. Balloons also measure air pressure at known heights. Air pressure and temperature are closely linked by the *universal gas equation*. This is $pV = nR^*T$, where p is the pressure, V is the volume, n is the amount of gas in moles, R^* is the gas constant (8.31434 joules per kelvin per mole), and T is the temperature in kelvins. The air pressure at a specified altitude can be compared with the surface pressure and the temperature at that height calculated very accurately. Finally, weather satellites monitor atmospheric temperature.

Surface stations

Surface weather stations record the temperature at set times each day. The stations are located on land and also at sea. In addition to weather ships, which remain anchored in particular places, and automatic buoys, which drift with surface currents, about 7,000 merchant ships contribute weather observations as part of the voluntary observing ship scheme.

Obviously, merchant ships travel between trading ports along shipping lanes. They do not travel randomly over the entire ocean and from time to time routes have changed. The opening of the Suez and Panama Canals produced major changes. This means that certain parts of the ocean are monitored very thoroughly, while others are missed, although the increasing use of buoys dropped from aircraft is rapidly improving the situation. Even so, there is very little monitoring of temperatures over the ocean south of about latitude 45°S.

Measurements from land stations have been affected by changes in land use. The most significant of these results from the *heat island* effect (see "Urban heat islands" on pages 151–157). Many weather stations are located at airports. These were built in open countryside some distance from the cities they serve, but over the years the cities have spread outward until they surrounded their airports. These stations have shown a steady rise in temperature, but it is due to the influence of the urban area, not to a general climate change.

Weather balloons and satellites

Weather balloons are free from such types of interference. They use standard instruments, calibrated to recognized standards, and they measure temperature and pressure in air that is well clear of the surface. The measurements are very reliable, but their global coverage is poor and there have been changes in the instruments used and the way their data is processed that have left gaps in the record. Balloons are released from land-based stations and there are far more in North America and Europe than in other parts of the world.

Satellites began recording air temperatures during the 1960s, but the most accurate of all records began only in January 1979. That is when the first *microwave sounding unit* (MSU) began transmitting data. MSUs are carried on the TIROS-N series of United States satellites. They measure the emission of microwave radiation from oxygen molecules in the troposphere. The wavelength and intensity of these emissions are used to calculate the temperature with a claimed accuracy of ±0.02°F (±0.01°C).

Is the world growing warmer?

Measurements from surface stations record an increase in global temperature of about 0.27°F (0.15°C) per decade. Weather balloons and satellites both record a slight cooling, the balloons by 0.036°F (0.02°C) and MSUs by 0.018°F (0.01°C) per decade.

The discrepancies are real and probably reflect the true state of affairs. The air temperature is rising immediately above the surface, but it is remaining steady or falling slightly in the upper troposphere.

The Central England temperature record shows that since 1800 the temperature in the area covered has risen by about 1.26°F (0.7°C) and that most of this rise has taken place in winter. In other words, winters are becoming milder, but summer temperatures are changing very little.

The temperature in the stratosphere is falling by 0.9°F (0.5°C) at 49,000 feet (15 km), rising to 4.5°F (2.5°C) at 31 miles (50 km). This is due to the depletion of the ozone layer. Stratospheric processes by which ozone forms and is broken down again absorb shortwave solar radiation, warming the stratosphere, but cooling the troposphere by reducing the amount of radiation that penetrates to the surface (see "The radiation balance" on pages 135–142).

When people talk confidently about the rate at which the world is growing warmer, it is as well to bear in mind the complexity of measuring small changes. The scientists who summarize research findings for the Intergovernmental Panel on Climate Change are more cautious. In *Climate Change 2001: The Scientific Basis* (paragraph 2.2.4, page 123) they state that: ". . . it is very likely that the surface has warmed in the global average relative to the troposphere, and the troposphere has warmed relative to the stratosphere since 1979. However, the relative warming is spatially very variable and most significant in the tropics and sub-tropics." They also say the difference between the change near the surface and that at higher levels is still not understood and requires further research. Taking the temperature of the atmosphere is not a straightforward task.

URBAN HEAT ISLANDS

People who move from the city into the countryside often find conditions are far different from those they imagined. The weather is wetter. There is mud everywhere. What is more, it is often colder and usually windier. Disillusionment sets in, not helped by the suspicion that what they see and feel springs not from nature, but from the failure of their romantic expectations of life in a warm, sunny, rural idyll.

Perhaps it is a mistake to expect such a radical change to happen smoothly and to suppose that the difference between town and country life amounts to nothing more than the scenery. It is not a mistake, though, to suggest that the weather is different. Cities have a different climate from the countryside around them. It is warmer, wetter, and less windy than the adjacent rural climate, and there are more thunderstorms. The countryside may seem wetter, but that is because the rain is often driven by a strong wind and people are more exposed to it than they are in the city—and the ground is certainly muddier.

The first person to document this difference was Luke Howard (1772–1864), the English meteorologist who gave us the cloud names that we use to this day. In 1818–19 Howard published *The Climate of London* in two volumes, and in 1833 he published a second edition, this time in three volumes. It was a formidable achievement. In this work he made what is thought to be the first reference to a *heat island* and he produced temperature records to support it.

City air is drier, but rainfall is higher

City streets and squares are paved. This is the first and most obvious difference between the urban and rural environments. It means that rain does not soak into the ground, but is removed by storm drains. When the rain ceases the streets dry very quickly. Rainwater is removed too quickly for much of it to evaporate and there are fewer areas of standing water—ponds and lakes—than there are outside the city. Consequently, there is less evaporation in the city than there is in the countryside. There is also less transpiration, because there are fewer plants to move water from the ground into the air.

Combined with the warmer temperature, which lowers the relative humidity by about 6 percent compared to rural air (see the sidebar on page 152)—or sometimes by up to 30 percent on warm nights—reduced evaporation and transpiration suggest the urban climate should be drier than

Humidity

The amount of water vapor air can hold varies according to the temperature. Warm air can hold more than cold air. The amount of water vapor present in the air is called the *humidity* of the air. This is measured in several ways.

The *absolute humidity* is the mass of water vapor present in a unit volume of air, measured in grams per cubic meter (1 g m^{-3} = 0.046 ounces per cubic yard). Changes in the temperature and pressure alter the volume of air, however, and this changes the amount of water vapor in a unit volume without actually adding or removing any moisture. The concept of absolute humidity takes no account of this, so it is not very useful and is seldom used.

Mixing ratio is more useful. This is a measure of the amount of water vapor in a unit mass of dry air—air with the water vapor removed. *Specific humidity* is similar to mixing ratio, but measures the amount of water vapor in a unit mass of air including the moisture. Both are reported in grams per kilogram. Since the amount of water vapor is always very small, seldom accounting for more than 4 percent of the mass of the air, specific humidity and mixing ratio are almost the same thing.

The most familiar term is *relative humidity*. This is the measurement you read from hygrometers, either directly or after referring to tables—and it is the one you hear in weather forecasts. Relative humidity (RH) is the amount of water vapor in the air, expressed as a percentage of the amount needed to saturate the air at that temperature. When the air is saturated the RH is 100 percent (the "percent" is often omitted).

the rural climate—but it is not. Scientists are not sure why this is so, but it may be that the dustier air over the city produces a higher concentration of cloud condensation nuclei (see the sidebar "John Aitken and cloud condensation nuclei" on page 125). In calm weather with clear skies, city streets tend to trap warm air, and the air remains moist because the surfaces of streets and buildings are too warm for excess moisture to be deposited as dew.

Whatever the reason, there are six or seven more rainy days a year in European and North American cities than there are in the nearby countryside, suggesting the urban rainfall is up to 10 percent higher. Summer thunderstorms and hail are also more frequent in some areas, especially within and up to 25 miles (40 km) downwind of cities in the Midwestern states.

Cities are less sunny

One reason people find the countryside attractive may be that they believe it to be sunnier. They are quite right. On average, city dwellers experience 5 percent to 15 percent fewer hours of sunshine over the year, 15 percent to 20 percent less solar radiation in total, and 5 percent less ultraviolet radiation in summer and 30 percent in winter. The drawing shows why this is so. Buildings shade the ground and the taller the buildings are, the deeper the shade that they cast. The extent of the shade depends partly on the height of the Sun in the sky. The streets are more shaded in winter when the Sun is low than they are in summer. This is also why there is such a large reduction in the amount of ultraviolet radiation reaching the ground in winter. A street that is shaded by the tall buildings on either side is known as an *urban canyon*. Depending on its orientation, the walls of the buildings lining the canyon may receive different amounts of solar radiation, or receive similar amounts but at different times of day.

Very little of the sunshine reaches street level, but as it is reflected back and forth most of the radiation is absorbed by the fabric of the buildings. As the buildings grow warmer they begin to radiate their heat. Where the buildings are tall, most of the absorption and radiation take place some distance above street level. It is shadier at street level, but the air is somewhat warmer than it would be otherwise, because the walls lining the street are

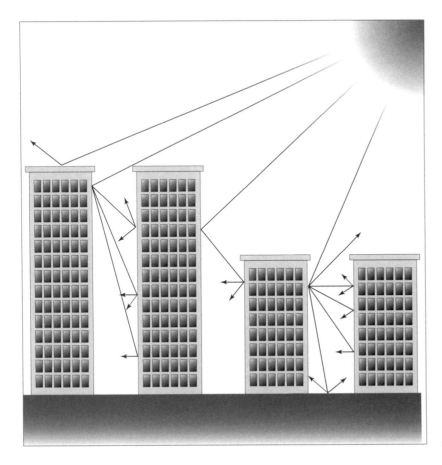

Solar radiation in the city

radiating heat. This effect is greater in summer than in winter, but in winter large amounts of warm air leaks from heated buildings, so the air on the street is still relatively warm.

The temperature difference is especially noticeable at night. Out in the countryside, as the night falls, the ground, plants, and other objects begin radiating the heat they absorbed during the day and the temperature drops sharply. This also happens in the city, but the warm air escaping from buildings offsets one-quarter or even more of the heat that is being lost by radiation.

Shading is the main reason for the reduced sunshine at ground level, but there is another. City air is much dustier than country air—it is more polluted. The extent of the radiation loss varies according to the height of the Sun because of the varying distance that solar radiation must travel through the polluted air. When the Sun is low in the sky the city may lose almost one-third of its incoming solar radiation. The most dramatic losses used to occur when coal was widely used for domestic heating, so city air contained large amounts of smoke. This used to reduce the duration of sunshine by about 44 minutes a day in the center of London, England. The smoke also absorbed infrared radiation from the surface, so it helped to make the nights warmer. Cities have been much sunnier since coal burning was banned.

Cities are less windy, except along urban canyons

Cities are less windy than the surrounding countryside. The average wind speed is up to 30 percent lower inside the city than it is outside and there are 5 percent to 20 percent more calm days. This is due to the friction caused by buildings. Wind blowing in from outside is deflected this way and that, so there are many eddies and the wind inside the city is gusty, but each of the structures it blows against absorbs some of its energy. The buildings slow the wind.

There are exceptions, however. Buildings block and deflect the wind quite effectively, but only provided that they are aligned at an angle to the wind direction. If they are aligned approximately in the same direction as the wind, the wind speed will increase. The effect is called *funneling* and it happens most often in urban canyons.

As the moving air approaches, the buildings guide it into the spaces between them—along the streets. The street confines the air into a narrower space than it occupied outside, but it must leave the canyon at the same rate as the air above it and to the sides, which was not funneled along it. If the air did not accelerate, air would accumulate on one side of town and there would be less on the opposite side. This means that the air must move faster along the street than it does elsewhere. The wind accelerates, just as wind accelerates when it is funneled through a natural canyon.

Heat islands and urban domes

Air escaping from heated buildings, atmospheric particles absorbing infrared radiation at night, the reduction in wind speed, and the heat from thousands of engines combine to make the city into an island of warmth surrounded by a cool, rural "sea." It is a *heat island*.

During the day the temperature rises rapidly. On a sunny day in summer it may rise by as much as 31°F (17°C) between dawn and the middle of the afternoon. It falls again at night, but in the early part of the night the city center may be up to 14°F (8°C) warmer than the surrounding countryside. The effect is so strong that urban heat islands are clearly visible in satellite photographs taken in infrared light.

On clear, calm nights the difference between the temperature inside and outside the city sometimes generates *country breezes*. Warm air rises over the city center, producing a local area of low pressure. Air from outside the city converges on the low-pressure region, entering as a cool, light wind.

A similar breeze occurs when city air becomes trapped beneath an *urban dome*. This happens when warm air lies above cooler air, producing a *temperature inversion* above the city. Warm air rises over the city, but cannot penetrate the inversion, because air in the inversion layer is less dense than the air rising from below. Trapped beneath the inversion, the city air spreads to the sides. As it moves, the warm air loses heat by radiating it upward, so the farther it travels from the center the cooler the air becomes. Its density increases as its temperature decreases and the air subsides just outside the city boundary. It then returns to the city center as a low-level

Urban dome

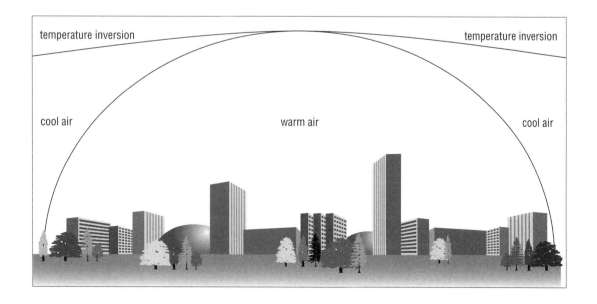

temperature inversion   temperature inversion

cool air   warm air   cool air

breeze. This establishes a cell-like flow of air, with air converging at ground level in the city center and diverging beneath the inversion. As the illustration on page 155 shows, the warm air then forms a dome above the city.

Heat islands and global warming

A weather station located in a large urban area will consistently show higher temperatures than a weather station located in the open countryside. If the temperature record is being used to detect signs of climate change, this is not necessarily important, because both sets of readings will change together. They will be in step, so that any warming or cooling trend should appear in both.

There is a problem, however, where a city spreads to engulf a weather station in a formerly rural area. The record from that station will then show a rise in temperature that has nothing to do with genuine climate change, but is caused by the urban heat island effect. Climatologists searching for evidence of climate change must remove this bias from the record.

They have been quite successful at this in many places. Where there are two reporting stations in the same area, one in an urban and the other in a rural location, their records can be compared. If the urban station reports a rise in temperature that is not detected at the rural station, the rise is attributed to the heat island effect and is ignored.

The method is more difficult to apply in areas that have become urbanized only recently. This is because a period of between 10 and 15 years must elapse before the heat island warming becomes evident against the natural variation in temperature. During this time the station may record a rise in temperature that cannot be clearly identified as due to urbanization. There is no way to remove this bias and therefore recent temperature trends have to be adjusted by an estimated amount. Studies have shown that urbanization has produced an apparent increase in temperature of approximately 0.09°F (0.05°C) in the period 1900–90 and the IPCC climate scientists have allowed a margin of error to produce an estimate of a heat island effect of 0.22°F (0.12°C) by 2000. This is an estimate, however, and some critics feel it is too low. They maintain that cities have spread faster and wider than the IPCC allows and that urban heat islands are contributing more than 0.22°F (0.12°C) to the warming trend.

Scientists know that any village with a population of more than about 1,000 will have a heat island, raising the average temperature to 3.6–4.5°F (2–2.5°C) above that of the surrounding countryside, and that even an out-of-town retail park will produce one. The magnitude of the effect is directly linked to the size of the population and can reach a maximum of almost 22°F (12°C).

A study based on measurements of infrared radiation by the Advanced Very High Resolution Radiometer carried on the NOAA-9 satellite and similar data from the NOAA-14 satellite revealed the scale of the urban heat island effect over the city of Houston, Texas. The data showed that between 1987 and 1999 the nighttime surface temperature at Houston increased by 1.46–1.49°F (0.81–0.83°C) and that the rate of increase was proportional to the 30-percent increase in population during this period. The warming was due to the urban heat island effect and not to any wider change in the climate.

Urban heat islands are real. They do increase the temperature above that of their rural hinterland and it may be that their influence on global temperatures is being underestimated.

IS THE SEA RISING?

Many of the world's great cities are very close to sea level and close to a coast or beside a tidal river. Baltimore, Maryland, is 13 feet (4 m) above sea level, for example, Charleston, South Carolina, is at 10 feet (3 m), and New Orleans, Louisiana, is a mere 6.5 feet (2 m) above sea level. London, England, is only 16 feet (5 m) above sea level, and Marseilles, France, 13 feet (4 m). The reason is obvious. Until railroad networks provided the means to move goods and people efficiently over long distances, the cheapest and most convenient way to travel was by water. Cities grew up in places that were easily accessible, beside navigable rivers or natural harbors.

If the sea level should rise by a large amount, many of these cities would be inundated. The economic and human consequences would be catastrophic. Some people fear that if the global climate grows warmer this is precisely what may happen. The evidence of what has happened in the past and the best scientific estimates of what may happen in the future suggest that the fears have been overstated.

The expansion and contraction of ice sheets

There are several reasons why sea levels rise and fall. The biggest changes are associated with the growth and disappearance of ice sheets during an ice age. Ice sheets represent a vast quantity of water. Even today, when we are living in an interglacial episode between ice ages, the Greenland and Antarctic ice sheets contain between them about 6.85 million cubic miles (28.56 million km^3) of ice. Add to this the smaller valley glaciers and ice caps, and the total amount of ice is approximately 6.90 million cubic miles (28.74 million km^3). This accounts for about 75 percent of all the fresh water on Earth. During the coldest part of the most recent ice age, the total volume of ice is believed to have been 18.89–19.61 million cubic miles (78.74–81.74 million km^3).

The ice is made from water that originally came from the oceans. Its accumulation as ice means that water has been removed from the oceans and not returned to them. It is sea water that is being stored on land. There are places near to many coasts where the extent of this storage can be seen in the form of *raised beaches*. A raised beach is a layer of beach material—sand or well-rounded pebbles mixed with seashells—that is now some distance above the present shoreline. It used to be a beach at a time when the sea level was higher than it is today. In Papua New Guinea there are layers of coral—the skeletons of animals that live in shallow seas—that lived about 125,000 years ago. These layers are now 1,312 feet (400 m) above sea level.

If the present ice were to melt, it would release enough water into the oceans to raise sea levels by about 230 feet (70 m). This would drown many cities.

Isostasy and glacial rebound

Ice sheets have a second effect. Ice is very heavy and the present Greenland ice sheet is an average 10,000 feet (3,000 m) thick and the Antarctic ice sheet 6,900 feet (2,100 m). During an ice age, ice sheets of this thickness cover a much greater area. The immense weight of ice depresses the crust beneath it.

The Earth's crust is made from solid rocks that lie above the hot, slightly plastic rocks of the *mantle*. The mantle behaves like a liquid with respect to the solid rocks of the crust, so effectively the crust floats on the mantle. When any object floats in a liquid it experiences an upward force, called *buoyancy*, that is equal to the weight of the liquid it displaces—this is *Archimedes' principle*. The body will find an equilibrium and this will determine whether it floats on the surface, sinks to the bottom, or floats at the surface only partly immersed. Ice, for example, has a density that is 90 percent of the density of liquid water. Consequently, ice floats with 10 percent above the surface. Geologists call buoyant equilibrium *isostasy*.

Crustal rocks, floating on the mantle, also achieve isostasy. The rocks are partially immersed in the mantle, to a depth that is proportional to the difference in density of the rock and mantle material. The mantle, despite being like a liquid in this respect, is made from denser material than crustal rock. Mountains have roots that project down into the mantle. If the mass of the crust increases, as it does when a thick sheet of ice accumulates on the surface, the rocks sink into the mantle under the weight, like a ship when it is loaded with a cargo, achieving a new equilibrium, called *glacioisostasy*. As the continents sink into the mantle, the sea rises by the same amount. When the ice age ends and the ice sheets melt, the crust rebounds. It is a slow process, but gradually the crust rises to its former level, and the sea level—the position of the sea surface relative to the land—falls. The rebound affects only the regions that lay beneath the ice or very close to its edges, and it continues to this day.

The melting of the ice releases water into the ocean, returning it from the ice sheets where it was stored. This raises the sea level and so the overall effect is equal to the extent of glacial rebound of the crust, minus the sea-level rise due to the release of meltwater.

The net effect is considerable. There are raised beaches in places bordering the Baltic Sea and Hudson Bay that are nearly 1,000 feet (300 m) above the present sea level. Material in them has been dated and is less than 14,000 years old, so this is the extent by which the land has risen by glacial rebound over this period. Parts of Scandinavia have risen about

1,700 feet (520 m) since the end of the ice age, but geologists believe that when the ice was thickest the crust was depressed by about 3,000 feet (1,000 m), so Scandinavia will continue to rise for some time yet. Scotland is also rising from the sea by glacial rebound, but at a rate that is not much different from the rate of sea-level rise from the melting of the ice sheets, so there is little overall change.

There are also places where the coast is eroding. Erosion by the action of the sea allows the sea to encroach further inland. At the same time, material eroded from the land is deposited on the seabed, raising it. Coastal erosion raises the sea level.

Thermal expansion and storage

Sea level is also affected by changes in temperature. Water expands when it grows warmer and contracts when it cools. If the average global air temperature rises, this reflects a rise in the surface temperature, because air is heated from below, by contact with the surface. If the oceans become warmer, the water will expand and sea levels will rise. This *thermal expansion* is estimated to account for about one-third of the observed rise in sea level during the 20th century.

Human activities can also lower the sea level. Nowadays we store large amounts of water in reservoirs and we pump water below ground, into abandoned mine workings, for example, to store it for future use. Without this intervention, the water would have returned to the sea and so storage causes the sea level to fall. In some parts of the world, however, we are doing the opposite by "mining" underground water—removing it faster than it is being replenished. The water we use eventually finds its way back to the sea, and so the mining of groundwater raises the sea level.

These changes illustrate the fact that the sea level is not constant. It changes slowly due to entirely natural causes over which we exert no influence whatever. Coastal erosion is a natural, continuing process. Engineering can control it to some extent, through building sea walls, for example, but many scientists believe the safest course is to allow it to happen, except where it threatens communities. In order to determine whether our own activities or climate change are affecting sea level, scientists need to monitor the sea level very precisely over a long period and deduct the natural variations from the changes they have observed.

Records of sea level

There are records of sea level, but few of them extend very far into the past. Sea levels are monitored by instruments called *tide gauges*. There are several types, but most record the movement of a float in a well fed from the sea, or by the pressure of sea water acting on a bubble of air. They record the rise and fall of the tides as a line on a chart drawn by a pen on paper fixed to a rotating drum, or as a digital record fed to a computer. The average height the water reaches—the *mean tide level*—can be calculated from the tide record, and so changes in it can be identified.

There are a few other, older records, including a benchmark carved in a rock at the Isle of the Dead, off Port Arthur, Tasmania, to mark the mean tide level as it was in 1841 (see the sidebar). This seems to show a very small rise in sea level since the benchmark was carved. With these few exceptions, earlier changes in sea level must be calculated indirectly, mainly from the location of layers of sediment.

Will the sea rise in years to come?

Clearly there is much uncertainty about the extent to which the sea level is changing. The IPCC combines measurements and estimates based on

Isle of the Dead

In the middle of the 19th century the island of Tasmania, then known as Van Diemen's Land, was a British penal settlement. Thomas Lemprière, one of the officials in charge of the settlement, maintained careful records of tides and weather. In July 1841, the Antarctic explorer Sir James Clark Ross (after whom the Ross Sea is named) visited Tasmania and met Lemprière. The two men discussed Lemprière's meteorological and tidal records and the problem Lemprière had with tide gauges. Convicts vandalized the gauges and he had to keep moving them to new locations. In the course of their conversation, Lemprière and Ross hit upon a plan to make a permanent mark, called a *benchmark*, that would be carved into the rock, to show the height of the mean tide—the level halfway between the lowest and highest points reached by the tide, which they measured using a tide gauge. In *A Voyage of Discovery and Research in the Southern and Antarctic Regions During the Years 1839– 43* (John Murray, London, 1847), a book describing his explorations, Ross mentions that the benchmark was set at the mean tide level as he and Lemprière estimated it in 1841.

They decided this mark should be made on a small island, about two acres (1 ha) in area, in Port Arthur harbor, at a point sheltered from storm-driven waves. Convicts avoided the island, because it was used as a burial ground. For this reason it was known as the Isle of the Dead. The convicts found it spooky.

Lemprière and Ross set up a tide gauge on the Isle of the Dead on July 1, 1841, and carved a benchmark beside it. In the 1990s, John L. Daly, a Tasmanian with a keen interest in climatology, read about the benchmark and decided to explore the shore of the Isle of the Dead in search of it. He found the mark exactly where the records showed it should be.

Some controversy surrounds its significance, but the probability is that the height of the benchmark indicates that the sea level has risen one inch (2.5 cm) since it was last examined. This was in 1888 by the government meteorologist Commander J. Shortt. This change in sea level is consistent with present rates of sea-level change around the coast of Western Australia, ranging from a fall of 0.037 inch per year (0.95 mm yr^{-1}) to a rise of 0.054 inch a year (1.38 mm yr^{-1}).

computer models to conclude that between 1910 and 1990 the sea level throughout the world changed annually by an average between –0.032 inch (–0.8 mm) and +0.09 inch (+2.2 mm), with a central value of +0.06 inch (+1.5 mm) a year. The change has been due to a number of factors. These, and the contribution each is estimated to have made, are listed in the table.

Sedimentation refers to the effect of material transported to the sea and raising the seabed. Some is transported by rivers and some results from coastal erosion. Storage on land is more complicated and its value is less certain than the others. It consists of the water that is held in reservoirs and in groundwater, and that remains on land due to changes in land use. Storage on land is likely to lower the sea level, but changes in land use might not if, for example, ground water were "mined" for irrigation or other uses faster than the underground aquifers could recharge.

The best estimates therefore suggest that during the 20th century the sea level has been rising, perhaps by 0.03 inch (0.7 mm) a year—although it may have been falling by 0.03 inch (0.8 mm) or rising by 0.09 inch (2.2 mm a year). If this rate of change continues for a century, sea levels will be about 3 inches (8 cm) lower than they are now, or up to 9 inches (22 cm) higher.

Whether this is a realistic prediction depends on what happens to the global climate. If the climate continues to grow warmer at a constant rate, then this is the magnitude of sea-level change we might expect. If warm-

SEA LEVEL CHANGE 1910–1990

Cause	Minimum in yr^{-1} (mm yr^{-1})	Central value in yr^{-1} (mm yr^{-1})	Maximum in yr^{-1} (mm yr^{-1})
Thermal expansion	0.012 (0.3)	0.020 (0.5)	0.028 (0.7)
Melting glaciers and ice caps	0.008 (0.2)	0.012 (0.3)	0.016 (0.4)
Greenland ice sheet (20th century)	0.0 (0.0)	0.002 (0.05)	0.004 (0.1)
Antarctic ice sheet (20th century)	–0.008 (–0.2)	–0.004 (–0.1)	0.0 (0.0)
Ice sheets since coldest part of last ice age	0.0 (0.0)	0.010 (0.25)	0.02 (0.5)
Melting permafrost	0.00 (0.00)	0.001 (0.025)	0.002 (0.05)
Sedimentation	0.00 (0.00)	0.001 (0.025)	0.002 (0.05)
Storage on land	–0.04 (–1.1)	–0.01 (–0.35)	0.02 (0.4)
Total	–0.03 (–0.8)	0.03 (0.7)	0.09 (2.2)

(Source: IPCC Third Assessment Report)

SEA-LEVEL CHANGE 1990–2100		
Cause	Inches	Meters
Thermal expansion	4.3–17	0.11–0.43
Glaciers melting	0.4–9	0.01–0.23
Greenland ice sheet	−0.8–3.5	−0.02–0.09
Antarctic ice sheets	−6.7–0.8	−0.17–0.02
Total	4.3–30	0.11–0.77

(Source: IPCC Third Assessment Report)

ing were to accelerate, sea level would rise more than this, and if the rate of warming were to decrease there would be a correspondingly smaller change in sea level.

Based on results from a total of eight computer models, the IPCC estimates that between 1990 and 2100 the global sea level will rise by an average of 4.3–30 inches (0.11–0.77 m), with a best estimate of 19 inches (0.49 m). The table shows the contribution each factor makes to this estimate.

GLOBAL WARMING

In 1985, the International Institute for Applied Systems Analysis, based in Laxenburg, Austria, hosted a meeting of representatives from the United Nations Environment Program (UNEP) and the International Council of Scientific Unions (ICSU). The purpose of the meeting was to discuss global warming and to take the first steps in preparing an international climate treaty aimed at bringing it under control. At the time, climate scientists knew about the greenhouse effect (see "Greenhouse gases and the greenhouse effect" on pages 94–104) and they also knew that industrial expansion and transport systems in many parts of the world were powered by energy derived from burning fossil fuels. Combustion of fossil fuels releases carbon dioxide and so it was reasonable to suspect that as the chemical composition of the atmosphere changed, the natural greenhouse effect might be enhanced, leading to a general rise in temperature.

Scientific understanding was theoretically solid, in that the way carbon dioxide and certain other greenhouse gases absorb infrared radiation was well known. There were also two continuous records of the atmospheric concentration of carbon dioxide from 1958, obtained at the Mauna Loa Observatory, on Hawaii, and at the South Pole. These are especially valuable because of the remoteness of the sites from any industrial region, ensuring that the carbon dioxide concentration is typical of air throughout the world and is not affected by local emissions. Nevertheless, in 1985 the carbon dioxide record extended over only 27 years. That is not very long compared with the rate at which the climate changes, but data on concentrations in the more distant past are available from sediment and ice cores, although these sources do not provide a continuous record.

Much less was known about the way the atmosphere might respond to this change in its composition. It might warm, certainly, but atmospheric movements would also affect it, so the warming might not be distributed evenly and other factors, such as changes in cloud cover, might modify the effect.

The Intergovernmental Panel on Climate Change

The next development came in 1988, when UNEP and the World Meteorological Organization (WMO) jointly formed the Intergovernmental Panel on Climate Change (IPCC). The WMO is a United Nations agency and so the IPCC belongs to the UN "family" of organizations. It exists to advise governments on the basis of information obtained from scientists throughout the world. It does not conduct research itself. The word *panel* is slightly misleading, since it suggests a small number of individuals gathered around a table. In fact, the "panel" comprises several hundred individuals.

Following its inception, the IPCC formed three Working Groups. It is the task of Working Group I to assess the available scientific information on climate change. Working Group II assesses the environmental and socioeconomic impacts of climate change. Working Group III formulates strategies for responding to climate change. The ultimate aim of the IPCC is to provide the basis on which politicians can build a climate treaty. In other words, the IPCC was founded in the belief that climate change is occurring, that human activity is influencing it, and that the implications of that change are so grave as to necessitate a coordinated international response. Since the adoption of the United Nations Framework Convention on Climate Change (see the sidebar on page 183), the IPCC has also undertaken to provide advice, on request, to the Conference of the Parties to the Convention.

Since its inception the IPCC has produced three assessment reports, each report comprising separate volumes from the three Working Groups, a summary for policy makers, and an overall summary. These reports were published in 1990, 1996, and 2001, with an updated summary in 1992. The IPCC also publishes a range of other reports and technical papers.

The Third Assessment Report

Only Working Group I (WGI) is concerned with assessing the scientific evidence of climate change and the projections of ways the climate may respond in the future. That task is formidable. *Climate Change 2001: The Scientific Basis*, the WGI contribution to the IPCC Third Assessment Report, published in 2001 (by Cambridge University Press), comes to 881 pages. It comprises 14 chapters, seven appendixes, and an index. Each chapter is written by a team of "lead authors." The number of lead authors varies, but it took a total of 122 lead authors to write the entire report. In addition, 515 contributing authors submitted draft text. When the draft was ready, it was sent to 420 reviewers. Once their comments had been noted, the revised draft was sent for comment to several hundred government officials. The report was modified in the light of their comments and the final version was adopted by WGI at a meeting in Shanghai on January 17–20, 2001.

The 2001 report states that the average temperature increased by 0.72–1.44°F (0.4–0.8°C) over the course of the 20th century and that the 1990s were very likely to have been the warmest decade. Two-thirds of the temperature increase occurred at night and one-third during the day. This means that the diurnal temperature range—the difference between daytime and nighttime temperatures—has decreased. It reports that the area permanently covered by snow has decreased by about 10 percent since the 1960s, that Arctic sea ice has become thinner and covers a smaller area. Precipitation has increased during the 20th century, by 0.5–1.0 percent per decade over middle and high latitudes of the Northern Hemisphere and by 0.2–0.3 percent per decade in the Tropics, although no increase has been observed in tropical areas in the last few decades of the century. Rainfall decreased by about 0.3 percent per decade between latitudes 10° N and 30° N. Sea levels rose by 3.9–7.9 inches (10–20 cm) during the century.

The report also points out that some areas experienced no warming. These were mainly in the Southern Hemisphere, including parts of Antarctica. The area covered by Antarctic sea ice has not changed since accurate satellite monitoring began in 1978.

Criticisms

In order to estimate what will happen in the future, the report uses four "story lines" that lead to four families of "scenarios." In all there are 40 scenarios, of which 35 contain complete data on all emissions. Each of them is based on assumptions about changes in global population size, economic growth, relative economic development among regions, and the technological and economic driving forces that affect emissions of gases and particles into the atmosphere. The overall summary of future climate change is derived from just six of these scenarios. The authors of the report consider all six to be equally plausible. The estimate of temperature change uses data from all 35. It suggests that between 1990 and 2100 the average global temperature will rise by 2.52–10.44°F (1.4–5.8°C). Sea levels are projected to rise by 4.3–30 inches (11–77 cm).

The very high temperature increase, of 10.44°F (5.8°C), is the result of assumptions about emissions of sulfur dioxide (SO_2), and although several models of emission scenarios predict it, when the models are combined the figure is reduced to 8.1°F (4.5°C). Sulfur dioxide forms sulfate aerosols that have a cooling effect, but there are uncertainties over the magnitude of their effect. All of the six illustrative scenarios used in the IPCC report predict a large drop in SO_2 emissions, thus reducing their cooling effect and leading to greater warming.

This reduction is based on the observation that SO_2 emissions have fallen sharply throughout the industrialized world, and especially in the European Union and United States, and are likely to continue falling. They have been curbed because of their link to acid rain. The rise in emissions of greenhouse gases that causes the temperature to rise happens throughout the world, however, and the IPCC projections assume fairly rapid economic growth throughout the industrializing countries of Asia, Latin America, and, with a time lag, Africa, powered by increasing consumption of fossil fuels. It seems less than certain that this development will be achieved using low-sulfur fuels or technologies to remove sulfur from exhaust gases before they are released. Such technologies exist and are used to limit sulfur emissions in the industrial countries, but they do not remove all the SO_2. Even if they were adopted everywhere, the predicted increase in fossil-fuel combustion might still lead to higher global emissions of sulfur. If the projected fall in sulfur emissions errs on the side of optimism, then the high figure for temperature rise will err on the side of pessimism.

The IPCC assumes that carbon dioxide emissions will increase by 1 percent each year exponentially. This means the increase will follow the pattern of compound interest. Each annual increment is calculated as 1 percent of the value for the previous year, added to that value, and the total is used as the basis for next year's calculation. At this rate of growth the atmospheric concentration of carbon dioxide will double after approximately 70 years. Observation shows that carbon dioxide is accumulating at a linear or simple interest, not exponential rate. This is much slower and means the amount will double in about 120 years.

The slower rate of accumulation is due to the fact that fuel use is becoming steadily more efficient, allowing us to obtain more in the way of products for each unit of fuel consumed. Decades ago a typical European family car might travel about 25 miles on a gallon of fuel (11 km 1^{-1}). Today a similar car is likely to travel about 35 miles on the same amount of fuel (15 km 1^{-1}) and fuel economy is still improving. New domestic appliances use energy more efficiently than those they replace and their efficiency rating is a selling point—the more efficient they are, the cheaper they are to run. Manufacturing industry also seeks to improve its efficiency, in order to hold down costs. As newly industrializing countries expand their manufacturing, they often use obsolescent machines bought from European or American companies that are replacing them. They can afford to do this because low labor costs mean their products are still competitive, but this is an advantage that will diminish as their economies expand and wages rise. They will then use more efficient equipment and their carbon dioxide emissions will increase more slowly—although they will nevertheless increase, of course.

Certain other greenhouse gas emissions are likely to decrease. CFCs (chlorofluorocarbons) and related compounds, for example, are being withdrawn from use because they break down in the stratosphere, yielding chlorine that breaks down ozone. They are also powerful absorbers of infrared radiation. Atmospheric concentrations of them have already begun to fall. The IPCC report assumes that atmospheric concentrations of methane will increase, but in fact the rate of increase began to slow in the early 1980s and it is now close to zero.

Doubts about economic growth

Critics also point out that the projections of economic growth, on which emissions of greenhouse gases are based, may be flawed. This is not a criticism of the climate science, but of the economic techniques the scientists have used in order to develop the scenarios. Projections of future global warming are based on the assumption that economic growth, especially in the countries that are still industrializing, will lead to increasing emissions of greenhouse gases. The rate of economic growth therefore makes a considerable difference to the outcome.

There are two ways to measure economic growth. The first begins by assessing the gross domestic product (GDP) of a country and converting it into a universal standard currency—usually U.S. dollars—at the market exchange (MEX) rate. GDP is the total value of all the goods and services produced in a country during one year, valued at current market prices and taking account of taxes and subsidies, divided by the number of people living in the country. This is the method used in most of the climate models (see "Modeling the atmosphere" on pages 169–174) on which the IPCC report is based. Consequently, it is the method the IPCC authors were constrained to adopt. Its disadvantage is that it takes no account of actual purchasing power in different countries. Most economists, including those at the U.N. Statistical Commission, have abandoned it for this reason. Instead they measure purchasing power parity (PPP). This compares the cost of the same goods in two different countries. The two methods sound very similar, but PPP is not tied to fluctuations in exchange rates and so it provides a more reliable comparison. Most important, it is a much more reliable guide to the actual purchasing power people possess. By undervaluing purchasing power, MEX leads modelers to assume unrealistic rates of growth if economies are to reach the predicted levels—in some scenarios of $70,000 per person at 1990 values, approaching the levels for industrialized countries of $100,000 or rather more. When PPP is substituted for MEX in the economic growth forecasts, the projected temperature increases in all six of the "marker" scenarios fall by about 15 percent. If the very high rates of economic growth are scaled back to a more credible level, the temperature rise is reduced still more.

Population size also affects greenhouse gas emissions. No one can know just how many people there will be in the world by 2100, so the scenarios use United Nations estimates. These offer high, medium, and low variants. Some scenarios follow each of the variants. This may introduce errors.

The difficulty the IPCC authors face is that no matter how well scientists understand how the atmosphere works, predictions depend crucially on how humans will behave in the future. This is much more difficult to predict. If greenhouse gases continue to accumulate at the present rate, it seems likely that by 2100 the average global temperature rise will be at the lower end of the IPCC projections, at around 2.7–3.6°F (1.5–2.0°C).

MODELING THE ATMOSPHERE

When climate scientists need to know the answer to "What would happen if . . .?" questions, they cannot change the world in order to find out. In this sense climate science is unlike most other scientific disciplines. A geologist, for example, can find out how much stress a particular type of rock can withstand before fracturing by placing a sample of the rock in a device which subjects it to increasing stress while displaying the amount of stress. Even an ecologist can perform experiments by changing the conditions on an experimental plot and comparing the effects with a control plot where the conditions remain constant.

Life is more difficult for climate scientists because the phenomena they study are so large and impossible to isolate. Even a minor summer thunderstorm is the size of a small town in horizontal area—8–20 square miles (21–52 km^2)—and extends vertically to about 35,000 feet (10.7 km). It is hardly something a scientist could study in a laboratory and even if that were possible, the thunderstorm is not really an isolated event. It draws in air from its surroundings and moisture from the surface beneath it, and its development is strongly influenced by the winds in the upper atmosphere.

Constructing models

Faced with this dilemma, scientists construct *models*. A model is a representation of some aspect of the real world. All of us construct models and carry them in our heads. They help us to make sense of the world around us and to predict how events will unfold. When you look to see whether the road is clear before crossing, you are using a mental model that tells you that an approaching car that is a certain distance away will reach a point halfway across the road at the same time you do. It also tells you that if it collides with you, the car may kill you. So you wait. You are making mental calculations based on your model of the way cars move and the effect of being hit by one. None of us would live very long if we lacked such models.

Climate models simulate the way the weather behaves, and they do so mathematically. Air is a mixture of gases and the temperature, pressure, and volume of a gas are related by a set of *gas laws* (see the sidebar on page 170). The rate at which the temperature changes with height—the *lapse rate*—is also known (see the sidebar on "Lapse rates and stability" on page 171).

The gas laws

The temperature, pressure, and volume of a gas are linked by a number of physical laws. Together these are known as the *gas laws* and they can be combined into a single *equation of state*.

In 1662 the Irish physicist Robert Boyle (1627–91) discovered that when a gas is compressed, its volume decreases by an amount proportional to the pressure acting on it. This is expressed as:

$$pV = \text{a constant}$$

where p is the pressure and V is the volume. In English-speaking countries it is known as *Boyle's law*.

About 15 years later the French physicist Edmé Mariotte (*ca.* 1620–84) made the same discovery, but noted that pV = a constant is true only if the temperature remains constant, because a gas expands when it is heated. In French-speaking countries Mariotte's more complete version of the law is known as *Mariotte's law*.

In 1699 the French physicist Guillaume Amontons (1663–1705) described *Amontons's law* relating the pressure, temperature, and volume of a gas. With the volume held constant, this is expressed as:

$$p_1 T_2 = p_2 T_1$$

where p_1 and T_1 are the initial pressure and temperature, T_2 is the temperature after it has been changed, and p_2 is the resulting pressure.

Jacques Alexandre César Charles (1736–1823), the French physicist and mathematician, repeated Amontons's experiments in about 1787 and discovered the amount by which the volume of a gas changes in response to a change in its temperature, provided the pressure remains constant. This is *Charles's law*, expressed as:

$$V \div T = \text{a constant}.$$

Charles discovered that for every temperature rise of one degree Celsius the volume of a gas increases by $1 \div 273$ of the volume it occupies at 0°C. It follows that at −273°C the volume of the gas must reach zero and no lower temperature is possible. This is *absolute zero*, equal to 0 kelvin (0K) and now known to be −273.15°C (−459.67°F).

The *pressure law* is derived from Boyle's (or Mariotte's) law and Charles's law. It states that provided the volume remains constant, the pressure within a gas is directly proportional to its temperature.

These laws are combined into a single equation of state from which a *universal gas equation* is derived:

$$pV = nR^*T$$

where n is the amount of gas in moles and R^* is the gas constant (8.31434 J K^{-1} mol^{-1}). It is not feasible to consider part of the atmosphere in isolation, because it is unconfined, but the volume of a gas is equal to its mass (m) multiplied by its density (ρ). Substituting the *specific gas constant for air* ($R = 10^3$ $R^* \div M$, where M is the relative molecular mass) for R^* allows the equation to be:

$$p = \rho RT.$$

Comparing the actual rate of temperature change with height with the dry and saturated adiabatic lapse rates allows scientists to measure the stability of air. The humidity of the air (see the sidebar on page 152) is proportional to the temperature. These relationships provide a basis for representing, or modeling, the atmosphere mathematically.

Air and the moisture it contains are in constant motion, and vaporization, condensation, sublimation, and deposition absorb and release latent heat (see the sidebar on page 32). Modeling these aspects of the atmosphere is much more complicated and involves solving difficult equations. The chemical composition of the air also changes through the emission of gases, such as sulfur dioxide and nitrogen oxides, that interreact to produce aerosols that affect climate. Changes in land use alter the surface albedo and cloud formation alter the planetary albedo (see "How bright is the Earth?" on pages 113–120). All of these influences must be taken into account.

The development of climate models

Modeling begins by imposing an imaginary, three-dimensional grid over the surface of the Earth. A picture of such a grid would resemble a cage, with lines running parallel to the equator and at right angles to it—like lines of latitude and longitude—but repeated at different heights.

Lapse rates and stability

Air temperature decreases (or lapses) with increasing height. The rate at which it does so is called the lapse rate. When dry air cools adiabatically (without exchanging energy with the surrounding air), it does so at 5.5°F for every 1,000 feet (10°C per km). This is known as the dry adiabatic lapse rate (DALR).

When the temperature of the rising air has fallen sufficiently, its water vapor will start to condense into droplets. This temperature is known as the dew point temperature and the height at which it is reached is called the lifting condensation level. Condensation releases latent heat, which warms the air. Consequently, the air cools at a slower rate, known as the saturated adiabatic lapse rate (SALR). The SALR varies, but averages 3°F per 1,000 feet (6°C per km).

The actual rate at which the temperature decreases with height is calculated by comparing the surface temperature, the temperature at the tropopause (about –67°F; –55°C in middle latitudes), and the height of the tropopause (about 7 miles; 11 km in middle latitudes). The result is called the environmental lapse rate (ELR).

If the ELR is less than both the DALR and SALR, rising air will cool faster than the surrounding air, so it will always be cooler and will tend to subside to a lower height. Such air is said to be *absolutely stable*.

If the ELR is greater than the SALR, air that is rising and cooling at the DALR and later at the SALR will always be warmer than the surrounding air. Consequently it will continue to rise. The air is then *absolutely unstable*.

If the ELR is greater than the DALR but less than the SALR, rising air will cool faster than the surrounding air while it remains dry, but more slowly once it rises above the lifting condensation level. At first it is stable, but above the lifting condensation level it becomes unstable. This air is said to be *conditionally unstable*. It is stable unless a condition (rising above its lifting condensation level) is met, whereupon it becomes unstable.

The modeler will then measure the conditions at every intersection on the grid. For each intersection, the modeler must supply data—numbers—describing the state of the atmosphere at that point. The data are fitted to the equations and all the equations are solved to show how the situation at each grid intersection affects the adjacent intersections. This operation must be performed for every intersection in the grid, and it is repeated, usually to represent intervals of 30 minutes. The model thus depicts the development of weather systems throughout the world as a series of 30-minute snapshots.

Obviously it is a huge task and much too large to be undertaken by individual scientists working with calculators. Modeling the atmosphere became feasible only with the introduction of powerful computers.

The first models considered only the atmosphere. They ignored changes in the land surface and the influence of the oceans. Climatologists knew that these were extremely important, of course, but they lacked the computing power to include them and, in any case, the relationship between the atmosphere and oceans was not well understood, making it impossible to provide reliable equations. Despite their limitations, these models, developed in the middle 1970s, were the first *general circulation models* (GCMs). They aimed to represent the general circulation of the atmosphere (see "General circulation of the atmosphere" on pages 10–17).

Ten years later, computer power had increased and new models were developed that took account of the land surface. They were still unable to include the influence of the oceans, but the ocean circulation and heat transport were the subject of separate models that also included sea ice. The two could be combined, up to a point, by using the output of one model as input to the other. By the early 1990s, with further increases in computing power, the ocean and atmospheric models were fully integrated. They were now known as *atmosphere–ocean general circulation models* (AOGCMs).

It was becoming possible to begin taking account of certain aspects of atmospheric chemistry. A model of the sulfur cycle was constructed in the early 1990s and by the end of the decade it had been merged with the AOGCMs. The carbon cycle (see "The carbon cycle" on pages 105–112) was also being modeled, at first with two models, one representing the carbon cycle on land and the other the cycle in the oceans. These were merged into a single model by the late 1990s and have now been added to the AOGCMs, as has a section of the model dealing with the effect of non-sulfate aerosols. The full modeling of atmospheric chemistry began in the early 1990s. It now exists as a separate model and scientists hope it will be added to the big models early in the 21st century.

The effect of vegetation is also being modeled and in time that model will be added to the overall model. Vegetation is affected by climate. Drier weather favors grasses rather than trees, for example, and extreme aridity produces deserts. Vegetation also affects the climate. Transpiration is the process by which plants take water from the ground and release it into the air, so changing the amount and type of vegetation affects the water cycle. Changes in the type of vegetation also alter the albedo.

Models have limitations

Climate models are now very detailed, but they still have limitations. Some climate processes are not yet fully understood and so assumptions have to be made about the way they function. Models are also limited by computing power. This affects the size of the grid. At present, the best models of the atmosphere over land use a grid with a side that is about 155 miles (250 km) long. Above the *boundary layer*—the lowest layer of air, extending to about 1,700 feet (519 m), in which the air is affected by surface conditions—there is a space of about 0.62 mile (1 km) between grid levels. The eight corners of a grid "box" thus enclose about 15,000 cubic miles (62,200 km²) of air. Over the ocean, the grid is usually 78–155 miles (125–250 km) horizontally and 0.12–0.25 miles (0.2–0.4 km) vertically.

Events that are calculated to occur must occur throughout the box and over land the box covers, approximately the same area as the state of West Virginia. This means that when there is a thunderstorm, it occupies that entire area. No thunderstorm was ever the size of West Virginia. Even when clouds form, the model assumes they cover the whole of their box. Many other atmospheric processes also occur on scales much smaller than the model grid and so they cannot be described accurately.

In fact, the models deal with the problem by *parameterizing* these processes. This means they give them average values and include them as approximations. Parameterization is the best solution possible, but it is not really satisfactory, especially with respect to clouds. Clouds are especially important because they both reflect and absorb energy, so they have a major effect on climate. Convection in the ocean is also important. It mixes surface waters and carries dissolved carbon dioxide to lower depths, but it, too, is a process that takes place on scales smaller than the model grid.

Additional factors have to be added to make model predictions match and to make them match the observed climate. This has been necessary to adjust for the fact that the early models predicted a much greater warming than has actually occurred, and it involved increasing the cooling effect of aerosols.

It is impossible to forecast weather, even approximately, for more than about two weeks ahead. This is because the development of weather systems is *chaotic*—differences in the initial conditions that are too small to measure dramatically affect the way the system develops. Climate models are less seriously affected by chaos because climate change develops much more slowly, so the equivalent of two weeks in a forecast might be several years in a climate model. Nevertheless, model predictions are checked by repeating their runs many times, using different models and different initial conditions, and comparing the results.

Other approaches to modeling

Smaller, simpler models produce very approximate results relating to particular parts of the climate system. They are useful for teaching and also for checking the big models. Their use results in there being a hierarchy of climate models, each with its own uses. The big models are so complicated that only the most powerful computers in the world are able to run them. There are a limited number of computers adequate to the task and access to them is necessarily restricted. Simpler models that will run on a PC allow scientists to explore specialized aspects of the overall climate.

Some climatologists adopt an entirely different approach to predicting the future development of climate. They belong to the "empirical school," which means they rely on observation rather than theory. They also use models, but theirs are *historical analog models* that use data from the past to predict the likely outcome of future changes.

In the case of the enhanced greenhouse effect, the empiricists point out that the present atmospheric concentration of carbon dioxide, of about 0.037 percent, is considerably greater than the 0.028 percent that was present in the air in about 1750. In fact, there is approximately one-third more carbon dioxide in the air now than there was then and we are already two-thirds of the way toward doubling the preindustrial concentration. This increase is enough to account for the general rise in temperature over the past century or so, but if there are to be other effects, some of those should also be evident by now. Yet, they point out, no harm seems to have ensued thus far.

Climate models are improving rapidly. The latest ones take account of the monsoons and several of the natural climate oscillations, such as the North Atlantic (or Arctic) Oscillation, although they are not yet able to include more than an approximation of the El Niño–Southern Oscillation (ENSO) phenomenon. Improvement of the models requires deeper scientific knowledge about several aspects of the global climate system. This requires research and takes time. It also requires advances in computing power, and present digital computers may be approaching an absolute limit in their power and speed that is imposed by the laws of physics. Eventually, the development of climate models may call for an entirely new type of computer, using quantum events, perhaps.

IS CLIMATE CHANGE ALL BAD?

Warmer weather sounds pleasant. A return to the climate of the medieval warm period (see "The medieval optimum" on pages 79–86) would make farming thrive. Barley and wheat would ripen much farther north than they do today. Farming communities could return to Greenland for the first time in more than 1,000 years.

Unfortunately, the global climate is complicated and the effects of a general rise in temperature are not easy to predict. The most important changes are those affecting agriculture and wildlife.

Evaporation and effective precipitation

Higher temperatures mean higher rates of evaporation, leading to increased cloudiness and higher rainfall. Indeed, the climate models predict increased rainfall for the Tropics, and also for latitudes higher than about 40° N and 40° S. Rainfall may decrease in the subtropics—the belt approximately between latitudes 30°–40° N and 30°–40° S. If this prediction proves correct, the Sahara, Arabian, Syrian, Thar, Kalahari, and Australian Deserts, all of which lie in the subtropics, will become drier.

Rainfall is projected to increase in temperate latitudes, but this does not necessarily mean that conditions will become wetter. What matters is not the amount of precipitation, but the amount of precipitation compared with the rate of evaporation—the *effective precipitation*. This is calculated by dividing the mean annual rainfall (with snow converted to its rainfall equivalent) by the mean annual temperature. If the temperature rises sufficiently, the increase in evaporation will exceed the increase in rainfall and the ground will become drier, despite receiving more rain. The climate models predict that this will be the case in summer in the interior of continents. Rainfall will increase, but in summer the ground will be drier, because moisture will be capable of evaporating faster than it falls as rain.

The Asian summer monsoon rains will become more variable. The models suggest that their intensity will vary within individual rainy seasons and also from one year to the next.

Effects on agriculture

All of these changes will have an adverse effect on farming, but only if the effective precipitation decreases. This will not happen if the rise in temperature is fairly modest—less than about 3.6°F (2°C). An increase by this amount would not increase the rate of evaporation sufficiently to reduce the effective precipitation. Instead of harming agriculture, the rise in temperature would then be beneficial. Crops would grow and ripen faster under slightly warmer conditions and the growing season would become longer, with fewer late and early frosts. Even the deserts would benefit, and some forecasts suggest the area of desert, especially the deserts of continental interiors and the semi-arid desert margins, will decrease by 4 percent to 20 percent.

The increased amount of atmospheric carbon dioxide would also benefit many crops, especially cereals other than corn (maize), root crops, leaf vegetables such as cabbages, and fruits. This is because the present concentration of carbon dioxide is so low that it limits plant growth. It is standard horticultural practice to increase the amount of carbon dioxide in the air inside greenhouses in order to stimulate growth. Some plants, such as corn and sugarcane, have evolved a modified version of photosynthesis (see the sidebar "Photosynthesis" on page 106) to use carbon dioxide more efficiently. These are the plants that would not benefit from an increase in atmospheric carbon dioxide, but plants lacking this modification would grow more vigorously.

It is possible, therefore, that agricultural output will continue to increase rather than decreasing. At present no one knows, but this is the effect the rise in temperature is having currently. Two-thirds of the rise has taken place at night. Minimum temperatures have risen more than maximum temperatures. This has had very little effect on the rate of evaporation, but the warmer nights and slightly warmer days, combined with the fertilizing effect of more carbon dioxide, are benefiting plant growth. The growing season is longer than it was. In North America, spring now begins four to 12 days earlier than it did in about 1980 and the growing season ends one to seven days later. In Europe the growing season commences four to eight days earlier and ends 14 to 22 days later.

Effects on wildlife

Wildlife is also responding to the change, but in more complex ways. Tree swallows (*Tachycineta bicolor*) in North America are breeding five to nine days earlier than they used to do, and American robins (*Turdus migratorius*) are migrating from their low-level wintering grounds to their high-altitude feeding grounds an average of two weeks earlier than they did in 1980. The change has allowed some plants and insects to move into more northerly regions or higher elevations that were previously too cold or dry for them. Butterflies are being seen in places that were once outside their range.

This can cause problems. The temperature has not risen over much of eastern North America, but the annual precipitation has increased. This means there is often more snow in winter and, because it lies deeper, the snow takes longer to melt. Robins, migrating earlier than they did, sometimes arrive at their feeding grounds before the snow has melted, so they are unable to start feeding and nesting. Marmots (*Marmota marmota*) hibernate high up in the mountains for eight months of the year, but they are emerging from hibernation nearly 40 days earlier than they did in 1980 in response to the warm spring sunshine. Unfortunately, they are emerging before the snow has melted, and they risk starving because they are still too weak to be able to walk down to lower levels that are free from snow.

Other effects are altering ecosystems. Gray wolves (*Canis lupus*) in the Isle Royale National Park, Minnesota, for example, have responded to the increased snow by hunting in larger packs. This has allowed them to kill three times more moose (*Alces alces*) than they did when they worked in smaller packs. Their increased predation has reduced the moose population. Moose feed on balsam fir (*Abies balsamea*) and so these trees are able to flourish. The ecosystem has changed slightly. It now has fewer moose and more balsam fir.

Most warming in high latitudes

The climate models suggest that warming will be most marked in the Arctic. Already there is less sea ice and the strongest warming signal of all comes from northwestern North America, including Alaska, and northeastern Siberia. Winters in these places are milder than they were.

This is the expected response to increased carbon dioxide. It occurs because during the Arctic winter the surface radiates its absorbed heat, and the temperature plummets. Cold, dense, subsiding air produces large anticyclones. Air flows outward from the anticyclones, and the extreme cold means that the air contains little moisture. Water vapor is the most powerful of all greenhouse gases, but the air over the Arctic is so dry in winter that the greenhouse effect is very small. Consequently, adding another greenhouse gas—carbon dioxide—has a disproportionately large effect. This is why all climate models predict a strong warming effect over the Arctic.

Warming in the Arctic and in northern Canada and Eurasia will affect the wildlife of these regions. The area of tundra will decrease, perhaps by 40 percent, and the ranges of animals that move freely in winter across the frozen sea will be more restricted, because the area of sea ice will also decrease, probably by about 25 percent. Migration routes, for example of caribou (*Rangifer tarandus*, known as reindeer in Europe), may change.

As the winters become milder and the summers warmer and longer, many species of plants and animals will begin to move. Seeds from the trees of temperate deciduous forests will germinate and grow in higher latitudes than they do today. Grasslands will replace forests in areas that become drier. Animals will follow the plants on which they depend for food and shelter. This is a natural process that has accompanied every climate change in the past. This time, though, there is a difference. People now manage much of the land, and this may make it more difficult for species to adapt.

On the other hand, people may encourage wildlife. The forested area is expanding throughout most of the temperate regions of the Northern Hemisphere. Forests are valued as public amenities for recreation, for the variety of wildlife they sustain, and because they absorb and store large amounts of carbon. If agricultural productivity continues to increase, the food we need will be produced from a smaller area and there will be more space for wildlife. Wildlife conservation is worthwhile whether the climate changes or not, of course. We need not wait for warmer weather before deciding to make more room for other species.

Exotic diseases

Among the species that may find new territories to colonize, some are insects that transmit diseases. Fears have been expressed that tropical diseases may spread into countries of the temperate regions. Malaria is the most dreaded of these.

Such fears are greatly exaggerated. Indeed, the risk may be nonexistent. Malaria was once common in parts of Britain. Known as "ague," it occurred in marshy areas in the east of the country, along parts of the Thames Estuary, and in the low-lying marshes of Somerset in the west of England. The last recorded case of English malaria was in 1911. True, the *Anopheles* mosquito that transmitted ague was of a different species from those that transmit tropical malaria, but the disease was the same and it was caused by the same protozoan parasite, *Plasmodium*. Malaria was prevalent in England during the centuries when the climate was distinctly cooler than it is today (see "The Little Ice Age" on pages 87–93).

It disappeared for a number of reasons. People moved away from the marshy areas, and these were largely drained. Public health provision improved and living standards rose. Draining the marshes destroyed the habitat in which mosquitoes breed. Better living standards included better housing, with fewer opportunities for mosquitoes to enter homes and feed on people while they slept. Better health provision included better education in preventing disease.

Malaria has also vanished from the other industrialized countries of the temperate regions and for the same reasons. It is difficult to see how the disease could return. Warmer weather will not restore the marshes, and without these wetlands migrating mosquitoes will lack breeding sites. If the *Plasmodium* parasite should be discovered, the public health authorities would have no difficulty in dealing with it.

In July 2000 there was an outbreak of dengue fever in El Salvador. For several years this disease slowly advanced northward through Central America. It is thought of as a tropical disease—the same "dengue" is from a Swahili word—and another of those that warmer weather might bring to temperate regions. Interestingly, though, the disease advanced as far as the United States border, but no farther. Its advance was checked by the efficiently organized U.S. health authorities, which were ready for it and took the appropriate steps to prevent its spread.

Dengue fever is also spread by mosquitoes, and it used to be well known in Europe. In England it was known as "breakbone fever" or "dandy fever." This referred to its most distressing symptom, which is pain and stiffness in the joints, leading to a peculiar, "dandified" gait with the neck and shoulders held stiffly. Although it is temporarily incapacitating, dengue fever is very rarely fatal. It disappeared from Europe, just as malaria did, and it is just as unlikely to return on a large enough scale to present a serious threat to public health.

Nowadays the most serious health risks arise from the extent and speed of travel. Even in the days before widespread commercial air transport, a global pandemic could have devastating consequences. The outbreak of influenza in 1918 swept across the world. Fewer than 3 percent of its victims died, but so many people caught the illness that it killed more than 20 million people. Health experts fear that a new infection, such as severe acute respiratory syndrome (SARS), also with a low mortality rate, might cause similar devastation. This risk is far more serious than that of a tropical illness moving because of warmer weather and overwhelming the health services.

Sea levels and storms

Some of the most dramatic consequences that have been predicted to accompany climate change also turn out to be exaggerated. There have been warnings of a rapid rise in sea level, of more and fiercer hurricanes, more tornadoes, and even of more blizzards.

Sea levels have risen, but the rise predicted by the models, of 4.3–30 inches (0.11–0.77 m), is modest (see "Is the sea rising?" on pages 158–163). Coastal erosion is serious in some places, but it is not due to global warming.

The frequency of tropical cyclones has not increased in recent decades and there has been a significant reduction in the average wind speeds of hurricanes—the tropical cyclones that develop over the Atlantic and

Caribbean. Some climate models predict an increase in both frequency and intensity of these weather systems, but so far there is no evidence that this is happening. It is possible, however, that hurricane frequency may increase in coming years to the level that obtained in the 1950s as part of a natural cycle of hurricane frequency that has nothing to do with climatic warming.

Climate models do not predict an increase in the frequency of tornadoes. Almost certainly there will seem to be more, however, for the same reason that has seen a sharp increase in the number in recent years. This has been due to better reporting of tornadoes. More of them are observed than was the case years ago and no doubt more will be reported in years to come. When the number is restricted to the most severe tornadoes, there is no recorded increase over the years and the number of *tornado days*—days when tornadoes are reported—has remained constant or even fallen slightly.

Blizzards may become more frequent, because precipitation is likely to increase and some of it will fall as snow. At the same time, extremely cold winters are expected to become rarer and winters generally will be shorter. More snow, but over a shorter winter, may mean more blizzards over a shorter period, but milder winters may make blizzards less likely. All in all, blizzards are more likely to become rarer than more frequent.

It is impossible to be certain, but the evidence at present suggests that many of the effects of climate change are likely to be mild and that the others, especially the effects on wildlife, can be ameliorated. This projection could turn out to be incorrect if the increase in temperature falls in the upper part of the range. Then there could be serious agricultural difficulties and the rapid rate of change could have an adverse effect on biodiversity.

While bearing in mind the risks, though, it is worth remembering that the climate models explore the implications of raising the atmospheric concentration of greenhouse gases to double the pre-industrial value. Two-thirds of that doubling has already taken place, yet so far there has been no sign of the more extreme consequences some people have predicted.

CAN WE PREVENT CLIMATE CHANGE OR MUST WE ACCEPT AND ADAPT TO IT?

Faced with the prospect of a change in our living conditions, we have two choices. We can adapt to the change, seeking to ensure that it causes as little disruption as possible to the way we live. Alternatively, we can choose to confront the change and seek to avert it. The choice sounds straightforward. Unfortunately, it is not.

The most obvious difficulty arises from our lack of information. It is not enough to know that releasing greenhouse gases into the air is likely to cause a general rise in temperature. We need to know what the consequences of that rise are likely to be. It is impossible to calculate these in detail, of course, but at least we should have a general picture of the way each region of the world will be affected. Without this knowledge we cannot prepare to adapt, because we do not know what it is we must adapt to, and neither do we know whether we face a threat so serious that we must take whatever steps we can to avert it.

Working Group II of the IPCC has attempted to work out the regional consequences of the degree of climate change predicted by the climate scientists of Working Group I, but the conclusions are still very approximate. The IPCC is now concentrating on this aspect of its work and its Fourth Assessment Report should provide more substantial guidance.

The precautionary principle

There is considerable disagreement about the effects of global warming. Few climate scientists doubt that releasing greenhouse gases will cause temperatures to rise, but they do not agree about the extent of the rise. This depends on the sensitivity of the climate to small changes in greenhouse gas concentrations. If the climate is very sensitive there will be a relatively large temperature rise. If it is not so sensitive the rise will be smaller—and perhaps too small to cause any harm. It also depends on the extent to which the atmospheric concentration of carbon dioxide changes and this depends on many factors. It is not impossible that the concentration might peak before it produces any major climate change and then remain constant or even fall.

This is not the first time politicians have been asked to make decisions on the basis of inadequate information and they have devised a way to deal with the issue. They invoke the *precautionary principle*. This states that if a proposed innovation or change might possibly prove harmful to human health or to the natural environment, then it should be forbidden. Critics of the precautionary principle warn that it is capable of preventing any kind of change and that it would be more sensible to balance the harm against the benefit the innovation or change is likely to bring. Clearly the principle has to be implemented with caution.

In the case of climate change, the decision to apply the precautionary principle was taken at the United Nations Conference on Environment and Development—the "Rio Summit" or "Earth Summit"—held in Rio de Janeiro, Brazil. That conference led to the adoption of the United Nations Framework Convention on Climate Change, an agreement by governments to devise ways of preventing or at least limiting climate change. After several further meetings, this led to a protocol to the convention that set targets for reducing emissions (see the sidebar).

Reducing emissions

Carbon dioxide is the most important greenhouse gas we emit. It is a by-product of burning fossil fuels. Therefore reducing greenhouse gas emissions consists primarily in reducing our reliance on fossil fuels. This is not something we can do quickly, because we cannot simply close factories and power plants and ban automobiles. We must find practical and affordable alternatives to fossil fuels.

These are being developed. Nuclear power generation releases no greenhouse gases. It is unpopular with environmental groups, but it is clean and could make an important contribution. Fusion power—a form of nuclear power based on the fusion of atoms rather than the fission of uranium or plutonium atoms—may one day provide abundant cheap, clean energy, but it will not be ready for commercial use until the middle of the century at the earliest. Wind power is being introduced widely and wave power is being developed. Passive solar heating, using solar panels, has been available for several decades for domestic water heating. Solar cells, generating electricity directly from sunlight, will also contribute if their generating costs can be reduced. Alternative fuels for vehicles are being sought. Hydrogen, used in fuel cells to produce electricity, is likely to be the fuel that is adopted.

In addition to actual reductions, countries are permitted to offset against their emissions some of the carbon that is absorbed within their territories, for example by planting new forests. They are also allowed to trade emissions. A country is permitted to exceed its emissions target either by buying emissions credits from a country that emits less than its target and has a surplus, or by financing a project that reduces emissions in another country. This is called the "clean development mechanism."

The UN Framework Convention on Climate Change and the Kyoto Protocol

In June 1992 the United Nations Conference on Environment and Development (UNCED) was held in Rio de Janeiro, Brazil. Variously nicknamed the "Rio Summit" and "Earth Summit," much of the discussion at UNCED centered on the risk of global warming and appropriate responses to it. At that time, although many climate scientists believed such a risk existed, there was little agreement on its extent, timing, or regional consequences. Nevertheless, one of the agreements reached in Rio was the outline of an international treaty to address climate change. The agreement was called the United Nations Framework Convention on Climate Change.

The Framework Convention accepts that climate change will produce adverse effects and its stated objective (Article 2) is:

". . . to achieve, in accordance with the relevant provisions of the Convention, stabilization of greenhouse gas concentrations in the atmosphere at a level that would prevent dangerous anthropogenic interference with the climate system. Such a level should be achieved within a time frame sufficient to allow ecosystems to adapt naturally to climate change, to ensure that food production is not threatened and to enable economic development to proceed in a sustainable manner."

The convention requires signatory nations to produce and publish inventories of their greenhouse gas emissions and of the amounts they remove from the air. They must develop means of reducing or preventing emissions, working in cooperation with other nations, and prepare to adapt to the consequences of climate change.

The convention was adopted on May 9, 1992, at a ceremony held at UN Headquarters in New York, and it came into effect six months after 50 governments had ratified it. This happened on March 21, 1994.

The Framework Convention is just that—a framework onto which detailed courses of action can be attached. It sets no targets for reducing greenhouse gas emissions and requires countries simply to collect information and meet to discuss the next steps. Several meetings were held, called "Conferences of the Parties." COP 1 took place in Berlin in March 1995, COP 2 in Geneva in July 1996, and COP 3 in Kyoto in December 1997. Each of these meetings was preceded by several preparatory meetings at which officials from the participating countries drew up drafts of the agreements that ministers would discuss at the COP.

The Kyoto COP set targets for reducing emissions. The overall aim was to reduce global emissions of greenhouse gases to 95 percent or less of their 1990 values during the "commitment period" of 2008–12. This was the Kyoto Protocol to the United Nations Framework Convention on Climate Change, usually known simply as the Kyoto Protocol, and it was agreed on December 11, 1997.

As well as setting an overall target, the Kyoto Protocol set targets—negotiated after many hours of wrangling—for each country. Three countries were allowed to increase emissions above their 1990 values. Australia was set a target of 108 percent, Iceland of 110 percent, and Norway 101 percent.

Targets were set by the Kyoto Protocol only for the industrialized countries and those countries of eastern Europe that were in the process of changing to a market economy. Developing countries were excluded, on the grounds that imposing restrictions on their emissions would inhibit their economic development and that the great bulk of greenhouse gas emissions were from the industrialized countries.

Is Kyoto achievable?

At times the arguments at Kyoto were bitter and deep disagreements remain. The United States and Australia are among a group of countries that have rejected the Kyoto Protocol, saying it will harm their economies while achieving very little. Even among those that have accepted the protocol, it is not certain that every country will be able to meet its Kyoto target. If they do, the effect on the climate will be very small. If global warming is to be halted by this means, there will need to be much more drastic reductions. Many scientists believe emissions will have to fall more than 60 percent below their 1990 values and some believe we will have to reduce emissions to zero and abandon fossil fuels altogether.

This seems impossible, but all the calculations are based on two suppositions, both of which have been challenged. The first is that unless we take steps to reduce carbon dioxide emissions, the atmospheric concentration of this gas will continue to rise exponentially—by compound interest. In fact, though, carbon dioxide emissions, vary from year to year and the atmospheric concentration is increasing at a slower rate than is fed into the climate models.

The second is that the climate is very sensitive to small changes in the concentration of greenhouse gases. This may be so, but at present the rate of warming is modest, amounting to about $3°F$ ($1.7°C$) a century, suggesting the climate is not especially sensitive. The atmosphere takes time to respond to changes in its composition, however, and the oceans respond to temperature changes very slowly indeed. It is possible, therefore, that the climate is still lagging behind the change in atmospheric chemistry and that the rise in temperature will accelerate once it catches up. At present no one knows.

We must live with the uncertainty as best we can, and adapting to change may be easier than it seems. Many of the innovations that would reduce carbon dioxide emissions will probably occur anyway in the natural course of our technological development. Conserving energy makes sense, because it increases efficiency and reduces pollution. Alternatives to gasoline and diesel engines will also reduce pollution—and the considerable harm it does to our health. Imagine what the center of your town would be like if there were no traffic fumes and the cars, buses, and trucks purred along quietly, driven by electric motors and emitting nothing into the air except water vapor. Imagine what it would be like if, one by one, all the chimneys were to be dismantled—except for a few kept as a reminder of the way things used to be, but not used, of course. Chimneys would not be needed in a world powered by cleanly produced electricity.

Perhaps the climate change will not be so bad after all. Meanwhile, as we struggle to understand climate change, we will learn more about how the Sun, the Earth, the atmosphere, and the oceans interact to produce the climates of the world. This knowledge will increase our sense of wonder at the movements and processes that bring us sunshine and rain, summer warmth, and winter cold.

SI UNITS AND CONVERSIONS

Unit	Quantity	Symbol	Conversion
Base units			
meter	length	m	1 m = 3.2808 inches
kilogram	mass	kg	1 kg = 2.205 pounds
second	time	s	
ampere	electric current	A	
kelvin	thermodynamic temperature	K	1 K = 1°C = 1.8°F
candela	luminous intensity	cd	
mole	amount of substance	mol	
Supplementary units			
radian	plane angle	rad	$\pi/2$ rad = 90°
steradian	solid angle	sr	
Derived units			
coulomb	quantity of electricity	C	
cubic meter	volume	m^3	1 m^3 = 1.308 yards^3
farad	capacitance	F	
henry	inductance	H	
hertz	frequency	H_z	
joule	energy	J	1 J = 0.2389 calories
kilogram per cubic meter	density	kg m^{-3}	1 kg m^{-3} = 0.0624 lb. ft.$^{-3}$
lumen	luminous flux	lm	
lux	illuminance	lx	
meter per second	speed	m s^{-1}	1 m s^{-1} = 3.281 ft. s^{-1}
meter per second squared	acceleration	m s^{-2}	
mole per cubic meter	concentration	mol m^{-3}	
newton	force	N	1 N = 7.218 lb. force
ohm	electric resistance	Ω	

SI UNITS AND CONVERSIONS (*continued*)

Unit	Quantity	Symbol	Conversion
Derived units			
pascal	pressure	Pa	1 Pa = 0.145 lb. in.$^{-2}$
radian per second	angular velocity	rad s^{-1}	
radian per second squared	angular acceleration	rad s^{-2}	
square meter	area	m^2	1 m^2 = 1.196 yards^2
tesla	magnetic flux density	T	
volt	electromotive force	V	
watt	power	W	1 W = 3.412 Btu h^{-1}
weber	magnetic flux	Wb	

PREFIXES USED WITH SI UNITS

Prefixes attached to SI units alter their value.

Prefix	Symbol	Value
atto	a	$\times 10^{-18}$
femto	f	$\times 10^{-15}$
pico	p	$\times 10^{-12}$
nano	n	$\times 10^{-9}$
micro	μ	$\times 10^{-6}$
milli	m	$\times 10^{-3}$
centi	c	$\times 10^{-2}$
deci	d	$\times 10^{-1}$
deca	da	$\times 10$
hecto	h	$\times 10^{2}$
kilo	k	$\times 10^{3}$
mega	M	$\times 10^{6}$
giga	G	$\times 10^{9}$
tera	T	$\times 10^{12}$

Bibliography and further reading

Abysov, S. S., M. Angelis, N. I. Barkov, J. M. Barnola, M. Bender, J. Chappellaz, V. K. Chistiakov, P. Duval, C. Genthon, J. Jouzel, V. M. Kotlyakov, B. B. Kudriashov, V. Y. Lipenkov, M. Legrand, C. Lorius, B. Malaize, P. Martinerie, V. I. Nikolayev, J. R. Petit, D. Raynaud, G. Raisbeck, C. Ritz, A. N. Salamantin, E. Saltzman, T. Sowers, M. Stievenard, R. N. Vostretsov, M. Wahlen, C. Waelbroeck, F. Yiou, and P. Yiou. "Deciphering Mysteries of Past Climate from Antarctic Ice Cores." *Earth in Space* 8, no. 3, p. 9, November 1995. American Geophysical Union. Available on-line. URL: www.agu.org/sci_soc/vostok.html. Accessed November 13, 2002.

Allaby, Michael. *Basics of Environmental Science.* 2d ed. New York: Routledge, 2000.

————. *Dangerous Weather: Fog, Smog, and Poisoned Rain.* New York: Facts On File, 2003.

————. *Deserts.* New York: Facts On File, 2001.

————. *Encyclopedia of Weather and Climate.* 2 vols. New York: Facts On File, 2001.

American Geophysical Union. "Climate of Venus May Be Unstable." Available on-line. URL: www.agu.org/sci_soc/venus_pr.html. Posted April 7, 1996.

Barry, Patrick L., and Tony Phillips. "The Inconstant Sun." NASA. Available on-line. URL: science.nasa.gov/headlines/y2003/17jan_solcon.htm?list847478. Accessed March 21, 2003.

Barry, Roger G., and Richard J. Chorley. *Atmosphere, Weather & Climate.* 7th ed. New York: Routledge, 1998.

Bryant, Edward. *Climate Process & Change.* Cambridge, U.K.: Cambridge University Press, 1997.

Burroughs, William James. *Climate Change: A Multidisciplinary Approach.* Cambridge, U.K.: Cambridge University Press, 2001.

"Cahokia Mounds State Historic Site." UNESCO. Available on-line. URL: whc.unesco.org/sites/1298.htm. Updated November 17, 2002.

Catling, David. "Basic Facts about the Planet Mars." Mars Atmosphere Group, Space Science Division, NASA Ames Research Center. Available on-line. URL: Humbabe.arc.nasa/gov/mgcm/faq/marsfacts/html. Accessed November 11, 2002.

Cornish, Jim. "The Anasazi Theme Page." Gander Academy. Available on-line. URL: www. stemnet.nf.ca./CITE/anasazi.htm. Updated December 12, 2000.

"Cracking the Mystery to Venus' Climate Change." *Spaceflight Now.* Available on-line. URL: spaceflightnow.com/news/n0103/13venus/. NASA/JPL news release posted March 13, 2001.

Crossley, John. "Carlsbad Caverns National Park." "The American Southwest: A Guide to the National Parks and Natural Landscapes of Southwest U.S.A." Available on-line. URL: www.americansouthwest.net/new_mexico/carlsbad_caverns/national_park.html. Updated November 13, 2002.

Daly, John L. "Tasmanian Sea Levels: The 'Isle of the Dead' Revisited." February 2, 2003. Available on-line. URL: www.john-daly.com/deadisle.

————. "The Surface Record: 'Global Mean Temperature' and how it is determined at surface level." Report to the Greening Earth Society, May 2000. Available on-line. URL: www.greeningearthsociety.org/Articles/2000/surface1.htm.

Dutch, Steven. "Glaciers." Available on-line. URL: www.uwgb.edu/dutchs/ 202ovhds/glacial.htm. Updated November 2, 1999.

Emiliani, Cesare. *Planet Earth: Cosmology, Geology, and the Evolution of Life and Environment.* Cambridge, U.K.: Cambridge University Press, 1995.

Geerts, B., and E. Linacre. "Sunspots and climate." December 1997. Available on-line. URL: www-das.uwyo.edu/~geerts/cwx/notes/chap02/sunspots.html. Accessed March 20, 2003.

GISP2 Science Management Office. "Welcome to GISP2: Greenland Ice Sheet Project 2." Durham, N.H.: Climate Change Research Center, Institute for the Study of Earth, Oceans and Space, University of New Hampshire. Available on-line. URL: www.gisp2.sr.unh.edu/GISP2. Updated March 1, 2002.

Henderson-Sellers, Ann, and Peter J. Robinson. *Contemporary Climatology.* Harlow, U.K.: Longman, 1986.

Hoare, Robert. "World Climate." Buttle and Tuttle Ltd. Available on-line. URL: www.worldclimate.com/worldclimate. Updated October 2, 2001.

Hoffman, Paul F., and Daniel P. Schrag. "The Snowball Earth." Available on-line. URL: www-eps.harvard.edu/people/faculty/hoffman/snowball_paper.html. August 8, 1999.

Houghton, J. T., Y. Ding, D. J. Griggs, M. Noguer, P. J. van der Linden, X. Dai, K. Maskell, and C. A. Johnson. *Climate Change 2001: The Scientific Basis.* Contribution of Working Group I to the Third Assessment Report of the Intergovernmental Panel on Climate Change. Cambridge, U.K.: Cambridge University Press, 2001.

IndiaNest.com. "Indus Valley Civilization." Available on-line. URL: www.indianest.com/architecture/00002.htm. November 13, 2002.

Iseminger, William R. "Mighty Cahokia." *Archaeology,* vol. 29, number 3, May/June 1996. Archaeological Institute of America. Available on-line. URL: www.he.net/~archaeol/9605/abstracts/cahokia.html. Accessed March 19, 2003.

Johnson, George. "Social Strife May Have Exiled Ancient Americans." *The New York Times.* Available on-line. URL: www.santafe.edu/~johnson/articles. anasazi.html. August 20, 1996.

Kaplan, George. "The Seasons and the Earth's Orbit—Milankovich Cycles." U.S. Naval Observatory, Astronomical Applications Department. Available on-line. URL: aa.usno.navy.mil/faq/docs/seasons_orbit.html. Last modified on March 14, 2002.

Ladurie, Emmanuel LeRoy. *Times of Feast, Times of Famine: A History of Climate Since the Year 1000.* New York: Doubleday and Company, 1971.

Lamb, H. H. *Climate, History and the Modern World.* 2d ed. New York: Routledge, 1995.

LeBeau, Kara. "A Curve Ball Into The Snowball Earth Hypothesis?" Geological Society of America. Available on-line. URL: www.geosociety.org/news/pr/01-63.htm. December 3, 2001.

Lovelock, James. *The Ages of Gaia.* New York: W. W. Norton & Company, 1988.

Lutgens, Frederick K., and Edward J. Tarbuck. *The Atmosphere.* 7th ed. Upper Saddle River, N.J.: Prentice Hall, 1998.

Mandia, Scott A. "The Little Ice Age in Europe." Available on-line. URL: www2. sunysuffolk.edu/mandias/lia/little_ice_age.html. Accessed March 25, 2003.

Members.tripod.com. "The Indus Valley Civilisation." Available on-line. URL: members.tripod.com/sympweb/IndusValleyhistory.htm. Accessed November 13, 2002.

Michaels, Patrick J., and Robert C. Balling, Jr. "Kyoto Protocol: 'A useless appendage to an irrelevant treaty.'" Statement to the Committee on Small Business, United States House of Representatives, July 29, 1998. Available on-line. URL: www.cato.org/testimony/ct-pm072998.html. Accessed April 15, 2003.

———. *The Satanic Gases: Clearing the Air about Global Warming*. Washington, D.C.: Cato Institute, 2000.

Montfort, Tim. "Effects of Sunspots on Earth." University of Maine. Available on-line. URL: www.cs.usm.maine.edu/~montfort/ast100.htm. Accessed March 20, 2003.

NASA. "Earth's Fidgeting Climate." Science@NASA. Available on-line. URL: Science.nasa.gov/headlines/y2000/ast20oct_1.htm. Posted October 20, 2000.

———. "Environmental Treaties and Resource Indicators (ENTRI)—Full Text." Center for International Earth Science Information Network (CIESIN), Socioeconomic Data and Applications Center (SEDAC). Available on-line. URL: sedac.ciesin.org/pidb/texts/climate.convention.1992.html. Accessed April 15, 2003.

———. "Global Warming." Available on-line. URL: www.maui.net/~jstark/nasa.html. Accessed March 28, 2003.

———. "Hydrologic Cycle." NASA's Observatorium. Available on-line. URL: observe.arc.nasa.gov/nasa/earth/hydrocycle/hydro2.html. Accessed November 12, 2002.

———. "Mars' Chaotic Climate." Space Telescope Science Institute. Available on-line. URL: oposite.stsci.edu/pubinfo/pr/97/15/background.html. Accessed November 11, 2002.

———. "NASA Scientists Propose New Theory of Earth's Early Evolution." Ames Research Center. SpaceRef.com. Available on-line. URL: www.spaceref.com/news/viewpr.html?pid=5687. Accessed August 3, 2001.

Niroma, Timo. "Sunspots: The 200-year sunspot cycle is also a weather cycle." Available on-line. URL: www.kolumbus.fi/tilmari/some200.htm. Accessed March 20, 2003.

"Ocean Surface Currents: Introduction to Ocean Gyres." Available on-line. URL: oceancurrents.rsmas.miami.edu/ocean-gyres.html. Accessed November 12, 2002.

O'Connor, J. J., and E. F. Richardson. "Jean-Baptiste-Joseph Fourier." School of Mathematics and Statistics, University of St. Andrews, Scotland. January 1997. Available on-line. URL: www-gap.dcs.st-and.ac.uk/~history/Mathematicians/Fourier.html. Accessed March 27, 2003.

Oke, T. R. *Boundary Layer Climates*. 2d ed. New York: Routledge, 1987.

Oliver, John E., and John J. Hidore. *Climatology, An Atmospheric Science*. 2d ed. Upper Saddle River, N.J.: Prentice Hall, 2002.

Petit, J. R., D. Raynaud, C. Lorius, J. Jouzel, G. Delaygue, N. I. Barkov, and V. M. Kotlyakov. "Historical Isotopic Temperature Record from the Vostok Ice Core." *Trends: A Compendium of Data on Global Change*. Oak Ridge, Tenn.: Carbon Dioxide Information Analysis Center, Oak Ridge National Laboratory, U.S. Dept. of Energy, January 2000. Available on-line. URL: cdiac.esd.orn1.gov/trends/temp/vostok/jouz_tem.html. Accessed November 13, 2002.

Phillips, Tony. "The Resurgent Sun." NASA. Available on-line. URL: science.nasa.gov/headlines/y2002/18jan_solarback.htm?list154233. Accessed January 22, 2002.

Powell, Eric A. "Caves and Climate." *Archaeology* 55, no. 1. Archaeological Institute of America. Available on-line. URL: www.archaeology.org/magazine.php?page=0201/newsbriefs/caves. January/February 2002.

Rothhamel, Tom. "Isostasy." Available on-line. URL: www.homepage.montana.edu/ ~geo1445/hyperglac/isostasy. Last modified July 11, 2000.

Schlesinger, William H. *Biogeochemistry: An Analysis of Global Change.* 2d ed. San Diego: Academic Press, 1991.

Space.com. "Lunar Data Sheet." Available on-line. URL: www.space.com/ scienceastronomy/solarsystem/moon-ez.html. Posted on November 11, 1999.

Stephenson, David B. "Environmental Statistics Study Group." Available on-line. URL: www.met.rdg.ac.uk/cag/stats/essg. Accessed April 4, 2003.

Stern, David P. "Precession," in *From Stargazers to Starships.* Available on-line. URL: www.phy6.org/stargaze/Sprecess.htm. Last updated December 13, 2001.

United Nations. "Full Text of the Convention." Available on-line. URL: unfccc.int/resource/conv. Accessed April 15, 2003.

———. "Kyoto Protocol to the United Nations Framework Convention on Climate Change." Available on-line. URL: unfccc.int/resource/docs/convkp/ kpeng.html. Accessed April 25, 2003.

———. "United Nations Framework Convention on Climate Change." Available on-line. URL: unfccc.int. Accessed April 15, 2003.

University of New Mexico. "UNM Scientists Establish Link Between Climate and Cultural Changes." University of New Mexico, Public Affairs Department. Available on-line. URL: www.unm.edu/news/Releases/Oct5earthand planetary.htm. Posted on October 5, 2001.

Van Helden, Albert. "Sunspots." Rice University. Available on-line. URL: es.rice.edu/ES/humsoc/Galileo/Things/sunspots.html. Accessed March 20, 2003.

"Welcome to Cahokia!" Available on-line. URL: medicine.wustl.edu/~mckinney/ cahokia/welcome.html. Accessed March 19, 2003.

Index

Page numbers in *italic* refer to illustrations.